TAX PLANNING FOR INVESTORS

The Eighties Guide to Securities and Commodities
Investments and Tax Shelters, 1985 Edition

TAX PLANNING FOR INVESTORS

The Eighties Guide to Securities and Commodities Investments and Tax Shelters, 1985 Edition

Jack Crestol, CPA, J.D., LL.M.
and
Herman M. Schneider, CPA, J.D., LL.M.
Both Tax Partners of Coopers & Lybrand

DOW JONES-IRWIN Homewood, Illinois 60430

This publication is designed to provide accurate and
authoritative information in regard to the subject matter
covered. It is sold with the understanding that the
publisher is not engaged in rendering legal, accounting, or
other professional service. If legal advice or other expert
assistance is required, the services of a competent
professional person should be sought.

*From a Declaration of Principles jointly adopted by a Committee
of the American Bar Association and a Committee of Publishers.*

ISBN 0-87094-632-3
Library of Congress Catalog Card No. 84–73045

Printed in the United States of America

1 2 3 4 5 6 7 8 9 0 K 2 1 0 9 8 7 6 5

Preface

The investor's primary objective in investing in securities is to make a profit: buy low, sell high. Unfortunately, however, getting the *most* profit from a year's security transactions is not a simple matter of buying low and selling high, because the tax laws determine how much of the profit can be kept.

The informed investor measures his or her economic gain or yield in terms of aftertax dollars or the amount of additional cash available after considering all expenses including income taxes. It should be emphasized, however, that although the informed investor should be highly conscious of tax factors, he or she will rarely allow these tax factors to affect an economic decision. A short-term gain taxed at ordinary rates is still superior to a long-term capital loss, no matter how heavily the gain is taxed. Nevertheless, in many instances taxes can be minimized with little or no economic effect.

To aid investors in their understanding of how security transactions and other types of investments are taxed and the kind of planning measures necessary to maximize the aftertax gain, this book was first issued in 1966, and was revised several times, the last time being in 1983. It has again been revised to reflect new developments and recent changes in the tax law, including the Tax Reform Act of 1984, a part of the Deficit-Reduction Act of 1984 (1984 Act), which was enacted on July 18, 1984, the Tax Equity and Fiscal Responsibility Act of 1982 (1982 TEFRA), the Economic Recovery Tax Act of 1981 (1981 ERTA), and the Tax Reform Act of 1976 (1976 TRA). The book is subdivided into two sections; Section I contains a list of tax savings opportunities, and in Section II there is a summary of the tax rules an investor needs to know to plan effectively.

This book is not intended to show investors how to realize economic gains in securities and commodities transactions, but rather how to obtain the best tax advantages in recognizing gains or losses. To this end, tax savings opportunities are discussed in the form of objectives, such as postponing tax recognition of gain, converting short-term gains into long-term gains, and the like. For example, the investor may either defer capital gain until the following year by means of a short sale or by purchasing a Put, while at the same time retaining the potential for future appreciation on the stock.

The Tax Reform Act of 1984, which was enacted on July 18, 1984, has made extensive tax changes which will affect most investors. The principal changes in the securities area are (1) the holding period for long-term capital gains has been reduced to six months; (2) the market discount on newly issued bonds is taxed as ordinary income; (3) the interest expense incurred on short-term discount bonds (T-bills) is not currently deductible; (4) the deductions for payments on short sales have been tightened; (5) the mark-to-market rules have been extended to nonequity options, including broad-based stock index options; (6) the tax straddle rules have been extended to stock and Listed options; (7) the use of tax shelters has been further restricted, including an increase in the depreciable life for real estate from 15 to 18 years; and (8) donors may now be taxed on interest-free loans. Corporate investors may also find it more difficult to obtain the 85 percent dividends-received deduction.

This book is concerned primarily with the federal tax liabilities of an individual filing an income tax return on a cash basis. Although many of the ideas presented and the discussion of the relevant income tax provisions may also apply (with or without some modification) to nonresident aliens, traders, dealers, partnerships, trusts, estates, and corporations, the text does not consider such possible application. However, there are separate chapters summarizing the tax effects for dealers, nonresident alien investors, corporations, trusts, estates, and other types of investors. In addition, the discussion is confined primarily to transactions in securities of publicly owned corporations, and, although many of these provisions apply also to closely held corporations, it does not consider the special tax provisions relating to closely held or related corporations. In all the examples, it is assumed that the investor files a tax return on the calendar year basis. Furthermore, for the sake of simplicity, a capital gains tax of 20 percent is used, although for many investors the effective tax rate will be lower. Unless otherwise indicated, all examples are applicable under the Tax Reform Act of 1984.

For practical reasons, state and local tax liabilities are not considered herein. Such liabilities are usually small in relation to federal tax liabilities, are deductible in computing the federal tax liability, and are frequently computed on comparable bases. The investor is warned, however, that situations may arise where state or local tax liabilities may be large enough to influence an investor's tax planning, especially where the alternative minimum tax might be influenced by such state or local tax burden.

Each investor should acquaint himself with the nature and magnitude of such taxes as they apply to him.

For the convenience of the reader, the discussion of tax savings opportunities is cross-referenced to the discussion of tax principles. Official authorities are referred to in footnotes and indexed in the appendix, and both a detailed word index of subject matters and a detailed table of contents are provided. Many readers will prefer first to scan the tax savings opportunities for interesting suggestions and then to read the sections of Section II that apply.

The authors wish to acknowledge their appreciation of the invaluable assistance of their associates in the offices of Coopers & Lybrand, in particular, Andrew R. Ben-Ami, CPA, Mark A. Fichtenbaum, CPA, James B. Fish, Jr., CPA, and Warren G. Wintrub, CPA, who assisted in preparation of the earlier editions and/or this revision.

Jack Crestol
Herman M. Schneider

Contents

Tax Savings Opportunities

¶1

1 INTRODUCTION

The ideas discussed in this section are intended to present the investor with alternative legitimate methods of casting a transaction so that the investor can either reduce his tax liability or defer the tax to another year. Many of these ideas have been sanctioned by court decisions or by Treasury regulations or rulings. However, the investor should be aware that the Treasury may attack tax savings transactions on various grounds, sometimes despite court approval of the transaction.

The trading in Listed options on several exchanges has become a very popular form of investment. However, for many sophisticated investors, Unlisted options are still being utilized. Accordingly, portions of this section dealing with options will cover all options, but certain sections will be applicable to only Unlisted options. Under such circumstances, the limitations will be clearly indicated. In addition, there has been expanded trading in stock index options, both broad-based and narrow-based, and nonequity options, such as options on government obligations and on foreign currencies. Possible tax planning with these and other new investment products is also discussed in this section.

The illustrations generally do not take into consideration the transaction costs (i.e., commissions, applicable transfer taxes, and so forth). Accordingly, such costs must be considered in the overall economics of the transaction.

It is appropriate at this point to reemphasize the importance of the economics of a transaction, aside from the tax considerations. The

courts and the Internal Revenue Service more and more have been look-
ing into the pretax economics of the transaction. The investor will be
denied the tax benefits of a transaction he enters into solely for tax
reasons with no expectations of ever realizing a profit on the transaction.[1] In denying losses realized in T-bill options straddles, the Tax
Court stressed that losses from tax-motivated transactions which Congress did not intend to encourage will be disallowed unless entered into
primarily for profit.[2] Accordingly, the economic and profit potential of
the tax saving opportunities discussed below must be considered.

2 POSTPONE TAX RECOGNITION OF GAIN OR LOSS

The transactions discussed below will postpone the recognition of
the gain or loss, but will not change the character of the gain or loss
when recognized for tax purposes. Several of the ideas have general
application, while others are limited to specific types of investments.

.01 "Short against the Box"

An investor can sell a security but defer the recognition of gain
until the next year by selling short an equal number of shares and
covering the short sale in the following year with the shares originally
held. This is commonly known as "selling short against the box."
Ordinarily, the long-term or short-term nature of the gain will be determined at the time of the short sale and therefore will not be affected by the deferral. However, in the case of securities held for
more than the applicable long-term holding period, care should be
taken to ensure that long-term capital gain treatment will result. With
the reduction in the required long-term holding period from one year
to six months for securities acquired during the period June 23, 1984
through 1987, it is easier to qualify for long-term capital gain before
entering into the short sale. The amount of tax on the gain will depend on the taxpayer's other income, other tax preference items, and
the tax rates in effect in the year in which the gain is recognized.
Deferral of the gain, therefore, may result in a higher or lower effective tax rate on the gain, and should be taken into account in determining whether or not to go short against the box. A deferral of gain
may be particularly effective where there will be a prospective tax
rate reduction or an investor has a change in economic status (e.g.,
retirement). By delaying long-term capital gains until after retirement, there may be a drop in overall income.

[1] *Goldstein*, 364 F2d 734 (CA-2, 1966), cert. den. [2] *Fox*, 82 T.C. No. 75 (1984).

Example (a). An investor may wish to protect his profit in stock acquired on November 15, 1983 for $20 per share and which is selling on November 16, 1984 for $50. Instead of recognizing a $30 per share long-term capital gain in 1984, the investor could sell the stock short at $50 and defer the closing of the short sale until January of 1985, at which time the long-term gain of $30 per share (less transfer fees) will be recognized. If the stock was acquired on July 15, 1984, so that the holding period of the stock was not more than six months at the time of the short sale, the gain recognized upon the closing of the short sale would be a short-term capital gain. (See discussion of short sales, ¶37.)

Example (b). *Alternative minimum tax:* Due to tax preferences realized in the current year and the disallowance of the deduction for taxes and investment expenses, the alternative tax for the year is higher than the regular tax. The investor wishes to realize additional capital gain but does not want to increase his alternative minimum tax for the year resulting from the additional state tax burden on that gain. By selling short and closing the short sale in the following year, he will minimize his alternative tax for the current year and defer the gain on the short sale until the next year, when he expects to pay a lower effective tax rate on the gain.

The short against the box transaction can also be utilized when an investor has a gain on a Listed option and wishes to defer the gain into the succeeding year.

Example. On September 10, 1984, T purchased one ABC Call February 55s for a premium of $600. On October 15, 1984, the Call is selling for $2,000 and T wishes to lock in the gain but defer the short-term gain until 1985. T could write (sell) the identical Call for a premium of $2,000 and effectively be in a short against the box position. In February 1985, both positions will be collapsed, thereby resulting in a $1,400 short-term gain in 1985. Note that Listed options can now qualify for long-term capital gain if they meet the new six-month holding period requirements. However, the tax straddle rules (including short sale and wash sale rules) will now apply if T wishes to lock in a profit by writing a Call. To obtain long-term capital gains, the long Call position should be held open for more than six months before the Call is written. Any losses realized on the short Call position may be converted into a long-term loss under the tax straddle rules.

A short sale may also be used to sell a depreciated security but defer the recognition of the loss until the next year. Ordinarily it is more advantageous to deduct the loss in the current year. However, under certain circumstances, it may be more beneficial in terms of taxes to postpone recognizing the loss. The following are some examples in which the losses should be postponed.

Example (a). *Excess deductions:* T's deductions exceed his income, including $3,000 of capital gains, by $5,000. On December 1, T wants to sell a stock and realize a capital loss of $2,000. There would be no tax benefit if the capital loss is recognized in the current year because there is no taxable income and the excess deductions cannot be carried to another year. (See ¶20.) A short sale of the stock will enable T to apply the capital loss against his income in the year the sale is closed.

Example (b). *Long-term loss and short-term gain:* In 1984, T has realized $10,000 of short-term gains and $10,000 of long-term losses. He expects to realize short-term gains and long-term gains in 1985. T has suffered a $6,000 loss on a stock acquired late in 1984 and wants to sell it before there is a further drop in its value. By selling the stock short and closing it early in 1985, T can offset his 1984 long-term losses against his short-term gains and offset the postponed $6,000 short-term loss against his 1985 short-term gains. If he recognized the loss in 1984, the loss would be applied against his 1984 short-term gains. However, only $4,000 of the $10,000 long-term loss could be offset against the remaining 1984 short-term gains, and $6,000 of the loss would be applied against $3,000 of his 1984 ordinary income (see ¶32.03).

Example (c). *Income averaging:* As a result of the income averaging rules (see ¶63), T can pay a low tax on his capital gains in 1984. T expects short-term gains in 1985 and expects to pay a much larger tax on his 1985 gains. T has incurred a $5,000 loss in a security and wants to sell it before there is a further decline. By selling short in 1984 and closing in 1985, T can obtain a greater tax benefit from the loss.

Example (d). *Alternative minimum tax:* When a taxpayer is going to be subjected to alternative minimum tax for the current year, one planning technique is to try to increase taxable income which would effectively be taxed at a 20 percent rate. Thus, where short-term capital gains are in the alternative minimum tax computations and therefore effectively taxed at the 20 percent rate, the investor should avoid recognizing any short-term loss until the next year when it might produce a 50 percent benefit. Selling short against the box could be used to defer such a loss.

Under certain circumstances, the broker may release to the investor a substantial portion of the funds arising from the short sale or allow the purchase of other securities with the purchasing power created because of such short sale. However, interest will ordinarily be charged when the funds created by the short sale are used. The investor should determine the policy of his broker in this situation before making the short sale. Some brokers will pay over to the customer a portion of the fee received from the stock loan involved with the short sale. In essence, a payment is being made on the short sale proceeds. It may be possible to keep both positions open for a long period of time, have the use of the funds or additional purchasing power during this period, and still avoid recognition of gain.

With the repeal of the basis carryover provision, it is possible during the interim period to avoid tax on the unrecognized gain if the investor died before the short sale was closed. A determination should be made whether closing the short sale before or after death would result in a savings of overall taxes.

.02   Acquisition of a Put

The investor can defer the recognition of any gain on his stock and still minimize the possible reduction in the amount of his gain by acquiring an option to sell the stock (a Put). The advantage of this method as compared to the use of a short sale, discussed above, is that in the event the stock continues to rise, the investor obtains the benefit of such rise. However, the cost of acquiring this insurance against decline is normally in the area of 10 to 15 percent of the value of the underlying security. This varies in accordance with the period of time that the option will run, the volatility of the stock, and supply and demand for the Put. A tax disadvantage under either method is that, if the underlying security is held for less than the required period for long-term capital gains at the time of the short sale or acquisition of the Put, any gain on subsequent sale will generally be treated as short-term, since the holding period of the stock will not begin until the short sale is covered or the Put is exercised, expires, or is disposed of. (See the discussion of short sales in ¶37.03.)

Because Listed Puts have a duration of not more than nine months, long-term capital gain potential on the sale of the Listed Puts was not available prior to the 1984 Act. Puts held for more than six months can now qualify if they are not part of a straddle. Unlisted Puts, which can be issued for more than one year, can also be utilized to obtain long-term capital gains under both the applicable six-month and one-year holding period requirement.

Example. Assume that an investor owned stock acquired on June 27, 1984 at $20 per share, and that on December 28, 1984, when the stock is selling at $105 she purchased a one-year, 10-day Unlisted Put at $50 for the equivalent of $5 per share. The investor then has the right to "put" or sell the stock to the writer of the option at any time during the period for $50 per share, regardless of the selling price of the stock. If the market value of the stock rises, for example, to $75 per share and the investor wishes to close out the transaction, she can sell the stock in the open market, recognizing a $55 per share long-term capital gain. (The stock was held for more than six months at the time the Put was acquired.) A $5 long-term loss would be recognized on disposition of the Put, whether or not it was held for more than six months.

If the investor had sold the stock short at $50 per share in lieu of acquiring the Put, she would have limited her gain to $30 per share. Thus, for a cost of approximately $5 per share, the Put insures a minimum gain and allows potentially substantial gain possibilities for the one-year period in the event of a rise in the stock market.

If the stock value of the shares should fall, for example, to $30 per share by December 15, 1985, she could sell the Put for the equivalent price of approximately $20 per share ($50 option price less the market value of the stock of $30) and, therefore, recognize a long-term gain of approximately $15 per share ($20 per share proceeds less $5 per share cost of the Put). (Note that the Treasury may issue regulations under the straddle rules that would convert this to a short-term gain.) The stock would be sold for $30, resulting in a long-term capital gain of $10 per share. Note that if the shares were acquired before June 23, 1984, or were held not more than six months at the time the Put was acquired, the gain would have been short-term under the short sales rules. If the stock were sold instead for $15 per share, the loss of $5

> per share would be long-term. Even if the shares were held for less than six months at the time the Put was acquired, the $5 loss would be long-term since the short sales rules do not suspend the holding period where a loss is realized.

.03 Sale of In-the-Money Calls

An investor can also defer the recognition of a gain on his stock by selling an option to buy the stock (a Call). The use of an in-the-money Call will lock in the amount of the gain as long as the stock price remains above the Call strike price. However, granting an in-the-money Call may either suspend or terminate the holding period of the stock. Therefore, such a Call can not be used to convert a short-term gain into a long-term gain.

> **Example.** T acquired ABC stock on August 1, 1984, for $38 per share. On December 1, 1984, the stock is selling for $50 per share. T wants to sell his ABC stock, but defer recognition until 1985. By writing a January 35 Call for $17, T will lock in his $14 gain on the stock as long as the stock price remains above $35. However, unlike the case with the acquisition of a Put, in this instance, T cannot benefit from any subsequent rise in the stock price.

.04 Deferred Delivery under New York Stock Exchange Rule 64(3) (Seller's Option)

A discussion of the seller's option is found in ¶**5.02**. Selling via this route will enable the seller to take advantage of the current market price and still defer recognition of gain and add up to 60 days to his holding period. Thus, a seller who has held a security within two months of the applicable long-term capital gain holding period can convert a short-term gain into a long-term gain without further exposure to market risk.

.05 Year-End Sales

A cash-basis investor selling stock toward the end of his taxable year may control which year the gain is to be recognized. When stock is sold in the "regular way," as is the case in most instances, the settlement day will be the fifth business day following the trade date. A loss will be recognized in the year in which the trade date falls, but a profit is not taxable until the subsequent year in which the settlement date falls. The cash-basis investor may cause the gain to be recognized in the year of the trade by making the sale "for cash." (See ¶5.02 dealing with deferred delivery under N.Y. Stock Exchange Rule 64(3) for possible postponement of gain for up to 60 days.) For example, assume that an investor has recognized a $10,000 long-term capital gain and a $10,000 short-term loss in the current year and on December 29 has sold stock which will result in a short-term gain of $11,000. Under the regular rules the $11,000 short-term gain will be recognized in the subsequent year and the $10,000 short-term loss will offset the $10,000 long-term gain in the current year. By making the sale for cash or electing not to have the installment sales rules apply, the $10,000 short-term loss will be applied against the $11,000 short-term gain instead of against the $10,000 long-term gain. The result will be that the investor will be accelerating the time the $11,000 gain would ordinarily be taxed, but he has reduced his overall tax liability on his stock transactions by converting $10,000 of the $11,000 short-term gains into long-term gains.

When Listed options are sold "to close" (i.e., long position is sold), the settlement day is the next business day. The rules concerning the year of recognition are the same as with stock sales as discussed above.

The following table illustrates these rules:

Stock	Cost	Selling amount	Gain (loss)	Date of sale	Terms	Year transaction recognized for tax purposes
A	$10	$15	$5	12/28/84	Regular way	1985
B	10	15	5	12/28/84	For cash	1984
C	10	5	(5)	12/28/84	Regular way	1984
D	10	15	5	11/15/84	Deferred delivery (seller's option)–60 days	1985

Gain or loss on the purchase of stock to close a short sale (settlement five business days after trade date) and on the purchase of a Listed option "to close" the short or written option (settlement one business day after trade date) will be recognized on the settlement date only (see ¶32.01).

.06 Transitional Rules

While the dual long-term holding period rules apply, an investor who purchased the same security before and after June 23, 1984 should take advantage of the alternative holding period rules in order to obtain a long-term capital gain and/or a short-term capital loss.

> **Example.** T acquired 100 shares of ABC stock for $20 a share on May 1, 1984 and on June 29, 1984. He wishes to sell 100 shares on December 31, 1984 when the price per share is $30. By selling the shares acquired later, T will realize a long-term gain of $1,000 which will be recognized in 1985 unless T elects to report the gain in 1984. If the shares were selling at $15 per share on December 31, 1984, T can realize a short-term loss in 1984 by selling the shares acquired on May 1, 1984. Note that a short sale of the shares should be avoided because it will result in a short-term gain or a long-term loss under the short sales rules.

.07   Installment Sale of Securities in a Private Transaction

An investor who has a large security position with substantial un-realized appreciation, and is negotiating a sale thereof in a private transaction, with part or all of the sale price to be paid after the end of the current year, should consider the availability of the installment sales method of reporting the income realized as a way of deferring part or all of the capital gains tax. The proceeds received after the close of the year now will qualify for installment sale treatment even if payments in the year of sale exceed 30 percent of the selling price. The contract should provide for a minimum annual interest in order to avoid the current imputed interest tax provision. Some tender of-fers, where debt obligations are issued, have been arranged so as to enable the seller to use the installment method of reporting the gain. Note, however, that certain demand obligations or readily tradeable obligations received in corporate acquisitions are treated as cash pay-ments. (See ¶**46.10.**) An installment sale with the seller's spouse, other family members, or trusts for family members may be permit-ted under certain circumstances. (See ¶**53.**)

An installment sale can be used to convert interest income into capital gains by means of a private installment sale to a brokerage firm, with payment of the sales proceeds deferred for a period of less than one year.

> **Example (a).** T purchased ABC stock for $20 on July 1, 1984, and the stock is selling for $50 a share on October 1, 1984. T sells the stock to a brokerage firm for $55, the sales proceeds to be paid five months later. The amount of gain and the character of the gain is de-termined at the time of sale, but the $35 short-term gain is not re-ported until the sales proceeds are received on March 1, 1985.

Example (b). T purchased ABC stock for $20 on July 1, 1984, and the stock is selling for $50 a share on December 1, 1984. T sells the stock to a brokerage firm for $52 with payment and delivery to take place on February 1, 1985, pursuant to a trade similar to a deferred delivery under NYSE Rule 64(3). (See ¶5.02.) The intent is that title passes on the delivery date. Therefore, T will realize a long-term gain of $32 when the transaction is consummated on February 1, 1985. Presumably, a deferred delivery can be made with third parties where payment and possession are delayed until the final closing date, and the seller is entitled to vote and to receive any dividends paid on the stock during the interim period.

.08 Tax-free Reorganization

An investor in many corporate reorganizations is given the choice of receiving either cash or stock or both in exchange for his stock. Where his stock has appreciated in value, generally it is desirable to receive stock of the acquiring corporation, thereby deferring the unrealized gain until a subsequent sale of the stock of the acquiring corporation. If an investor has an unrealized loss on his stock, it may be more beneficial to ask for cash in the exchange and thus recognize the loss in the year of the exchange. Note that if there is a pro rata distribution of stock and cash to the shareholders of the acquired corporation in a tax-free reorganization, any loss on the exchange would not be recognized for tax purposes but the receipt of cash may be taxed as a dividend to the extent of any gain.

.09 Exchange of Bonds

Holders of certain U.S. Government bonds may have an opportunity to exchange such bonds for other governmental obligations without recognition of gain. The conversion of Series E bonds into other government obligations has the effect of deferring the interest element until disposition or redemption of the new bonds. Tax-free exchanges of other types of bonds are also permitted. (See ¶46.10 for discussion dealing with exchange of bonds.)

.10 Contribution or Bargain Sale of Securities

A taxpayer can permanently avoid recognition of gain on appreciated securities by giving them to a charity, or can substantially avoid tax on the appreciation by selling them to a charity for a price equal to his basis. The charitable contribution deduction in the former situation is the market value, and in the latter case is the difference between market value and the selling price. A tax on the appreciation can be avoided only for property that qualifies for long-term capital gains treatment. The new six-month holding period for capital assets acquired after June 22, 1984 will make it easier to make tax-free charitable contributions of appreciated property. (See ¶24 for a discussion of the benefits of charitable contributions of low-basis appreciated securities.)

.11 Offsetting Losses

In lieu of postponing gain on sale, an investor may prefer to offset the recognized gain by selling other securities at a loss or by entering into other types of transactions. The use of Listed options, commodities, or other types of options or securities is discussed below. In addition, an investor may prefer to enter into a tax shelter in order to obtain the desired losses. Substantial first year losses can be obtained by entering into cattle or oil transactions. Real estate shelters, on the other hand, will ordinarily throw off deductions over a period of years. (See ¶71 for a discussion of tax shelters.) A long-term capital gain can be offset by a capital loss in a corresponding amount or by an ordinary deduction equal to 40 percent of the long-term gain. However, an ordinary deduction may result in only a 20 percent tax savings if the alternative minimum tax is applicable. (See discussion in ¶61.) The use of a capital loss, however, will also reduce the long-term capital gain deduction tax preference for purposes of the alternative minimum tax, but the tax preference will remain if offsetting ordinary deductions are utilized. For example, assume an investor has long-term capital gains of $50,000 and is entitled to a capital gain deduction of $30,000, which is a tax preference item. The remaining taxable gain of $20,000 can be offset by an ordinary deduction of $20,000, thereby eliminating any taxable gain. There will, however, be an outstanding tax preference item of $30,000. If a $50,000 capital loss were realized in the taxable year, the long-term capital gain would be completely eliminated and there would be no tax preference because there would be no long-term capital gain deduction.

3 INSURE PROPER TIMING AND NATURE OF GAIN OR LOSS

An investor may be in a current security position where some positive action on his part will assure him the desired tax result.

.01 Nature and Timing of Capital Losses

Investors should consider taking capital losses within the applicable short-term period in order to have the loss sustained carried forward as a short-term loss. Long-term losses sustained are carried forward as long-term losses in succeeding years and must first offset long-term gains in the year to which carried before offsetting short-term gains. (See discussion of capital loss carry-overs ¶32.03.) It is important where possible to arrange the year's transactions so that long-term losses are deductible against short-term gains. To the extent that a capital loss offsets a long-term capital gain, the average investor is reducing income tax at an effective maximum rate of only 20 percent. By timing to offset the capital losses against short-term gains, the investor is reducing income that may otherwise be subject to an effective maximum rate of 50 percent.

Example:

	1	2	3	4
Current year long-term gain	$10,000	$10,000	$10,000	—
Current year short-term gain	10,000	10,000	10,000	$10,000
Loss carry-over long-term	—	(10,000)	—	(10,000)
Loss carry-over short-term	—	—	(10,000)	—
Net long-term gain	10,000	—	10,000	—
Net short-term gain	10,000	10,000	—	—
Tax (assume 50 percent bracket)	$ 7,000	$ 5,000	$ 2,000	—

Tax savings on $10,000 long-term capital loss carry-over (compare column 1 with column 2) is $2,000. If the loss carry-over was short-term, such savings would have been $5,000 (compare column 1 with column 3). The same savings can be achieved from a long-term loss carry-over (column 4) only if there are sufficient short-term gains and no long-term gains in the year.

.02 Identification of Securities

Where part of a position in securities is sold or transferred, adequate identification should be made so as to assure proper and desired tax consequences. (See ¶35.01.)

Example.　*Position in XYZ Co.:*

Date purchased	Shares	Basis
January 5, 1977	100	$1,000
March 10, 1978	100	3,300
March 15, 1983	100	1,500
September 30, 1984	100	2,800

On December 15, 1984, the investor sells 100 shares for $3,000. By identifying the shares sold, he will recognize either long-term gain (against purchase 1/5/77 or 3/15/83), short-term gain (against purchase 9/30/84) or long-term loss (against purchase 3/10/78). The choice is his. Without proper identification of the certificates delivered, the stock from the 1/5/77 purchase will be deemed the 100 shares sold. (See ¶35.02(c).)

.03　Worthless Securities—When and How to Take a Loss

It is frequently difficult to establish the worthlessness of a security in order to obtain a deduction. Generally, a sale for more than a nominal amount will show that worthlessness did not occur in an earlier year barred by the statute of limitations for refunds. Because of the difficulty of establishing a worthless stock deduction, it is preferable, where feasible, to sell the stock at a nominal price to an unrelated party, such as a broker. Where the year of worthlessness is in doubt, protective claims for refunds should be filed for each possible year. (See ¶47.)

.04　Create Wash Sales

Under certain circumstances it may be desirable to create a wash sale so as to add back, to the basis of the newly acquired security, the disallowed loss and holding period. This may prove advantageous where the investor, within 30 days after the sale of securities at a loss, realizes the disadvantageous timing of the capital transactions. (See the discussion of wash sale rules, ¶36.01.)

Example (a).　T, after holding ABC stock for 5½ months, liquidates his position in 1985 to realize a short-term loss. Subsequently, but within the next 30 days, ABC stock suddenly starts to rise. T now feels that ABC stock has potential appreciation. By repurchasing ABC stock within 30 days after the previous sale, under the wash sale provisions his loss is not recognized for tax purposes and, instead, such loss would increase the basis of the new shares acquired. What is more important is that the ABC stock will start off with a 5½ month holding period, thus according sudden substantial overall gain long-term capital gain treatment by merely holding ABC stock for an additional one-half-month period.

Example (b). T, on January 2, 1984 purchased 100 shares of ABC stock at $100 per share (Lot 1) and 11 months later on December 3, 1984, purchased an additional 100 shares at $70 per share (Lot 2). By December 20, 1984, ABC has substantially appreciated in value and is selling at $95 per share. If T sells the 200 shares of ABC at $95 per share, he will recognize a net short-term gain of $2,000 ($2,500 gain on Lot 2 less $500 loss on Lot 1).

If instead, T sold 100 shares (Lot 1) on December 20, 1984, the $500 loss sustained is not recognized for tax purposes since T acquired 100 shares of ABC stock (Lot 2) within 30 days prior to such sale. Thus, the $500 loss would increase to $7,500 the basis of the 100 shares acquired on December 3, 1984. More relevant is the new holding period of the remaining 100 shares of ABC stock. The 11-month, 18-day holding period of the Lot 1 shares is added to the 17-day holding period of the Lot 2 100 shares. Thus, for tax purposes, the remaining 100 shares of ABC stock are deemed to have been held for more than six months and a sale of such shares on the next day, December 21, 1984, for $9,500 will result in the $2,000 net gain being treated as long-term.[3]

Example (c). T sells ABC stock and realizes a short-term loss. Subsequently, he discovers that he would obtain a greater tax benefit if the short-term loss were taken in the next year since he has realized long-term gains in the current year and expects to realize short-term gains in the subsequent year. Therefore, he repurchases the shares within 30 days and resells the stock at a loss in the subsequent year. The short-term loss is then offset against short-term gains and any excess against ordinary income, subject to limitations.

Example (d). Assume T realized a long-term loss on the sale of stock, which could only be offset against long-term capital gains, or ordinary income at the rate of two dollars of loss for every dollar of

[3] Code: 1223 (4).

ordinary income. By utilizing the wash sales provisions, he can carry the long-term loss into the next year and apply it against short-term gains.

Example (e). T inadvertently sells shares to a related party and the loss is disallowed under Section 267. (See ¶53.) Within 30 days he repurchases the shares and later obtains an allowable loss by selling the shares to an unrelated person.

Example (f). T owns 100 shares of ABC stock for several years at $100 per share. ABC stock is currently selling at $40 per share and T wishes to sell his investment and recognize his loss. However, the sale would produce a long-term capital loss of $60 per share. If T had sold or written a Listed Call on ABC stock and now purchases the same Call "open" (i.e., creates what is tantamount to a short against the box in Listed options) and within 30 days sells ABC stock for $40 per share, the $6,000 loss would be disallowed under the wash sales rules and would be added to the basis of the Listed Call purchased open. (The holding period of the option should also include the holding period of the ABC stock. However, this point may be irrelevant.) Thereafter, the long Call is "delivered" against the "short" Call to close. Any gain or loss on the closing of a short Call would be short-term. Accordingly, the $6,000 loss, which otherwise would have been long-term, now may become short-term capital loss (see ¶39 for a full discussion of options and an analysis of the technical and administrative procedures concerning option trading).

Example (g). T has owned 100 shares of ABC stock for several years with a tax basis of $100 per share. T wishes to sell the 100 shares at the current market value of $40 and recognize a $6,000 loss. However, he wishes to convert the loss which otherwise would have been a long-term capital loss into a short-term capital loss. T could purchase a Call on ABC stock at a strike price of 40 and sell the ABC stock at 40. The $6,000 loss would be disallowed under the wash sale rules and should be added to the basis of the Call. In addition, the holding period of the stock should also be added to the holding period of the Call. T would exercise the Call and purchase the stock (i.e., ABC stock at $40 per share). The basis of the newly acquired stock would include the basis of the option (i.e., the disallowed loss in the stock sale, $6,000, plus the premium on the Call and the amount paid for the new stock, $4,000). However, the holding period should completely disappear, and thus the immediate sale of the newly acquired ABC stock would result in a capital loss, which should be accorded short-term capital loss treatment. The cost of accomplishing this objective might be too significant (i.e., commission costs on the exercise of the option and on the sale of the second lot of stock, and, in addition, the premium paid for the Call).

Example (h). T has owned 100 shares of ABC stock for almost six months with a tax basis of $100 per share. T wishes to maintain his position in ABC stock even though ABC is now selling at $40 per share, but does not wish the potential loss to mature to long-term status. T purchases a Put on ABC stock. It should not matter what the striking price of the Put is nor the duration of the Put, because the mere acquisition of the Put should cause the short sale rules to apply, resulting in the loss of the holding period on the 100 shares of stock. The subsequent disposition of the Put or lapse of the Put will start a new holding period for the stock (see ¶**37.03(d)**).

In 1984 and 1985, wash sales can be used under certain circumstances to reduce the necessary holding period for long-term capital gain treatment from 12 months to 6 months.

Example. T buys ABC stock on June 15, 1984, for $40 per share. On January 10, 1985, when ABC is selling for $38 per share, T sells his stock. However, on January 11, 1985, T buys back 100 shares of ABC for $38 per share believing that the stock will appreciate. As a result of such a subsequent purchase, the wash sale rules come into play. On January 18, 1985, T sells his ABC stock for $45 per share. T will realize a long-term capital gain of $5 per share on the sale. Since the stock was acquired after June 22, 1984, the six-month holding period rule applies for long-term capital gain treatment. To measure the holding period when the wash sale rules apply, the holding period for the first block of stock is added to the holding period for the stock acquired in the wash sale. Therefore, the holding period for the stock acquired on January 11, 1985 will also include the period from June 15 through January 10. Thus, the sale of the newly acquired ABC stock will result in long-term treatment since it has been held for more than six months and is property acquired after June 22, 1984.

.05 Option Spreads—Create Gain and Loss in Different Taxable Years

The economic as well as the potential tax consequences of various option spread techniques have and will become more important with the increased listing of many more options—both Puts and Calls—and with the closing of what was perceived to be a loophole by the use of commodity straddles (i.e., deferral of and possibly conversion of short-term gain).

Example (a). For purposes of this illustration, assume that in 1983, T realized $20,000 of short-term gains from other transactions. On October 1, 1983, when ABC was selling at $50 per share, T purchased 10 Calls on ABC with an exercise price of 45 expiring January 21, 1984 (January 45 Calls), for a cost of $7,000 ($7 per share) and sold (wrote) 10 Calls on ABC with an exercise price of 50 expiring January 21, 1984 (January 50 Calls), for a premium of $4,000 ($4 per share). T had invested $3,000 with a maximum possible gain of $2,000 if ABC was selling at 50 or more by January 21, 1984, or a maximum loss potential of $3,000 if ABC was selling at 45 or less by January 21, 1984. It is interesting to note that if the price of ABC remains stable, T would make $2,000 on a $3,000 investment in three and one half months. This transaction is referred to as a *bull spread* (i.e., bullish on ABC).

Assume ABC rose to 74 by December 30, 1983, in which case the January 45 Call and the January 50 Call would be selling at approximately 29 and 24 respectively (parity). T could have bought in the short January 50 Call for $24,000 and recognized a $20,000 short-term capital loss in 1983, offsetting the previously recognized capital gains. In order to protect the built-in gain in the January 45 Calls, T could have written a higher priced Call on ABC, sold the January 45 Calls, effectively short against the box, or employed other strategies. A sale in 1984 or even on December 30, 1983 (settlement in 1984) for $29,000 would cause the gain of $22,000 to be recognized in 1984.

This strategy would not be effective for positions entered into after 1983 where there is a substantial diminution of risk of loss under the new tax straddle rules (¶38.02). The above example illustrates an economically risky "near the money" bull spread with the primary intent being profit. The new straddle rules were intended to apply to deep-in-the-money spreads where there is little economic potential or exposure, but rather a primary objective of deferral of income. The authors question whether in the above illustration the subjective test of substantial diminution of risk of loss is met so that the tax straddle rules are applicable.

Example (b). Assume the same facts as in **Example (a)** except that on October 1, 1984, when ABC is selling at $50 per share, T purchases 10 ABC Calls with an exercise price of 50 expiring January 19, 1985 (January 50 Calls) for a cost of $3,000 ($3 per share) and sells (writes) 10 ABC Calls with an exercise price of 55 expiring January 19, 1985 (January 55 Calls) for a premium of $1,000 ($1 per share). In this example, T has invested $2,000 with a maximum economic gain potential of $3,000.

Further assume that ABC rose to 74 by December 28, 1984, in which case the January 50 Call and the January 55 Call would be selling at approximately 24 and 19 respectively. T could buy in the short January 55 Call for $19,000 and recognize an $18,000 short-term capital loss in 1984, offsetting the previously recognized capital gains. In order to protect the built-in gain on the January 50 Calls, T could write a higher priced Call on ABC, sell the January 50 Calls, effectively short against the box, or employ other strategies.

When compared to **Example (a)** above, this bull spread should be unaffected by the 1984 Act. This is because out-of-the-money covered options should not be subject to the loss deferral rules, since the positions do not substantially diminish risk, and, therefore, do not constitute a straddle. In addition, subsequent movement in the price of the stock should not cause the straddle rules to come into play.

.06 Qualified Covered Calls—Create Gain and Loss in Different Taxable Years

The ability to create gains and losses in different taxable years with option spreads, as discussed above, (**¶3.05**) may be available in certain covered writing situations.

Example (a). T owns ABC stock and has written a qualified covered Call option on ABC. Thus, T is not generally subject to the loss deferral rules with respect to these holdings. Assume that T closes out the short Call for a loss in December, and then writes a new qualified covered Call. The straddle rules require that a loss on a qualified covered Call be deferred if the underlying stock is sold at a gain in a later taxable year, and the stock is not held for 30 days or more after closing the option. For this purpose, holding period does not include the time the investor was the grantor (writer) of a Call unless the Call is a qualified covered Call.

Therefore, in the above example, closing the qualified covered Call at a loss followed by reestablishing the qualified covered Call position will not cause the loss deferral rules to come into play.

Example (b). T purchases ABC stock at $40 per share on July 31, 1984. On November 1, 1984, ABC is selling for $47 per share. At that time, T sells Calls at $50 for $2 per share. Since the Calls are out of the money, T's holding period for ABC stock will continue to accrue. If, at year-end, the stock price has risen to $60 per share, T can close out the Call for an $8 loss while deferring the gain on the ABC stock until 1985. Note that if T had originally sold a 45 Call (an in-the-money Call), T's holding period for the stock would have been suspended.

.07 Qualified Covered Calls—Suspend Holding Period

An investor who is holding stock with an unrecognized loss and a less than six-month holding period should consider the sale of a qualified covered Call to stop the holding period of the stock. Under the tax straddle rules, selling an in-the-money qualified covered Call will suspend the holding period on the underlying stock. Where the sale of stock would result in a loss, the investor may want to suspend the holding period before the loss has matured into a long-term loss. The investor can continue to hold the stock and have the choice of recognizing a short-term loss if the stock price does not increase, or of closing out the Call and letting the stock mature into a long-term gain if the stock price rises.

.08 Covered Writing—Transitional Rule

The expansion of the loss deferral rules to stock and stock options (¶39.11) is effective for positions established after December 31, 1983. It appears that stock acquired prior to 1984 can be offset with options or any other position without being subject to the loss deferral rules. The same should be true for any other pre-1984 acquisitions of property that were not subject to the tax straddle rules when acquired, but which would be if acquired after 1983 (e.g., Listed options).

.09 Obligations Issued at a Discount

A simple means of deferring ordinary income is to buy short-term obligations at a discount (e.g., a Treasury bill or one-year certificate of deposit). The discount is not included in the income of a cash-basis investor until the obligation is sold or matures. However, if the obligation is purchased on margin or with other direct financing, the net interest expense is deferred to the extent of the deferred accrued discount on the bond. An investor in a leveraged purchase may find it more beneficial to elect to include the accrued bond discount into income using the lower compound interest method and also currently deduct the interest expense. It is sometimes difficult to show a potential economic profit on these leveraged short-term obligation purchases. Repurchase agreements (Repos) executed on a 30-day basis with one-year Treasury bills are an example in which there is a potential economic profit on the assumption that interest rates remain constant. However, increases in short-term borrowing rates could cause a substantial economic loss. With current volatile interest rates, it should be easier to demonstrate a profit motive for shorter-term Treasuries. (See ¶46.09(b).)

An investor may elect in any taxable year to include in income annually the increase in the redemption value of certain non-interest-bearing obligations issued at a discount, such as Series E savings bonds. Thus, if it is advantageous to increase income of a given year, the election can be made. If an election is not made during his lifetime, it can be made on the deceased investor's final return. (See ¶19.02.)

.10 Sale of Municipal Bonds at a Loss (Bond Swaps)

Many tax-exempt bonds are selling far below their original offering price because of the increase in interest rates since the tax-exempt bonds were issued. Holders of these bonds have the choice of selling them at a loss or holding them until maturity and receiving the face value of the bonds upon redemption. A sale of these bonds gives the investor not only a capital loss, which can be offset against capital gains and to a limited extent against income, but also provides an opportunity to upgrade the investments or purchase bonds with proportionately higher yields. For example, T purchased $10,000 of 7 percent municipal bonds, which mature in 1989 and which are presently selling at 80, or $8,000 for all of the bonds. By selling the bonds T would recognize a $2,000 capital loss. The proceeds are then reinvested in 10 percent tax-exempts, thereby increasing the tax-free interest yield from $700 to $800. The current use of the capital loss plus the increased interest yield may more than offset the loss of $2,000 upon redemption of the bonds at maturity. Note that the wash sales rules do not apply to the losses where securities which are not substantially identical are acquired.

4 PROTECT APPRECIATION ON LONG-TERM POSITION WITH POSSIBILITY OF ADDITIONAL LONG-TERM CAPITAL GAINS

If the investor has held a profitable position for more than the applicable long-term holding period and wants to protect the long-term capital gain, he may consider selling the stock short against the box and simultaneously purchasing a Call. Thus, for the cost of a Call, he is both ensuring his present economic gain and also obtaining the benefit of any future appreciation in the stock.

Example. T, on June 1, 1983, purchased 100 shares of ABC stock at $20. On July 1, 1984, ABC stock is selling at $30. T could buy one Jan ABC 30 at $3 ($300) and sell short 100 shares of ABC at $30. If ABC declines below $30 by the middle of January 1985, the long position could be delivered against the short position resulting in a $1,000 long-term capital gain, and the worthless Call would result in a $300 long-term capital loss. If ABC should rise to $50, the 100 share long position could be sold, resulting in $3,000 long-term capital gain, and a $300 long-term capital loss would result under the short sale rules on the exercise of the Call and delivery of the stock to close the short position. The net long-term capital gain would be $2,700. Thus, T was able to insure a minimum long-term capital gain at a cost of $300, and, if successful, as in the example, obtain an additional economic gain of $1,700 for a total of $2,700 of long-term capital gain.

5 CONVERT SHORT-TERM GAIN INTO LONG-TERM GAIN

Investors owning appreciated securities or options for less than the applicable long-term holding period may wish to protect their economic gain and still maintain their position in order to have the recognized gain treated as long-term. The after-tax benefits that can be derived from converting short-term gains into long-term gains by means of the ensuing transactions are illustrated in the following chart.

Correlation between after-tax benefits of short-term and long-term gains

Tax bracket of investor (percent)	Short-term	Long-term
50%	$10	$6¼*
45	10	6¾
40	10	7⅛
35	10	7½
30	10	8

*A $6.25 long-term capital gain is equivalent to a $10 short-term capital gain when measured in terms of after-tax profit to the taxpayer in the 50 percent tax bracket. Thus, an investor could incur expenses or losses of more than $3 to obtain long-term capital gains and still retain more after-tax dollars than by realizing a $10 short-term gain.

.01 In General

Before passage of the 1984 Act, an investor who owned appreciated stock for less than one year could sell a Call on the stock which would not expire until the stock had been held for more than one year. The investor would thus give the purchaser of the Call an option to acquire the stock at a specific price within a specified period of time. If the stock moderately increased in value and the Call was exercised toward the end of its term, the investor would be assured of a long-term capital gain to the extent that the Call proceeds exceeded the basis of the stock. If the stock substantially increased in value, the investor could buy other shares in the open market to deliver against the Call or, if dealing in Listed Calls, buy the Call long in a closing transaction, recognize a short-term loss, and sell the long position for a greater long-term gain. Writing Calls may further increase gains or reduce losses to the extent of premiums received on the Calls if the investor expects that the stock will not appreciate much or may fall in the near future, but also expects the price to rise after a period of time. Under the 1984 Act, the holding period for stock not held for the applicable long-term holding period will either be terminated under rules similar to the short sales rules or suspended depending upon whether the Call is an in-the-money qualified covered Call. (See ¶39.11.) However, writing out-of-the-money qualified covered Calls to provide some protection against downside risk does not affect the holding period of the stock. In addition, termination of the Call at a loss will result in a long-term loss if sale of the underlying stock at that time would have given rise to a long-term gain.

.02 Deferred Delivery under NYSE Rule 64(3) (Seller's Option)

The investor may take advantage of the current market price and still prolong his holding period for up to 60 days. This is accomplished by selling at today's market price, and contracting that payment and delivery will take place on a specified date within 60 days following the date of contract, with all dividends to stockholders of record before the delivery date belonging to the seller. Special arrangements must be made to have the dividends accrue to the seller. Otherwise, under the normal deferred delivery transaction, dividends payable after the contract date would go to the buyer, which might affect the rule on when the sale takes place. The intent of the parties is that title passes on the delivery date. Thus, an investor who has a holding period that is within 60 days of the applicable long-term capital gain period could convert an unrealized short-term gain into a long-term gain without any economic risk. It is understood that the Treasury's position in such a case is that the contract date is not regarded as controlling, and that the sale does not take place until the delivery date. A slight reduction in sales price is generally required to obtain a purchaser for deferred delivery stock. The authors do not believe that the contract for sale should be considered a formal sale of stock until it is closed and, therefore, a "position" in stock so as to come within the tax straddle rules for offsetting positions.

Example. T acquired XYZ stock on February 1, 1984, at $30 per share. On December 15, 1984, the market value has risen to $64, at which time T wishes to liquidate his position and thereby protect his gain. By selling on a deferred delivery basis, for delivery on February 2, 1985, usually at a $1 to $2 discount (assuming no usual dividend record date falls in the interim), T will recognize in 1985 long-term gain of approximately $32 per share ($62 discounted selling price less $30 cost) in lieu of recognizing $34 short-term gain per share in 1984. T, who is in the 50 percent tax bracket, will earn in after-tax dollars, $25.60 per share under the deferred delivery sale, in lieu of $17 per share had he sold the stock in the regular way on December 15, 1984.

The authors believe that an extension of the holding period can also be obtained in a private sale. An executory contract may provide that the security holder will deliver the security for an agreed-upon price at a specified date. During the interim period, the holder is entitled to all dividends and may vote the shares. Theoretically, the holder is also free to sell the security and may purchase and deliver similar securities at the time the contract is executed. As indicated above, the tax straddle rules should not apply.

.03 Elect Not to Defer Installment Gains

An investor may have realized substantial long-term capital gains and short-term losses during the taxable year. In the same year, the investor may have also realized a short-term gain in a year-end sale or an installment sale with the sales proceeds to be received in the following year. If no election is made, the long-term gains will be offset against the short-term losses and the short-term gain will be recognized in the following year. By electing not to use the installment method, the short-term gain will be recognized in the year of sale. As a result, it can be offset by the short-term loss, leaving a long-term capital gain for the year. This can result in substantial tax savings when compared to a one-year deferral in paying the higher tax on the short-term gain. (See ¶50 for a discussion of installment sales.)

6 CREATE SHORT-TERM CAPITAL LOSS AND 60 PERCENT LONG-TERM CAPITAL GAIN

.01 Mixed Straddles—Stock and Broad-Based Stock Index Options

Investors are sometimes faced with selling their substantial stock portfolio (incurring large selling costs) because of poor market conditions and possibly suffering substantial economic losses. The introduction of stock index options gives the investor the alternative of leaving his investment virtually intact and selling short stock index options. If the expected decrease in stock prices occurs, the investor should have capital losses (short or long term, depending on the holding period) on his stock investments and a 60/40 capital gain on the broad-based options. Since these stock index options ordinarily are not substantially similar and may not fully hedge the risk on the long positions, it is questionable whether they could be treated as part of a mixed straddle. The issue is whether the portfolio "mimics" the stock index options, thus substantially reducing risk of loss. Short-term trading in both the long and short side of broad-based stock index options has the additional tax advantage of creating 60 percent long-term gains no matter how short the duration of the position. (See ¶38.04 and ¶39.10.)

.02 Mixed Straddles—Cash and Carry Transactions

Prior to the 1981 Economic Recovery Tax Act (ERTA), sophisticated investors could find economic opportunities in cash and carry transactions, and, if they were successful, the tax implications were interesting. For example, T, expecting gold to fall in value, purchases 100 ounces of spot gold at $450 per ounce (referred to as one warrant) and simultaneously sells one regulated Futures contract (Futures) three months out at $470 per ounce. (The spread represents an annual interest yield of 18 percent.) Assume that one week later, gold has fallen by $30 per ounce, such that the spot gold (or warrant) was worth $420, and the Futures (taking into consideration reduced value without any change in interest rates) was selling at $438 per ounce. By collapsing both positions, T would lose $3,000 on the spot commodity. (Interest expense for the one week that had to be capitalized on the spot commodity was disregarded for purposes of the illustration.) This would be a short-term capital loss. The repurchase of the short Futures would result in a gain of $3,200, of which 40 percent ($1,280) would be short-term and 60 percent ($1,920) long-term. Thus, a net short-term loss of $1,720 and a long-term capital gain of $1,920 would result from the transaction. Under the 1984 Act (generally effective after 1983), only the net gain or loss from the mixed straddle position will receive 60/40 long-term/short-term capital gain treatment. While the potential for short-term losses has been eliminated, the ability to obtain the 60 percent long-term gain treatment on the net gains should not be overlooked. The authors believe that short-term trading, both on the long and short side of commodity Futures, has become more advantageous after the recent changes in the tax law. This is also true of other Section 1256 contracts, especially broad-based index options.

7 CONVERT CAPITAL LOSS INTO ORDINARY DEDUCTION

An investor may have incurred a substantial capital loss and does not expect to realize offsetting capital gains in the near future. The capital loss may be offset against ordinary income, within limitations, but it may take many years before the investor could fully utilize the capital loss in this manner. He may be of advanced age and there may be a good likelihood that he will die before obtaining the full benefit of his capital loss. Any unused capital loss would expire with his demise. In addition, if the loss is long-term, it would require $2 of the long-term loss to offset $1 of ordinary income, so that the investor would in effect lose the benefit of one-half his loss. A capital gain created to offset the large capital loss would result, in effect, in "tax-free income," while the ordinary deduction would offset ordinary income. (See ¶9 for a discussion of creating capital gains and ordinary deductions.)

8 CREATE LONG-TERM GAIN AND SHORT-TERM LOSS

The ensuing transactions may create the desired short-term capital loss which will offset existing short-term capital gains, or short-term capital gains created from naked or covered option writing (see ¶9.01), or other similar transactions, and simultaneously create the desired long-term capital gain.

.01 Arbitraging Securities Not Substantially Identical

Long-term capital gains can be obtained in arbitrage situations if the long position is held open for the applicable long-term holding period and if the securities sold short are not "substantially identical" to the long securities for purposes of the short sale rules.[4] (See ¶37.04.)

> **Example.** X and Y corporations plan to merge and the stock of X corporation will be exchanged evenly for shares of Y corporation. Prior to approval by the shareholders, the two securities are not considered to be substantially identical. (See ¶37.04.) X stock is selling at $20 and Y stock is selling at $22. The investor buys X stock and sells Y stock short. It is immaterial that the X stock subsequently becomes "substantially identical" to the Y stock. It should also be immaterial that after an exchange for X stock, Y stock is now held in a long position. The exchange should not be deemed an acquisition of the Y stock bringing into play the short sale rules. (See ¶37.03.)
>
> The closing of the long position of the Y stock received in the exchange against the short position of Y after the requisite long-term holding period will result in long-term gain to the extent of the initial spread of $2 per share. If the value of Y stock at the time of delivery rises above $22 per share, then the Y stock received on the exchange should be sold in order to recognize long-term capital gains greater

---

[4] Rev. Rul. 62-153, C.B. 1962-2, 186. The Treasury may by regulations, treat certain arbitrage situations as falling under the tax straddle rules, but not solely stock arbitrages. If this is done, the short sales rules would apply to the holding period of the offsetting positions. Code: 1092(d)(3).

than the initial spread of $2 per share. The short position should be covered through the purchase in the open market of Y stock, resulting in the recognition of a short-term capital loss which could be utilized to offset short-term capital gains. The net economic gain will be equal to the initial spread of $2 per share, but the character of the gain and loss for tax purposes will be different.

9　CREATE CAPITAL GAIN AND ORDINARY DEDUCTION

Certain forms of investments discussed below, by their component steps and tax treatment, have created capital gain and ordinary deduction. Many investors have avoided these types of investments because of apparent complexities and oftentimes undesired short-term capital gain results. However, sophisticated investors have realized that the pure economics (i.e., the profit potential) is overriding, and have accepted these forms of investments as the most desirable from a risk-reward viewpoint. Until the change in the law, they looked to additional types of investments, such as the commodity straddle transactions to offset the short-term capital gains and create long-term capital gains.

Sometimes the separate tax treatment of each component of these transactions can be beneficial to the taxpayer without any further transactions. For example, investors with substantial capital loss carryovers will effectively have the short-term capital gain treated as tax-free income.

.01　Covered Option Writing

Covered option writing (i.e., writing one Call for each 100 shares of stock owned or, in the alternative, writing one Put for each 100 shares of stock sold short) may result in a reduction of risk of loss under adverse market conditions and increased economic yield on the investment position. Covered option writing on a fully margined basis will tend to further increase the economic yield under stable or positive market conditions. (See ¶39 for detailed discussion of options.)

> **Example.**　On September 28, 1984, T purchases 1,000 shares of ABC stock at $28½ and writes 10 ABC Calls, January 25s, for a premium of $650 each ($6½ per share) or a total of $6,500. Thus, T is selling to an investor the right to purchase 1,000 shares of ABC stock at $25 per share any time between September 28, 1984, and

January 18, 1985. The intrinsic value of the Call is $3½ per share (the difference between $28½ fair market value and $25 striking price of the Call), and the balance of the premium on the Call of $3 per share represents the time value portion. Assuming no change in price of the underlying stock, the time value generally diminishes as the Call approaches expiration. Disregarding commission expense, the maximum economic gain that T could realize, which will occur as long as ABC stock stays at or above $25 per share, is $3,000, which will be short-term capital gain in 1985 if the Call is exercised after December 21, 1984. This amount will be reduced by the interest cost on the borrowed funds of $14,250 by approximately $400, most of which will be deducted in 1984. The net cash amount invested by T is approximately $8,000 (50 percent of $28,500, less the Call premium of $6,500). T cannot incur an economic loss unless ABC stock falls below $22 per share ($28½ cost less option premium of $6½). The amount of the time value premium is a function of the volatility of the underlying stock (period of time to expiration and the relationship of intrinsic value to total premium). Generally, as the intrinsic value increases, the time premium will shrink, irrespective of time to expiration.

If the Call should expire unexercised (i.e., ABC stock is selling below $25), the $6,500 premium will be short-term capital gain in 1985. If ABC stock is also sold (e.g., sold at $24 per share), the resulting loss will be a short-term capital loss of $4,500.

If ABC should rise to $40 per share, T may wish to buy, in a closing transaction, the ABC January 25s for the equivalent of $15 per share ($15,000 for 10 Calls) and recognize a short-term capital loss of $8,500. T could write higher striking price and longer duration ABC Calls (e.g., October 35s) with a view toward obtaining additional yield. The holding period of the underlying stock would be suspended while the in-the-money qualified covered Call is outstanding. Therefore, the ABC stock would have no holding period, because the period is suspended while the in-the-money Call is outstanding.

.02 Selling Short before Ex-Dividend Date

An investor intending to establish a short position should enter into the short sale before the ex-dividend date in order to obtain an ordinary deduction for the amount paid as a dividend on the short sale and thus have the resulting equivalent amount potentially available as capital gain. To qualify for a deduction, the short sale must remain open for at least 46 days, and the dividend must not qualify as an extraordinary dividend (5 percent preferred stock dividend, 10 percent common stock dividend, 20 percent aggregate dividends in a 365-day period). The deduction will be subject to the investment interest expense limitations. (See **¶51.06.**) Generally, the market value of the stock on the ex-dividend date falls in an amount equal to the dividend paid. If the investor subsequently covers his short position and there is no other variation in the value of the stock, he will realize a short-term capital gain approximately equivalent to the amount paid as a dividend on the short sale. The same possibility may exist with respect to selling short a flat bond where significant arrearage interest will be paid in the near future. A short-term gain might be desired in order to offset short-term losses that would otherwise offset long-term gains. However, it should be noted that where the sole purpose of the transaction is tax avoidance, the deductibility of the dividend paid may be questioned. (See **¶51.06.**)

Example (a).   ABC stock is scheduled to go ex-dividend a $1 dividend on December 15, 1984. T wishes to sell the stock short at $60. If he establishes the short position prior to December 15, 1984, he will have to pay $1 per share for such a dividend, for which he becomes entitled to a $1 per share ordinary deduction by keeping the short position open for more than 45 days. Assuming there is no other change in market value, ABC stock should fall in price to $59, thereby creating a potential short-term gain of $1 per share. However, if T waits until December 15, 1984, he will establish his short position at a price of $59 per share, the market value on that day. T will not have any ordinary deduction or the built-in potential capital gain of $1 per share.

Example (b).   ABC 6½ percent debentures are trading flat at $86. An arrearage interest payment of 2½ years or $16.25 will be paid on December 1, 1984. T wishes to sell the debenture short on the assumption that the debenture, after the interest payment, will fall in price more than $16.25. Assuming no other changes in market value, ABC debenture should decrease in price to $69.75 thereby creating a potential short-term gain of $162.50 per $1,000 bond. T will have to pay $162.50 per $1,000 bond on the short side which should be an ordinary deduction (see **¶51.06**).

.03   Sale and Repurchase of Appreciated Bonds

Holders of taxable bonds which are selling at a premium and have appreciated in value, for example, because of changes in the going interest rate, should sell the bonds, and shortly thereafter repurchase an equal number of the same bonds. Gains on the sale of the bonds held for more than one year are taxed at the lower capital gains rate. The premium paid on the subsequent repurchase (not attributable to any conversion privilege) may be deducted against ordinary income through amortization usually computed to the maturity date.[5] (See ¶46.02(b).)

> **Example.** T owns $50,000 of 15 percent noncallable and nonconvertible XYZ bonds due January 1, 1990, which he acquired at par in 1983. These bonds on January 2, 1985, are selling at 105 and are therefore worth $52,500. If T sells these bonds, he will recognize a long-term capital gain of $2,500. Assuming he still wants to maintain his investment position in these bonds, he would repurchase them at 105 for $52,500. T should then elect to amortize the $2,500 premium over the remaining term of the bonds. Thus, T would be entitled to a deduction against ordinary income of $500 per year ($2,500 amortized over the period of 1985 through 1990). T, in the 50 percent tax bracket, may pay a capital gain tax of $500 in 1985, but would have available ordinary deductions each year, which might result in tax savings of $250 annually or $1,250 over the five-year period.

.04 Market Discount Bonds

When interest rates are high, many high-grade low-interest-rate bonds sell at substantial market discounts. Investors who anticipate a decline in the interest rates are in a position to make large gains by purchasing these deep discount bonds on the highest margin available. Before the 1984 Act, the spread between the purchase price and the amount received from sale or redemption was taxed at capital gain rates in the year of disposition, and any interest paid on the financing was currently deductible, subject to the investment interest expense limitations. (See ¶51.05.) The interest income received on the bonds is always taxable at ordinary income rates. Accordingly, the higher the income tax bracket of the investor, the greater his after-tax gain.

An investor may still obtain the benefit of capital gains treatment on the market discount by purchasing bonds issued before July 19, 1984. However, the purchase should not be made with borrowed funds or else the capital gains will be converted into ordinary income to the extent of the interest expense that cannot be deducted until the bond is sold.

---

[5]Rev. Rul. 55-343, C.B. 1955-1, 381.

While market discount on bonds issued after July 18, 1984 is generally taxed as ordinary income at the time of disposition, an election can be made to report the discount income currently by use of the compound interest method. This produces less ordinary income in earlier years than would be produced if the discount income were deferred. All of the interest income incurred in financing the purchase would be currently deductible, and any gain realized on disposition of the bond would be taxed as capital gains. This election may prove to be especially beneficial for investors with investment interest expense limitations. (See ¶**46.09(c)**.)

.05   Nondividend-Paying Stock

Long-term gain and ordinary deduction can also be obtained by purchasing on margin nondividend-paying stock of a corporation which plows all of the corporate profits back into the business. The average investor can deduct the interest paid on the margin and pay capital gains tax on sale of the stock. (See ¶**51.05** for discussion of limitations on the deductibility of investment interest expense.)

> **Example.**   On January 2, 1984, T purchases on 50 percent margin 100 shares of ABC stock for $50,000. T pays the maximum amount of deductible interest in 1984, and deducts this amount in the year paid. On January 3, 1985, the stock has appreciated in value to $60,000 and T sells the stock and pays a capital gains tax on the $10,000 gain.

.06   Tax Shelters

Certain types of tax shelters can also generate ordinary deductions and capital gains upon disposition. Real estate investments can still produce losses during the early years (but there are transitional rules limiting construction period deductions except for low-cost housing) and a gain on sale will be treated as capital gains after first recapturing certain depreciation in excess of straight-line depreciation. An oil and gas investment will throw off larger deductions in the first year, but under the new rules gain on a subsequent sale will be treated as ordinary income to the extent of excess intangible drilling expenses. Investing in a breeder cattle program for a period of approximately five years will also result in ordinary deductions in the early years and capital gains primarily from the sale of cattle born after commencement of the cattle breeder program. (See ¶**71** for a more detailed discussion of tax shelters.) One of the benefits of tax shelters is that income generally will be deferred for a longer period of time than through the use of securities or commodities. The economic risks involved, the costs of entering into the transaction, and the capital requirements must also be considered before a decision is reached as to the best type of investment to accomplish the desired economic and tax goals.

10   CREATE CAPITAL GAINS—OFFSET BY CAPITAL LOSSES

.01   Forward Conversions—Listed Options

With the expansion of trading in Listed Calls and Puts in recent years and high interest rates, an interesting opportunity exists for the sophisticated investor to generate annual income of 15 to 20 percent in the form of primarily capital gains. Those taxpayers who have capital losses will effectively generate tax-free income. In addition, those taxpayers who have current unrelated short-term capital gains might have an opportunity to generate short-term capital losses this year from conversion transactions and capital gain in the succeeding taxable year. Thus, a net economic gain in the form of capital gain, with the possibility of "timing differences," can be obtained from forward conversion investments for individual taxpayers.

Example.   On October 19, 1984, taxpayer purchases 1,000 shares of ABC at $51 per share, 10 Puts on ABC with an exercise price of 50 expiring January 19, 1985 (Jan 50 Puts), at a cost of $3,000 ($3 per share) and sells (writes) 10 Calls on ABC with an exercise price of 50 expiring January 19, 1985 (Jan 50 Calls), for a premium of $6,000 ($6 per share). The taxpayer will be guaranteed a net economic profit of $2,300 irrespective of the price of the stock in January 1985, resulting in an annual yield of 19¼ percent as shown below. The Put (a "married" Put) will protect him in the event of a decline in price, whereas the stock will be called away if the price of the stock rises.

Cost of 1,000 shares of ABC at $51	$51,000
Cost of 10 ABC Jan 50 Puts	3,000
Estimated total transaction costs	300
Total	$54,300
Less: Premium received—sale of 10 ABC Jan 50 Calls	6,000
Net out-of-pocket cost	$48,300

Profit on close of transaction:
Put or Call proceeds, 1,000 at $50	$50,000
Net out-of-pocket cost	48,300
Net profit	$ 1,700
Estimated dividend income for quarter	600
Total profit	$ 2,300
Effective Annual Yield	19¼%

The $2,300 net economic profit consists of $600 dividend income in 1984 or 1985 with the balance of $1,700 considered to be short-term capital gain taxable in 1985.

In the event that the price of ABC moves substantially at year-end, the taxpayer might collapse the loss side of the transaction, recognizing the capital loss in 1984 and the gain side in 1985 while still earning approximately the same effective annual yield. The ability to create a loss in one year and a gain in the next might be frustrated by the applicability of the new loss deferral/straddle rules.

The new, complicated tax straddle rules and the reduction of the holding period for long-term capital gains to six months make the forward conversion transactions discussed above a more interesting opportunity under the new law. If the covered Call written is an out-of-the-money qualified covered Call, the suspension of the holding period and the loss deferral rules should not apply. However, one could argue that a technical reading of the statute dealing with loss deferral rules would cause the married Put to be considered a position that substantially diminishes the risk of loss on the stock and, accordingly, the covered Call is no longer excluded from the loss deferral rules.

11   OBTAIN LONG–TERM GAINS IN A DECLINING MARKET—ACQUISITION OF A PUT IN LIEU OF SELLING SHORT

If the investor is bearish with regard to a particular stock, he should consider the purchase of a more-than-six-month Listed or Unlisted Put in lieu of selling the stock short. In the event his expectations of a falling market are realized, he may sell the Put just prior to its expiration (or after a six-month holding period), recognizing long-term gain. (See ¶12.01 and ¶39.04(b).) The investor's gain will be lower, as compared to a short sale of the stock (by the cost of the Put), but the gain will be taxed at substantially lower rates. On the other hand, had the investor sold the stock short, any gain on the closing of the short sale would be short-term. (See ¶37.) If the stock should rise in price, the investor should sell the Put prior to the six-month holding period in order to have the loss sustained treated as short-term. (See ¶39.04(b).) His loss would be limited to the cost of the Put. However, with a short sale, his loss could be substantially greater. In view of the fact that the amount of funds necessary to acquire a Put may be substantially less than the funds necessary to margin a short sale, greater economic leverage may be obtained by acquiring a Put. The economic leverage may be further increased through the acquisition of an out-of-the-money Put (the option price of the stock is below the current market price) at a substantially reduced cost, but with the potential profit also reduced to the extent of the discount.

Example. T expects XYZ stock selling at $30 per share to fall in price. T purchases a more-than-six-month Put for $400, which gives him the right to sell 100 shares of XYZ stock at $30 during the term of the option. Assume that at the end of six months, XYZ stock is selling for $20. T would then sell the Put for approximately $1,000, realizing a net long-term gain of $600 ($1,000 less the $400 cost of the Put). If T had sold short 100 shares of XYZ stock, he would have realized an approximately $1,000 economic gain, which would be treated as short-term.

If T were in the 50 percent tax bracket, the long-term gain of $600 would produce $480 in after-tax income, while the short-term gain of $1,000 would produce $500 in after-tax income. If XYZ stock had instead risen to $50 at the end of the six-month period, T would sustain a $400 short-term loss (assuming he had sold the Put just prior to the six-month holding period) as compared to a $2,000 short-term loss had he sold short 100 shares of XYZ stock. T's investment in the Put would be lower if he acquired an out-of-the-money Put (e.g., $100 for a Put on XYZ stock at $25 where the market value of the stock was $30 per share).

---

12 OBTAIN LONG–TERM GAINS ON APPRECIATED OPTIONS

.01 Sale of a Call or Put

Where the investor holds a Call, which has appreciated in value, for more than six months, and he does not wish to maintain an interest in the stock, the Call should be sold in order to convert the recognized gain into a long-term gain. If the Call is exercised and the underlying stock is sold within six months, the resulting gain would constitute a short-term gain. (See ¶39.04(d).)

Similar action should be taken with respect to a Put held for more than six months. Although the acquisition of a Put is considered a short sale for purposes of applying the short sale rules, under other tax provisions dealing with options the Put is treated as a capital asset in the hands of the investor and its sale results in long- or short-term capital gain or loss depending upon the holding period.

> **Example.** An investor on June 27, 1984, purchased a more-than-six-month Call on 100 shares of XYZ stock at $30 per share for $400. On January 2, 1985, XYZ stock is selling at $50 per share. The investor should sell the Call in lieu of exercising it and then selling the stock. The sale of the Call will produce a long-term capital gain of approximately $1,600, while the sale of the stock received on exercise of the Call will result in approximately the same amount of short-term gain.

.02 Adjustments to Unlisted Put or Call Option Price— Dividends, Rights, Etc.

Where the option price of an Unlisted Put or Call is to be adjusted because of any dividends, and the like, the time the option is exercised may be an important consideration. For example, where an extraordinary fully taxable dividend has been declared, the exercise of the Call after the ex-dividend date would reduce the acquisition price to the investor with a possible greater capital gain upon subsequent disposition. The dividend in this instance would be taxable to the previous holder of the stock, not the investor. Similarly, an investor should exercise a Put prior to the ex-dividend date in order to produce a greater long-term capital gain (assuming the stock was held for the applicable long-term holding period prior to the acquisition of the Put so as to avoid the short sales rules). If the Put is exercised after the ex-dividend date, the investor receives dividend income with a corresponding downward adjustment in the selling price of the stock resulting in reduced long-term capital gain. (See the discussion of Puts and Calls in ¶39.)

> **Example.** T acquires a 30-day Unlisted Call on December 1, 1984, for $200 to buy 100 shares of XYZ stock at $30 (the current market price). XYZ stock will go ex-dividend an extraordinary fully

taxable dividend of $5 per share on December 15, 1984. On December 14, 1984, XYZ stock is selling at $36 per share. If T exercises the Call prior to December 15, 1984, his basis in XYZ stock will be $32 per share ($30 purchase price plus $2 per share paid for the Call). The market value of XYZ stock, assuming no further fluctuation in price, will drop to $31 per share after the stock goes ex-dividend the $5 dividend distribution. Then T will be taxed on the $5 per share dividend distribution and have a potential capital loss of $1 per share (basis of $32 less market value of $31). However, if T waited until December 15, 1984, to exercise the Call, the exercise price would be adjusted downward to $25 because of the dividend distribution. Thus T would be holding XYZ stock having a fair market value of $31 per share with a basis of $27 per share ($25 purchase price plus $2 per share paid for the Call). T would now have a potential $4 capital gain and no dividend income.

13   LIMIT LOSS IN VOLATILE STOCK AND RETAIN POTENTIALITY OF LONG–TERM GAIN

.01   Acquisition of a Put Simultaneously with the Purchase of Stock

The simultaneous purchase of a Put and the underlying stock under certain circumstances (described in ¶37.03(d)) will prevent the Put from being treated as a short sale. This exception to the short-sale rules allows the investor to limit any loss in the transaction to the cost of a Put, without sacrificing the possibility of long-term gain in the event the stock increases in value. The practical use of this transaction is limited to volatile securities which may have a substantial swing in market value in either direction. A literal interpretation of the tax straddle rules now applicable to stock and options would indicate that this transaction could cause a loss of holding period in the stock. However, the "married Put" rule should be the controlling rule where there is an inconsistency.

Example. On July 1, 1984, T purchases 100 shares of ABC stock at $70 per share and at the same time buys a more than six-month Put on ABC stock at $70 for $1,000 ($10 per share). If the market value of the stock should fall to $30 per share, T could sell the stock for $70 by exercising the Put. Thus, T's loss is limited to the cost of the Put, $1,000. (It would appear that T could sell the Put for $4,000, recognizing a gain of $3,000, which should be given long-term capital gains treatment, provided the Put was held for more than six months.) The stock could be sold immediately prior to meeting the six-month holding period requirement, resulting in a $4,000 short-term capital loss. (See ¶37.03(d) for further discussion of this alternative.)

However, if the Put and stock positions are deemed to be offsetting positions subject to the tax straddle rules (see ¶38.02), then the holding period of the long Put should be terminated under regulations to be promulgated by Treasury, resulting in a short-term capital gain. (As indicated above, however, the holding period of the stock should not be terminated.) If this is the rule, then generally, it would not make sense to sell the Put separately.

Should the stock rise substantially, for example, to $100 per share, T could sell his position, recognizing a gain of $2,000 (the cost of the unexercised Put must be added to the basis of stock), which would be given long-term gain treatment if the stock was held for more than six months. If T had sold the "worthless" Put prior to the six-month holding period, there is a possibility that the $1,000 paid for the Put would result in a short-term loss and that the long-term gain on the subsequent sale of the stock would be correspondingly increased.

Thus, T has limited any loss on the transaction to $1,000, the cost of the Put, and still has a potential economic gain (long-term capital gain after six months) if there is a rise in the price of ABC stock.

14 OBTAIN LONG–TERM GAIN ON SALE OF APPRECIATED WHEN–ISSUED CONTRACTS

An investor who has held "when-issued" stock for more than six months should consider, where practical, the private sale of the when-issued stock (technically the sale of a contract to buy stock when and if issued) prior to settlement date, in lieu of either receiving the new stock and the immediate sale thereof, or selling the when-issued stock through a stock exchange. Gain realized on the private sale will be long-term while the sale of the new stock received, or of the when-issued stock through a stock exchange, will cause the gain to be short-term (see discussion in ¶40.05). This is similar to the sale of a Call held for more than six months as compared to the exercise thereof and selling the stock. (See ¶39.04(d).)

Example. T bought 100 shares of ABC stock "when-issued" on November 1, 1984, at $30 per share. The when-issued stock is scheduled to "go regular" on December 15, 1985. Assume that on May 2, 1985, ABC when-issued is selling for $50 per share. If T sells the when-issued through the stock exchange, which is the usual transaction, the $2,000 gain will be considered to be recognized on the settlement date, December 15, 1985, as a short-term gain, even though the when-issued contract had been held for more than six months. If T waits until December 15, 1985, to receive the "regular" stock of ABC, and then sells the stock at $50 on the next day, his $2,000 gain will still be short-term. T should sell the *when-issued contract* on May 2, 1985, in a private sale, in which case the $2,000 gain recognized will be treated as long-term.

With respect to when-issued stock sold short (technically entering into a contract to sell stock for a fixed price when and if issued), the investor should sell or assign the contract right rather than close out the short position. However, in this instance, it is questionable whether long-term gain will result even though the contract was held for more than six months. (See ¶**40.05.**)

15 PROTECT GAIN ON EXERCISE OF A STOCK OPTION

A corporate executive or employee must not dispose of stock received upon exercise of an incentive stock option until the stock has been held for more than one year and two years from the date the options were granted.[6] (Under a qualified stock option plan the stock must be held for three years.)[7]

The possibility of loss during the required holding period after exercise may be eliminated by purchasing an Unlisted Put concurrently with the exercise of the option.[8] However, the cost of a Put for the required one-year holding period for incentive stock options may be so high as to preclude this method of protecting the gain.

Another possible way of locking in the profit on stock acquired under an incentive or qualified stock option plan and still meet the requisite holding period, is to sell short a comparable number of shares of the stock ("short against the box"—see ¶**2.01**). For determining the time when gain or loss on the short sale is recognized, the stock is not deemed sold until the short sale is closed. Thus, under this rule a disqualifying disposition should not take place until the closing of the short sale. However, the Treasury has ruled that a short sale is considered a disposition of the stock for purposes of meeting the holding period requirement.[9] Another disadvantage to the use of a

---

[6]Code: 422A.
[7]Code: 422(a). Qualified stock options exercised after May 21, 1981 will be treated as nonqualified stock options un-

less an election is made to convert them into incentive stock options.
[8]Rev. Rul. 59-242, C.B. 1959-2, 125.
[9]Rev. Rul. 73-92, C.B. 1973-1, 208.

short sale is that the underlying stock must be held for more than six months before a short sale is made, so as to avoid the short sale rule denying long-term gain treatment. (See ¶37.03(a).) If shares of another corporation in the same industry have had a similar price movement, the executive may consider hedging his investment by selling short the other stock. However, additional funds required for margin purposes may cause this hedge to also be impractical.

Officers, directors, and 10 percent or more shareholders of listed corporations and other corporations required to file periodic reports with the SEC are apparently forbidden by the Securities Exchange Act of 1934[10] to sell short the stock of their corporation or to go "short against the box" for more than a limited period.

16 CREATE CAPITAL GAINS ON SALE OF EX-DIVIDEND STOCK "FOR CASH"

Assuming no other market fluctuations, the price of stock that goes ex-dividend is generally reduced by the amount of the dividend. The investor should sell the stock before, not after, the ex-dividend date, in order to produce greater capital gain by the amount of the dividend payment. Where the stock is sold after the ex-dividend date, but prior to the record date, the sale should be made "for cash." (See ¶2.05.) The dividend under these circumstances belongs to the purchaser. However, the selling price of the stock is increased by the amount of the dividend and will thus result in greater capital gains to the seller.

.01 Acquisition of Shares in a Mutual Fund

An investor in a high tax bracket may welcome an opportunity to obtain capital gain treatment on dividends rather than on ordinary income by investing in a regulated investment company (mutual fund) rather than in a regular corporation. The investor should consider buying shares in a mutual fund immediately prior to a large capital gain distribution. However, a long-term loss will be realized whether or not the shares are held for more than six months.[10a] By selling just before a large income distribution, the investor will also realize a capital gain rather than dividend income. A long-term loss on a sale within six months would not be detrimental if the shares are acquired

---

[10] Section 16(c).

[10]a—Code Section 852(b)(4) necessitates a more-than-six-month holding period (a 31-day holding period was required before 1984); otherwise, the loss on the sale up to the amount of the capital gain dividend would be treated as long-term. Similar treatment is available by investing in a real estate investment trust. Code: 857(b)(7).

before year-end and the loss could be offset against short-term capital gains in the following year. Of course, the investor is subjected to the vagaries of the market during the holding period. The "loading" charges of some mutual funds would increase the loss on the sale to such an extent as to make this transaction uneconomical. However, shares of a so-called no-load fund may be available. Shares of a "closed-end" mutual fund could also be utilized in a similar manner; however, a commission expense will be incurred upon acquisition and subsequent sale of such shares.

> **Example.** On November 14, 1984, T purchases 1,000 shares of ABC Fund (a no-load fund) for $20 per share. ABC distributes a $2 long-term capital gain to holders of record on November 15, 1984. T will recognize long-term capital gains on the receipt of the $2,000 distribution even though he was a holder of record for one day. The value of ABC Fund will fall to $18 per share. Assuming that there are no changes in the value of ABC Fund for the balance of the year, T will sell the 1,000 shares after January 7, 1985 and realize a long-term capital loss of $2,000 (cost of $20,000 less the selling amount of $18,000) which could be offset against expected short-term capital gains in 1985.

17 ACCELERATE INCOME

Sometimes an investor may have sustained business or capital losses, or may have incurred investment expenses or other deductions, such as medical expenses or casualty losses, which exceed his projected income for the year. Under the tax rules, many of these excess expenses cannot be carried to other years, and a failure to generate additional income will see these losses expire without tax benefit. In addition, the investor might be in the alternative minimum tax trap for the year. Additional income will be taxed at 20 percent. Income can be generated by entering into a commodity forward straddle and selling the profit position in the earlier year. However, a capital loss is created in the later year rather than an ordinary loss. Entering into a regulated Futures straddle will not produce income in the earlier years because the offsetting position would have to be marked-to-market at year-end. A mixed straddle could be used to accelerate gains provided the investor has elected not to use the marked-to-market rule for the offsetting regulated Futures contract.

Other possible actions are a sale of bond coupons (see ¶**46.09 (f)**), a sale of future dividends (see ¶49 for a general discussion of assignment of income), or elect not to defer gains in transactions qualifying for installment sale treatment (see ¶50.)

18　AVOID WASH SALE RULES

.01　Short Sale—"Short against the Box"

In order to deduct a loss on securities for tax purposes and still maintain the same long position, a method frequently used in the past in order to avoid the wash sale rules was the simultaneous purchase and short sale of the same security, and 31 days thereafter, the covering of the short position with the original shares held. The expected results were a recognition of the loss, and maintenance of the same long position with the lower basis. The Treasury has issued regulations[11] which, if upheld by the courts, would prevent this method of obtaining a deduction for the loss. (See ¶36.08.) However, a variation of this short sale transaction might still be used effectively to accomplish the same objective of deducting the loss and maintaining the same long position. (See ¶36.01 for discussion of wash sale rules.)

.02　Other Methods

Investors sometimes avoid the wash sale provisions by replacing securities sold with securities in another corporation in the same industry. Another method frequently utilized is "doubling up" or buying an equivalent amount of the same issue, holding both lots for 31 days, and then selling the original holding and recognizing the loss. This latter method has the disadvantage of tying up and risking additional capital. Of course the investor could sell the loss securities, wait 31 days, and repurchase them. However, he is now without any economic interest in the securities for the 31-day period. A sale of the loss securities in January may result in greater proceeds than a sale in December if the securities are expected to drop further in value, because of tax-loss selling at the end of the year, and then recover. Tax factors alone should not affect economic decisions.

.03　Sale of "In-the-Money" Puts

The wash sales provisions, disallowing a loss deduction, is triggered when within the 30-day period the taxpayer has acquired, or

---

[11] Reg. 1.1091-1 (g).

has entered into a contract or option to acquire, substantially identical property. The sale of the stock at a loss with a simultaneous sale of an "in-the-money" Put, where effective economic interest in the movement of the price of the stock (up to a certain point) remains with the investor, should not come within the technical requirements of the wash sales rules so as to disallow the loss deduction.

Example. T owned 100 shares of X stock with a basis of $50 per share for several years. The current market value of X stock is $20 per share. T wishes to recognize a $3,000 long-term capital loss deduction without giving up his economic interest in the stock. Simultaneous with a sale of X stock for $20 per share, T could write a Put, with an expiration date of more than 30 days and with a strike price of $30. T will receive approximately $1,000 for the sale of this in-the-money Put. As long as X stock is selling at a price below $30, T will be assured that the stock will be sold to him at $30 near the expiration date of the Put. T's tax basis will be the $30 per share paid less the $10 per share premium received on the sale of the Put, or a net of $20 per share. The 30-day acquisition period rule under the wash sales provisions will not have been violated. The sale of the in-the-money Put (whether Listed or Unlisted), should not be considered as the acquisition of an option or absolute right to acquire the stock unless the option is so deep-in-the-money that it is absolutely certain that the Put will be exercised. If X stock should rise in value above $30 per share during the period of the outstanding Put, T's economic interest will disappear. He will not receive back the stock because the worthless Put will be allowed to expire unexercised, resulting in a short-term gain of $1,000. Therefore, T should make sure that the intrinsic value of the Put (the amount of dollars that the Put is in-the-money), is of sufficient size to take into account the possibility of a reasonable sudden rise in the value of the stock during the Put period.

Unlisted in-the-money Puts might also be used with securities (including tax-free municipals) to accomplish the above stated objective.

---

19   AVAILABLE TAX ELECTIONS

.01   Allocation of Basis to Stock Rights Received

Where the fair market value of stock rights received is less than 15 percent of the value of stock, no allocation of the basis of such stock to the rights is made unless the investor so elects. If the investor intends to sell only the rights, or to exercise the rights with a view toward selling the newly acquired stock within six months, or before selling the old shares, an election to allocate the basis should be made in order to reduce the amount of gain recognized on the sale of the rights or the new shares. An election should also be made if the investor intends to sell both his old and newly acquired shares in order to maximize the long-term gains on the old shares and reduce the amount of short-term gains on the new shares. If the old shares are sold at a loss, an election should be made so as to reduce the amount of long-term losses. Where the investor intends to retain the stock acquired on exercise of the rights, there may be an advantage in not making the election if such action results in creating widely different bases which permit selective gain or loss on later sales. Where stock dividends are received, part of the basis of the old stock *must always* be allocated to the stock dividends. (See ¶33.04 for discussion of the method of making the allocation to either dividend stock or rights.)

Example.   T owns 100 shares of X stock with a basis of $100 per share. He receives 100 rights to purchase more shares. The market value of the stock, on the first day traded ex-rights, is $180 per share and the rights are then worth $20 per right (less than 15 percent of $180). If T sells the rights at $20 each and makes no election, he will recognize $2,000 of gain (long-term or short-term depending upon the length of time the 100 shares of X stock were held). However, T may elect to allocate a portion of the basis of the $100 per share of X stock to the rights. Thus $10 ($100 times $20/$200) of basis would be allocated to each right. The gain that is recognized on the sale of such rights will thus be reduced to $1,000.

.02   Bond Discount

Discounts on bonds or other obligations can arise when a short-term obligation is issued *(acquisition discount)*, or on purchase of an obligation with a value that has declined due to market conditions *(market discount)*. The amount of accrued bond discount, whether acquisition discount of short-term obligations or market discount, is computed using the straight-line or ratable method. This generally results in more accrued discount income and may be detrimental if an election is made to currently report the discount income. An election to compute the discount income by means of the compound interest method will, in the early years, reduce the accrued market discount or, if an election to report the income currently was made, reduce the amount of current discount income. (See ¶46.09 (b) and (c).)

An investor may elect in any taxable year to include in income annually the increase in the redemption value of certain noninterest-bearing obligations issued at a discount, such as Series E savings bonds. Otherwise the entire discount element will generally result in ordinary income treatment in the year of redemption. The election is binding and applies to all such obligations owned and later acquired. All increases in value occurring in years preceding the election must be included in taxable income in the year of election. Investors, such as minors or retired persons with little or no taxable income, may find this election to be most advantageous.

Recognition of gain on the increased value of certain U.S. Government obligations not previously recognized as income in the years earned may be further deferred by exchanging them for other similar obligations. (See ¶46.10.)

Example. W purchased a $100 Series E savings bond for $75 in June, 1975. In 1977, she elects to include the increased annual redemption value in her income. At the end of 1977, between 2½ and 3 years have passed since the issuance date so W will recognize approximately $9.50 of interest income, which represents the full increment in value from date of purchase to the end of the year in which the election is made. (The amount of the increment depends upon the date of issuance of the savings bond and may be affected by an increase in rates of return on such bonds.) Without such election, W would recognize $25 of interest income upon redemption of the bond at initial maturity. She could, based upon past precedents, continue holding such bond without recognizing income, as Congress has not permitted any U.S. savings bonds issued since 1941 to finally mature unless the bonds have a 40-year maturity. W could exchange the Series E bond for certain Series H bonds (which pay current interest) without being required to recognize any interest income represented in the increased value of the Series E bond and not previously reported as income. The interest represented by the increment in value would have to be reported when the Series H bonds were redeemed.

.03 Amortization of Bond Premiums

Taxpayers in all tax brackets generally will find it advantageous to elect to amortize premiums paid upon the acquisition of taxable bonds. The allowable deduction for amortization operates to decrease ordinary income and to reduce the basis of the securities. The alternative is the maintenance of basis and a consequent capital loss or reduction of capital gain upon redemption or sale. (See ¶**46.02** for method of computation and restrictions.)

Example. T purchases on January 21, 1977 a $5,000 10 percent ABC bond due January 2, 1987, for $5,500. T elects to amortize the premium of $500 over the 10-year term of the bond, thus obtaining annually a $50 ordinary deduction. Upon redemption in 1987 for $5,000, T will recognize neither gain nor loss, since the basis will have been reduced to $5,000. However, without such election, T would sustain a $500 long-term capital loss upon redemption ($5,500 cost less redemption amount of $5,000). Thus the election gives T annual deductions against ordinary income and may prevent capital loss upon subsequent sale or redemption of the bond.

.04 Elect Not to Use the Installment Sale

Under the revised installment sale rules (see ¶**50**), any gains on payments received in the year following the year of sale of securities are automatically deferred until the year of payment unless an election is made not to use the installment method. An investor may have expiring losses or credits and could only use these tax attributes if the entire gain is recognized in the year of sale. The investor may have already realized long-term gains and short-term losses and may wish to apply the short-term gain to be realized on the sale against the short-term losses rather than pay a higher tax on the short-term gain in the subsequent year. Another possible situation is that he expects to be in a much lower tax bracket in the year of sale and the tax savings would be greater than the benefits from deferring the payment of tax. Other items, such as income averaging or alternative minimum tax, may also make it more beneficial for the investor to elect to report the entire gain in the year of sale.

20 UNDESIRABILITY OF LONG–TERM GAIN IN CERTAIN SITUATIONS

Normally an investor would prefer to have recognized gains on securities treated as long-term and losses treated as short-term. If an investor had large capital losses in the year, it is immaterial whether he realizes long-term or short-term capital gains, since the losses will offset any capital gain on a $1 to $1 basis. Therefore, an investor need not risk his potential gain by retaining the security until long-term gains can be obtained. Similarly, if an investor has only short-term gains or long-term gains, it is immaterial whether the losses are long-term or short-term because either type of loss can be fully offset against the capital gains. In this situation an investor should realize his long-term losses and save his short-term losses, if any, for use in future years. However, if the capital losses exceed the capital gains, it is preferable to have short-term losses that can be offset against ordinary income on a $1 to $1 basis, whereas $2 of long-term losses are required to offset $1 of ordinary income. In a case where an investor has recognized short-term gains and long-term losses, there is no benefit from realizing the long-term gains in that year. The long-term losses will merely offset the long-term gains, leaving short-term gains subject to tax at regular rates. Where possible the long-term gains should be deferred until the subsequent year, possibly by means of a short sale. (See ¶37.02.) Realization of long-term capital gains, in lieu of short-term gains, is not advantageous where an investor has excess personal deductions (e.g., medical expense, charitable contributions, investment expenses) which cannot be carried to other years and the capital gains are less than the excess deductions. If the capital gains exceeds the excess deductions then it may be more advantageous to recognize long-term capital gains. There would also be no benefit in holding the securities for long-term capital gains treatment if the investor expects to compute his tax liability under the alternative minimum tax (see ¶61). The capital gain deduction is added back in determining the minimum tax.

Example. T has excess deductions of $10,000. His XYZ stock, which he has held for several years, has unrealized appreciation of approximately $10,000. He also owns ABC stock on which he has unrealized short-term gains of approximately $10,000. In this situation it would be preferable to sell the ABC stock since the ordinary deductions would offset the short-term gain. The long-term gain on the XYZ stock could be taken in a subsequent year. There would be no benefit in selling the XYZ stock in the loss year since the $6,000 capital gain deduction would be wasted because it cannot be carried over to another year. However, if the unrealized gain on the XYZ stock were $25,000, then the full $25,000 of long-term gain would not be subjected to tax because it would be offset by the $15,000 capital gain deduction and the $10,000 of excess ordinary deductions. The possible effects of the alternative minimum tax should be considered before completing the transaction.

21　STOCK TRANSFER TAXES

Investors are no longer subject to any state transfer tax on the sale of stock. Previously, transfer taxes were deductible as a tax and not merely as a sales expense in computing gain or loss in the transaction.

22　INTEREST ON MARGIN ACCOUNTS

Interest charged on a stock brokerage margin account is deductible by a cash-basis taxpayer in the year in which credits such as dividends, cash deposits, or proceeds from the sale of securities are made to the account sufficient to absorb the interest charge.[12] Therefore, a payment should be made into the margin account towards the end of December in order to assure the deduction of interest charges of that month and prior months where there have been no recent credits to the account of adequate amounts. This may be accomplished by mailing a check before December 31, although received by the broker in January, indicating the payment is for the unpaid interest. Prior to the 1976 TRA, additional deductions could be created by prepaying the next year's interest on the margin accounts.[13] This is no longer permissible. (See **¶51.05**.) It should be noted that interest expense incurred on the purchase of taxable securities on margin may be partially disallowed if an investor owns or purchases tax-exempt securities for cash or through another account. Where an investor has also purchased a home, automobile, or other large personal item, it is preferable for tax purposes to incur a liability for the personal expenditure rather than on the purchase of taxable securities. There would not be an disallowance of interest expense in the latter situation. Also note that the investment interest expense deduction may be subject to limitations or may be disallowed under the alternative minimum tax computations. (See **¶61**.) In the latter situation, it may be more beneficial to defer the interest expense to a subsequent year.

23　PREPAYMENT OF STATE INCOME TAXES

Where large capital gains are subject to state income tax, it may be advisable to prepay the state income tax in order to obtain the current deduction of such taxes. Otherwise, the deduction of the state income tax on the federal income tax return for the following year may produce a much smaller benefit.

---

[12]Rev. Rul. 70-221, C.B. 1970-1, 33.　　　　[13]Rev. Rul. 68-643, C.B. 1968-2, 76.

24 CONTRIBUTION OF APPRECIATED SECURITIES

Contributions to public charities and certain private foundations of appreciated long-term securities will result in a contribution deduction (subject to a 30 percent limitation with the excess carried forward for five years) equal to the fair market value of the property at the time of the gift. The appreciation in value escapes taxation. An election may be made to apply the 50 percent limitation rather than the 30 percent limitation to the contribution, but only 60 percent of the appreciation would be deductible. Taxpayers who normally make charitable donations each year should still consider giving appreciated securities or sell securities to the charity at a discount in lieu of giving cash. The cash can be used to purchase the same or similar stock and thereby to obtain a high tax basis for the stock. A gift of stock should be made before any final agreement of merger or liquidation or the donor will be taxed on the appreciation.[14] Donations of short-term securities should be avoided since no charitable deduction will be allowed for the appreciation. Also, depreciated securities should not be donated but sold to establish a tax loss.[15] The taxpayer would then donate the proceeds if there are no appreciated long-term securities which could be contributed. A current deduction is not allowed on the transfer of an option on property owned by the taxpayer to a charity. Instead, a deduction will be allowed in the year of exercise to the extent the market value of the property exceeded the option price at the time of exercise.[16]

Example. T normally makes $1,000 of charitable contributions each year. T has owned for more than six months 100 shares of ABC stock with a fair market value of $10 per share, which cost him $1 per share. T should contribute these securities to a qualified charity. In this way, $900 of appreciation would escape tax. (See ¶25 for "bargain sales" of appreciated securities.)

An investor who has received tax-free public utility stock dividends can contribute these shares to charity and obtain a charitable deduction for the full value of the shares if held more than one year prior to the contribution. However, the charitable deduction will be disallowed to the extent the investor received any tax-free stock distributions within one year of the contribution. For example, assume

---

[14]*Jones,* 531 F. 2d 1343 (CA-6, 1976);   [15]*Withers,* 69 T.C. 900. (1978).
Kinsey, 477 F. 2d 1058 (CA-2, 1973).   [16]Rev. Rul. 82-197, C.B. 1982-2, 72.

an investor receives 10 shares of qualified public utility stock on January 1, 1984, and on March 1, 1984. On February 1, 1985, the investor donates the 10 shares received on January 1, 1984. He will not be entitled to any charitable deduction because the March 1, 1984, shares were received within one year of the time of the donation. Note the charitable deduction will be allowed if the investor does not elect to treat the March 1, 1984, stock distribution as a tax-free dividend. (See ¶55.01 for discussion of public utility dividends.)

Prior to 1979, taxpayers in the top tax brackets could have realized a greater profit by contributing shares with a low tax basis to charity rather than selling the shares and keeping the after-tax proceeds. This would not be true for post-1981 taxable years, because the maximum tax rate on long-term capital gains has been reduced from 28 percent to 20 percent and the maximum rate has been reduced from 70 percent to 50 percent.

Example. T, who was in the 70 percent tax bracket in 1978, owned 100 shares with a market value of $50,000 and a basis of $100. A sale before November, 1978 would result in net proceeds of approximately $32,500, assuming an aggregate capital gains tax and minimum tax of 35 percent. By donating the shares to charity, T would receive a charitable deduction which would increase his after-tax income by $35,000. Thus, a gift to charity enabled T to realize an additional profit of $2,500. In addition, the charity of his choice received property worth $50,000. If the contribution was made in 1984, when the maximum rate on ordinary income is 50 percent, T would be entitled to a charitable deduction which would increase his after-tax income by $25,000. A sale of the property in 1984, when the maximum tax in capital gains is 20 percent, would result in net proceeds of $40,000, or $15,000 more than a contribution to charity. Thus, the reduced maximum tax on both ordinary income and capital gains will make it more expensive to make gifts of securities to charity. Any intended gift to charity should be with appreciated long-term stock that would otherwise have been sold, rather than cash, in order that the gain escape tax. This is true irrespective of the tax bracket of the taxpayer.

---

25   BARGAIN SALES OF APPRECIATED SECURITIES TO CHARITIES

A sale of appreciated securities to a qualified charity at their tax basis will also result in a contribution deduction (subject to percentage limitations) equal to the amount of appreciation. However, the sales are subject to tax. The amount of gain is determined by subtracting from the sales price a portion of the donor's basis, in the ratio of the sales price to the market value of the security.[17] Despite being partially taxable, a bargain sale of the security may result in greater after-tax dollars than an outright contribution of the security or a sale of the security followed by a cash contribution. Note that the effect of the bargain sales provision is to place the taxpayer in the same position as a sale of shares equal in value to the tax basis and a charitable contribution of the remaining shares. Use of the latter method, however, would result in additional sales commission (especially if there is an odd lot sale), and a possibly reduced sales price if there is a small market for this amount of shares.

> **Example.** T owns 100 shares of XYZ stock, purchased in 1978 at $40 per share. On February 1, 1984, this stock is selling at $100 per share. T, who is in the 50 percent bracket, wishes to close out his position and make a charitable contribution of $6,000. A sale would produce a $6,000 long-term gain and a tax of $1,200. His after-tax proceeds will be $8,800 ($10,000 selling amount less $1,200 in taxes). After donating $6,000 to charity and thereby reducing his tax by $3,000, he will retain $5,800 after taxes. However, if T sells the 100 shares to a qualified charity for his cost of $4,000, he would be entitled to a $6,000 charitable deduction which would reduce his income taxes by $3,000. A $500 tax would be paid on the bargain sale (20 percent of $4,000 sales price less allocated basis of $1,600). Thus, T's after-tax proceeds would be $6,500 ($4,000 selling amount plus $2,500 net savings of income taxes), or $700 more than if the security was first sold and $6,000 of cash was donated to charity.

26 CHARITABLE LEAD TRUST

Deductions for charitable contributions can be accelerated by creating a trust for less than 10 years, fund the trust with tax-exempt bonds, and provide for annual guaranteed payments of income to charitable organizations. See ¶67 for detailed discussion of charitable lead trusts and other tax benefits that can be obtained by the use of short-term trusts.

---

[17]Code: 1011(b); Reg. 1.1011-2.

27 CAPITAL GAIN OR NONTAXABLE DIVIDENDS, AND TAX–EXEMPT INTEREST

A high-bracket investor should measure the income yield on invested capital in terms of after-tax dollars earned. Consideration should be given to investments offering tax-sheltered yields, such as securities in certain public utilities,[18] natural resources corporations, and trusts where part of the yield is considered a return of capital.

The investor should also compare his after-tax yield on savings bond interest, industrial bond interest, and other income with interest income from tax-exempt state or municipal bonds, or tax-exempt savings certificates.

The tax factors are recognized in the securities market in that variations in values do exist because of different tax treatment. For example, a U.S. Government obligation selling at a discount will sell at a price which produces a lower pretax yield than a U.S. Government obligation selling at par. This occurs because the discount on bonds issued before July 19, 1984 will be treated as a capital gain upon subsequent retirement.

28 TRANSFER OF APPRECIATED SECURITIES TO RELATIVES

High-bracket taxpayers may effectively avoid the income tax on sales of appreciated securities by transferring them, at cost, to relatives, such as children, in lower tax brackets. The relatives, in turn, could, after a period of time, sell the securities at the market value, recognizing (and paying tax on) the full appreciation. If the donor is of advanced age or there is no intent to sell the security in the immediate future, a step-up in basis could be obtained if the donor dies owning the shares. (See ¶33.06.) A gift of the securities could result in gift tax liability if the amount of the gift exceeded available exemptions and credits. The basis of the securities may be increased by the payment of gift taxes.[19]

Example.   T owns 100 shares of ABC stock purchased November 1, 1984, at $10 per share. On December 15, 1984, this stock is selling at $30 per share. If T, who is in the 50 percent bracket, sells such securities for full value, he will recognize $2,000 of short-term capital

---

[18] These tax-free dividends have been reduced in many instances after June 30, 1972. Code: 312(k).

[19] Code: 1015(d).

gain and pay a tax of $1,000. However, T could sell the 100 shares to his son for $1,000 and make a gift of the balance of the value. If there were no other gifts to his son during the year, there would be no gift tax on this transfer. Assuming the son is in the 11 percent tax bracket, he would pay only $220 of income taxes on the $2,000 short-term capital gain recognized by him upon the sale of the stock, as compared to $1,000 of tax that would have been paid by the father.

If the relative sells the securities as soon as he receives them, the Treasury may attempt to impute the gain to the high-bracket taxpayer, on the theory that the relative acted as his agent in making the sale. Therefore, it is helpful to be able to show that the relative acted as a free agent in his own behalf. This is usually easier to show in the case of an adult relative, and more difficult if the transfer is made to a minor for whom the high-bracket taxpayer is guardian.

29 TRANSFER TO RELATIVES OF INCOME FROM SECURITIES

A high-bracket investor who is currently providing for the needs of an elderly or indigent relative, or is saving for the future needs of the younger members of the family, should consider interest-free loans[20] or setting up a 10-year support trust.[21] A taxpayer in the 50 percent tax bracket must earn $4,000 in order to give his needy relative $2,000. By placing securities in trust for at least a 10-year period with the income distributed annually, the trust income would be taxed to the trust beneficiary and not to the grantor. As a result of the beneficiary's personal exemption, zero bracket amount (standard deduction) if the beneficiary is not a dependent of the grantor or another person, and $100 dividends received deduction, at least $3,400 could be received by the beneficiary free of tax. If the beneficiary is a dependent of the grantor or another person, and, therefore, cannot utilize the standard deduction, then the amount of tax-free dividend and other income would be at least $1,100. Any additional income will be taxed at the lowest tax brackets. Alternatively, an investor can avoid the expense of creating a support trust by taking advantage of the current high yields on tax-exempt bonds. By receiving the tax-free interest and giving it to his dependent, the investor can also claim a deduction for the dependent's personal exempion and any medical expenses paid in his behalf.

---

[20] A lender may be subject to income and gift taxes on interest-free loans to family members when the loans are tax motivated. Code: 7872.

[21] Code: 673(a).

Example. T, who is in the 50 percent bracket, gives his elderly mother $2,000 annually from his dividends and interest. To obtain the $2,000 after-tax amount, T must receive $4,000 of income and pay a $2,000 tax on the income. If T sets up a trust for his mother for a period of 10 years or his mother's life, whichever is shorter, with the trust principal reverting to T at the end of the period, the income would be taxed to T's mother and not to T. T's mother is entitled to a personal exemption of $2,000 (over age 65), a standard deduction of $2,300 and a dividend exclusion of $100. Instead of paying a $2,000 tax on the income, T's mother would pay no tax and would have $4,000 for her personal needs. Approximately 60 percent of the value of the securities placed in trust would be subject to gift tax, but with the greater annual gift tax exemptions ($10,000 per donee, $20,000 for joint gifts) and credits for gifts made after 1981, in most cases no gift tax liability will arise.

30 GOVERNMENT OBLIGATIONS ACCEPTABLE IN PAYMENT OF FEDERAL ESTATE TAXES

Certain U.S. Treasury bonds ("flower bonds") selling at a discount are redeemable at face value in payment of federal estate taxes. With the reduced maximum estate tax rates for post-1981 years and the depressed bond market due to the high interest rates, substantial savings in estate tax can be accomplished by the purchase of these bonds by an individual with a short life expectancy. (See ¶**46.11.**)

31 DEATHBED PLANNING

Both economic conditions and changes in the tax law have substantial effect on "deathbed" actions. As indicated previously, individuals with a short life expectancy should consider purchasing "flower bonds." As a result of the repeal of the basis carry-over rules and the enactment of an unlimited marital deduction for post-1981 years, a taxpayer can save both income taxes and estate taxes by deferring the sale of appreciated property until after death and bequeathing his property to the surviving spouse. The surviving spouse will obtain a higher tax basis for the securities, except for one half of the securities held in joint name (see ¶**33.06**). However, the surviving spouse may not qualify for joint return or head of the household treatment in subsequent years. Consequently, the income received by the spouse may be subject to the higher separate return rates. The unneeded assets can be bequeathed to other family members in lower tax brackets or to a discretionary trust, at least to the extent of the applicable unified estate tax credit. This could result also in income tax and estate tax savings during the life of the surviving spouse and at the time of the spouse's death. There are other tax benefits that can be obtained from deathbed planning for securities.

An investor with depreciated securities should sell the securities before death to offset any capital gains for the year and to obtain the maximum deduction for capital losses that can be offset against ordinary income ($3,000 for years after 1977). At death, the lower fair market value will become the tax basis of the securities in the hands of the decedent's estate or beneficiaries. (See ¶33.06.)

A conflict on whether to sell before death or to get a basis step-up at death but risk a decrease in the value of the stock can be resolved by "selling short against the box." (See ¶2.01.) A short sale will preserve the economic value of the stock and the gain on sale can be averted by delaying the closing of the short position until after the death of the investor. (See ¶37.05.) An alternative to a short sale would be an installment sale. Gain on the sale could be deferred until the sales proceeds are received by electing the installment method. (See ¶2.07.) Thus, if the decedent's estate or beneficiaries would be in a lower tax bracket, the deferral of the sales proceeds would result in the estate or beneficiaries paying less taxes on the gains. In addition, they would be entitled to a deduction for the estate taxes payable on the unpaid installment gain.

If an investor has capital losses or net operating losses from his business, he could realize capital gains before death to take advantage of these losses since they will expire at death even if he files a joint return with his surviving spouse. Of course, with the repeal of the basis carry-over rules, his estate or beneficiaries would also escape tax on the appreciation since the new tax basis of the inherited stock generally would be its fair market value at time of death. Again, the decedent may wish to sell the appreciated securities because he anticipates a downturn in the market. As an alternative the surviving spouse can make use of the capital losses or net operating losses by selling her appreciated securities. These sales can occur before or after the death of the investor, provided they take place in the year of death and a joint return is filed for such year.

Principles of Taxation of

Securities and Commodities

Transactions

¶32

32 INTRODUCTION

A general coverage of the income tax provisions applicable to transactions by an individual investor, on a cash basis, in publicly traded securities is given in this section. Also included is a summary of the tax provisions affecting other types of investors. The existence of complex tax rules necessitates a limited discussion of some types of securities transactions. In addition to a thorough analysis of the Tax Reform Act of 1984 (1984 Act), a review of previous tax acts, including the 1976 Tax Reform Act (1976 TRA), the Economic Recovery Tax Act of 1981 (1981 ERTA), and the Tax Equity and Fiscal Responsibility Act of 1982 (1982 TEFRA), that may have a direct or indirect effect on securities transactions, is also included in this section.

.01 Time of Reporting Income or Deductions

A cash-basis investor generally will include dividend income, interest income, and gains on the sale of securities in his gross income in the year in which cash or other property is received.[22] Thus, dividend income is not included in income at the time the dividend is declared, or when the dividend check is issued by the distributing corporation, but is included when the check is received by the shareholder even if the check is received in the following year.[23] A divi-

---

[22]Reg. 1.446-1(c)(1).

[23]Reg. 1.451-2(b); Rev. Rul. 68-126, C.B. 1968-1, 194.

dend of property other than cash, however, is valued at the date of distribution although it is received at a later date.[24] Gain on the sale of securities generally is also taxed in the year the sale proceeds are received and not on the day the transaction was entered into ("regular way" sales). In the case of stock sold on an exchange, the settlement date and not the trade date is controlling.[25] Ordinarily, the settlement date will be the fifth business day following the trade date.

Interest expense, investment advisory fees, and other deductible investment expenses are also deductible when paid, rather than at the time they are incurred. Commissions paid by an investor in buying or selling securities are not deductible as investment expense, but are added to the cost of the securities purchased or for years prior to 1983, were subtracted from the selling price.[26] For compliance purposes, starting in 1983, the Treasury has required the gross sales price to be reported, and the selling expenses are added to the adjusted tax basis of the security. This has no effect on the net gain or loss on the sale of the security.

Losses on the sale of securities generally are deductible on the trade date even though delivery and receipt of the proceeds occur in the subsequent year.[27] The fact that the funds used to buy the securities were borrowed from a bank will not delay the current deduction of the loss.[28] However, in one court case, an investor was denied a loss until his notes were repaid. In this case, securities were purchased and sold through a margin account, but instead of posting the required margin, the investor gave his notes to the broker.[29] In a subsequent case involving losses in commodity futures trading, the speculation losses were deductible in the year they were incurred although the funds were borrowed from a joint venturer and the investor did not have sufficient funds to pay the entire debt.[30]

A cash-basis investor may cause the gain to be recognized in the year of the trade by making the sale "for cash" or electing not to use the installment sale method.[31] (See ¶19.04.) However, gain or loss on the closing of a short sale of securities, or on the closing of a short (or written) Listed option, will be reflected in the year the settlement date occurs because the controlling event is the delivery of the securities.[32]

---

[24]Reg. 1.301-1(b).

[25]*Harden F. Taylor*, 43 B.T.A. 563 (1941); Rev. Rul. 72-381, C.B. 1972-2, 233.

[26]*Helvering* v. *Winmill*, 305 U.S. 79 (1938); *Spreckles* v. *Helvering*, 315 U.S. 626 (1942).

[27]Rev. Rul. 70-344, C.B. 1970-2, 50.

[28]*Larkin*, 46 B.T.A. 213 (1942).

[29]*Page* v. *Rhode Island Hospital Trust Co.*, 88 F. 2d 192 (CA-1, 1937); *Bramer*, 259 F. 2d 717 (CA-3, 1958).

[30]*Eric D. Hirsch, Est.*, T.C. Memo 1983-371.

[31]Rev. Rul. 82-227, C.B. 1982-2, 89.

[32]Code: 1233 and 1234.

.02   General Rules for Capital Gains and Losses

All securities held by investors, except acquisitions before June 24, 1981 of short-term U.S. or other government obligations issued at a discount without interest, are considered capital assets.[33] Capital gains or losses are determined by taking the difference between the sales price or proceeds received and the tax basis of the security (usually the cost of the security). Sales, exchanges, or redemptions of publicly traded securities will, in general, result in capital gains or losses, which are divided into two basic classifications: long-term and short-term. Capital assets acquired during the period June 23, 1984 through 1987 qualify for long-term capital gain or loss treatment if they are held for more than six months. Other securities sold or exchanged after 1977 will generally result in long-term gain or loss if the security was owned for more than one year.[34] A shorter holding period (see ¶34.01) would result in a short-term gain or loss.

In the case of binding contracts entered into in one year where part or all of the proceeds of sale are received in a subsequent year, the holding period rule for the year the gain or loss on the sale is realized—rather than the year the gain or loss is recognized or reported for tax purposes—is generally used in determining whether the amounts received are subject to long-term or short-term capital gain treatment.[35] The reinstatement of the six-month holding period for capital assets acquired during the period June 23, 1984 through 1987 and a one-year holding period for capital assets acquired before or after this period represents a deviation from the general rule. Thus, short- or long-term recognition will depend on the asset chosen for sale rather than the year of sale. For example, if an investor acquired 100 shares of ABC stock on April 1, 1984 and 100 shares on July 1, 1984, a sale of the April shares in January of 1985 will result in a short-term gain or loss, whereas a sale of the shares acquired later will receive long-term treatment.

Note that in the case of a short sale,[36] the gain or loss will be recognized in the year the short position is closed, but whether the gain or loss recognized on the short sale is short-term or long-term may depend upon the time the underlying stock was acquired and whether it

---

[33]Code: 1221(5), repealed by 1981 ERTA: 505. A sale of securities by a trader, who is not a dealer in the securities, results in capital gain or loss. *H. M. Adnee,* 41 T.C.40 (1963); *L. J. Kabernat,* TC Memo 1972-1320; *Van Suetendall,* 152 F. 2d 654. (CA-2, 1946). Even a predominant business motive cannot preclude the stock from capital gain or loss treatment, as long as there was substantial investment motive for acquiring or holding the stock. Rev. Rul. 78-94, CB 1978-1, 58.

[34]Code: 1222.

[35]1976 TRA: 1402(c).

[36]Reg. 1.1233-1(a)(1).

was acquired during the special six-month holding period. Thus, if in the above example, there was a short sale in January 1985, any gain realized would be short-term and any loss would be long-term.

The six-month holding period remains in effect for Futures transactions in any commodity subject to the rules of a board of trade or commodity exchange even if the transaction was not made during the special six-month holding period ending before 1988.[37] However, this rule will have no effect on regulated Futures contracts acquired after June 23, 1981 that are subject to the mark-to-market rules. (See ¶41.03(b).) The applicable six-month or one-year holding period requirement will still apply to the gain or loss realized on sale of a commodity, as distinguished from a regulated commodity Futures contract. If a commodity is used to close a Futures transaction, the general straddle provisions may apply to the mixed straddle[38] and adjustment must be made for gains or losses recognized under the mark-to-market rule. For example, if in July 1984 an investor buys a spot commodity contract and sells a Futures contract which requires delivery after the seventh month, the closing of the Futures contract with the spot commodity will be treated as a termination of the Futures contract with gain or loss recognized on the Futures contract based on its market value at time of termination. Sixty percent of the gain or loss will be long-term and 40 percent will be short-term. Any gain or loss on disposition of the commodity, based on the value of the commodity at the time of delivery, will be short-term. The 60/40 capital gain or loss must be netted with the gains and losses on other offsetting positions for mixed straddles established after December 31, 1983.

A sale of a Call, Put, or similar stock option that is not part of a straddle will also fall under the general rules. Sales of nonequity options, such as T-bill options or commodity options, will receive 60/40 long-term/short-term treatment. See ¶39.10 for a discussion of rules applicable to nonequity options.

Capital gains dividends from mutual funds or real estate investment trusts will also receive capital gain treatment even if the shares were held for only one day.[39] A sale of these shares at a loss after they were held for not more than six months will be treated as a long-term capital loss to the extent of the capital gain dividend received by the shareholders.[40] (See ¶16.01.)

---

[37]Code: 1222; IR 1787 (3/30/77).

[38]Code: 1092. (See ¶41.03(c) for a discussion of tax treatment of mixed straddles.)

[39]Code: 852(b)(3)(B) and 857(b)(3)(B).

[40]Code: 852(b)(4) and 857(b)(7). The at-risk rules of Section 246(c) are to be applied in determining the six-month holding period.

All long-term transactions are netted to produce a net long-term gain or loss. Short-term transactions are similarly netted. Net long-term gains are reduced by net short-term losses (referred to in the Internal Revenue Code as "net capital gain"); net short-term gains are reduced by net long-term losses.[41]

A deduction of 60 percent is allowed against net capital gains (net long-term gains less net short-term losses) realized on sales or exchanges after October 31, 1978, or proceeds from prior sales received after such date.[42] Note that the capital gains deduction is a tax preference item[43] that is included in the alternative minimum tax computation.[44] (See ¶61.) Individuals can no longer use the alternative capital gains tax of 25 percent on the first $50,000 of net capital gains for post-1978 years. An alternative tax will not be necessary for post-1981 years because the maximum effective rates in those years has been reduced from 28 percent to 20 percent (50 percent maximum rate times 40 percent of capital gains). Low-bracket investors may find that their capital gains rates may in some cases be less than five percent because of the recent reductions in the tax rates. Net short-term gains in excess of net long-term losses are taxed as ordinary income. Income averaging may also be used for both types of capital gains if it will result in a lesser tax. (See ¶63.)

.03 Capital Losses and Carryovers

Where there is a net capital loss sustained in or carried to taxable years beginning after 1977, the amount of the loss allowed as a deduction against ordinary income is limited to $3,000 or the taxable income for the year, whichever is smaller.[45] Previously, the deductible amount was $1,000 for taxable years beginning before 1977, increased to $2,000 for years beginning in 1977.[46] Married persons filing separately can deduct only one half of the otherwise deductible amount against their ordinary income.[47] Thus, for the year 1984, each spouse could apply up to $1,500 of his or her net capital loss against ordinary income. Short-term capital losses, including short-term loss carryovers, are to be first deducted against ordinary income up to the applicable amount for the year.[48] If there are no short-term losses or

---

[41]Code: 1222.

[42]Code: 1202; Rev. Rul. 79-22, C.B. 1979-1, 275. A 50 percent deduction was allowed for pre-November 1, 1978 net capital gains.

[43]Code: 57(a)(9)(A).

[44]Code: 55.

[45]Code: 1211(b)(2); Reg. 1.1211-1(b).

[46]Code: 1211(b).

[47]Spouses filing separately for pre-1977 taxable years could each carryover and apply $1,000 of their pre-1970 capital losses against their ordinary income. Post-1969 capital losses are limited to the $500 maximum in effect for those years. Rev. Rul. 72-105, C.B. 1972-1, 228.

[48]Code: 1211(b)(1).

they total less than the applicable amount, then long-term losses may be deducted to the extent of the difference. For years beginning after 1969, only 50 percent of an investor's net long-term losses may be deducted from ordinary income subject to the above-mentioned applicable limitation.[49] The ratio of $2 of long-term capital loss against $1 of ordinary income has not been changed despite the fact that the net capital gains deduction has been increased to 60 percent for post-October 31, 1978, transactions. Thus, for 1984, long-term losses of $6,000 must be used to obtain a $3,000 ordinary deduction. Any amount in excess of $6,000 may be carried over to succeeding years, but the nondeductible half of the $6,000 will be lost.[50] Note also that long-term losses may be deducted in full against short-term gains. For this purpose long-term losses incurred in the current year would be applied first against short-term gains.

Capital loss carryovers are now allowed for an unlimited period, but the losses retain their original character. Capital losses sustained after 1963 are carried over separately as long-term or short-term losses, depending upon the nature of the losses in the year sustained and are combined with the losses of the same category for the succeeding year as if they had been incurred in such succeeding year.[51]

Treasury regulations provide specific rules for allocating capital carryovers between husband and wife where a joint return is filed in one year and separate returns are filed in another year.[52] Generally, spouses are treated as separate taxpayers who are permitted to combine their capital gains and losses as though they were one individual by filing a joint return. Thus, capital losses from separate returns may be carried over and applied in a joint return. Excess capital losses may be carried from one joint return to another. Where separate returns are filed in a subsequent year, however, the long-term and short-term capital losses are each separately apportioned between the spouses in accordance with the amounts of such losses each contributed. For example, if the husband had $2,000 of long-term gains and $2,000 of short-term losses, and the wife had $2,000 of long-term losses and $3,000 of short-term losses, the husband would be entitled to 40 percent ($2,000 short-term losses over $5,000 total short-term losses) of the short-term capital loss carryover even though on a separate return basis he would have no excess capital loss for the year. Upon the death of a spouse the decedent's share of the unused capital losses in the final joint return cannot be carried over by the surviving spouse, nor by the decedent's estate or beneficiaries.[53]

---

[49]Code: 1211(b)(1)(c)(ii).
[50]Code: 1212(b)(2)(B).
[51]Code: 1212(b)(1).

[52]Reg. 1.1212-1(c).
[53]Rev. Rul. 74-175, C.B. 1974-1, 52.

.04   Section 1256 Loss Carryback

Under the 1984 Act, net losses from Section 1256 contracts may be carried back three years and offset against net profits from Section 1256 contracts in such years.[54] Prior to the 1984 Act, only net losses incurred on regulated Futures contracts that were marked-to-market could be carried back and offset against net gains on regulated Futures contracts.[55]

It is unclear whether net losses from all types of Section 1256 contracts (see ¶38.03) can be carried back to a period prior to the 1984 Act, during which only regulated Futures contacts were subject to the mark-to-market rules of Section 1256. It would appear that this carryback would be available under the literal language of the statute.

33   BASIS

.01   In General

The investor has the burden of proof in establishing the basis of a security sold. The Treasury may be able to impose a lesser or zero basis in the event the burden is not met.[56] Thus the importance of accurate record-keeping is self evident.

.02   Purchase

The tax basis of securities acquired by purchase is ordinarily the cost of acquisition, including the commissions paid. Interest equalization tax, if applicable for purchases before July 1, 1974, is added to the basis of the security. Distributions received in excess of the earnings and profits of the distributing corporation will reduce the basis of the stock in the hands of the investor.[57] A bond purchased at a premium will have its basis reduced when the bond premiums are deducted.[58] The basis of an original issue discount bond is increased when the discount income is reported by the bondholder.[59] Similarly, if an election is made to currently report market discount income, the basis of the market discount bond will be increased by the amount of the taxable market discount income.[60] A basis increase must also be made for the acquisition discount income that must be currently taxed if an election was made to currently report the discount on short-term obligations.[61]

---

[54]Code: 1212(c), as amended by the 1984 Act: 102.

[55]Code: 1212(c), prior to amendment by the 1984 Act.

[56]*Eder,* 9 TCM 98 (1950); Biggs, T.C. Memo, 1968-240; see ¶33.05 for spe-

cial rule when property is acquired by gift.

[57]Code: 301(c)(2). See ¶55.01.

[58]Code: 171(a)(1). See ¶46.02.

[59]Code: 1272(c)(3). See ¶46.09(b).

[60]Code: 1276(b)(2). See ¶46.09(c).

[61]Code: 1282(b)(2). See ¶46.09(b).

Securities received in exchange for other securities in a corporate reorganization or other nontaxable exchange will generally take the same basis as the securities exchanged. On the other hand, if the exchange is taxable, the fair market value at such time becomes the basis of the securities.[62] Reference to published Capital Changes services will ordinarily provide the information necessary to establish basis for any publicly held security received in an exchange or distribution.

.03 Taxable Distribution

The basis of securities received by the investor in a taxable corporate distribution is the fair market value at such time.[63]

.04 Stock Dividends and Stock Rights

The general rule is that a portion of the basis of the "old" stock is allocated to a nontaxable stock dividend (or right).[64] The allocation is based upon fair market values of the stock or rights received in relation to the fair market value of the "old" stock at the time of distribution. Where a stock distribution is taxable (e.g., is treated as a cash dividend[65] or consists of stock of another corporation), the basis of the stock will be the same as the amount of the dividend income to the shareholder. Reference to published Capital Changes services will provide the necessary percentage of allocation.

Where the fair market value of rights at the time of distribution is less than 15 percent of the value of the stock, no allocation is made and the basis of the rights is zero, unless the investor elects to make the allocation under the general rule.[66] The allocation *must always* be made where stock dividends are received, regardless of the market value of the properties.

.05 Gift

Securities acquired by gift (after 1920) have a basis for purposes of determining gain equal to the donor's basis. For the purpose of determining loss, the fair market value of the property at the time of the gift, if less than the donor's basis, is used.[67] Thus it is possible under certain circumstances that neither gain nor loss will be recognized. Where it is impossible to determine the basis of the donor, the fair

---

[62]Rev. Rul. 55-757, C.B. 1955-2, 557.
[63]Code: 301(d); Reg. 1.301-1(h).
[64]Code: 307; Reg. 1.307-1.
[65]Code: 305.
[66]Code: 307(b); Reg. 1.307-2.
[67]Code: 1015(a); Reg. 1.1015-1.

market value at the time the donor acquired the property will be the basis to the donor for purposes of determining the donee's basis.[68]

The donee's basis for securities received as a gift before 1977, as determined under the above rules, is increased by the amount of gift tax paid with respect to the gift, but not above the fair market value at the time of the gift.[69] With regard to gifts received after 1976, the donee's basis is increased only by the portion of the gift tax paid on the net appreciation in the value of the gift (i.e., the excess of fair market value at time of gift over donor's basis).[70] For example, if a gift tax of $2,000 was paid on a gift of $100,000, of which the net appreciation was $10,000, the donor's basis would be increased by $200 (10 percent of $2,000). Where the donor died before 1982 and the securities received as a gift are included in the donor's taxable estate, the basis of the securities to the donee is generally the value used for estate tax purposes.[71] For post-1981 years, these gifts generally are no longer includible in the decedent's estate, and the basis of the securities in the hands of the donee will not change because of the death of the donor.[72] (See ¶34.02(f) for effect on holding period.) If an election was made to use the carryover basis rules for a death after 1976 (see following paragraph), the donee would retain the holding period of the donor.[73]

.06 Inheritance

Securities received by inheritance take a basis equal to the value used for estate tax purposes (fair market value at date of death or if alternate value is elected, the value six months after death or at date of earlier disposition).[74] An heir, however, ordinarily is not bound by the valuation used for estate taxes and is allowed to use a correct valuation unless he is prevented from using another valuation because of his involvement in the estate tax valuation.[75] Since under the 1981 ERTA only one half of the property held in joint name with the surviving spouse is includible in the decedent's estate, there will be no adjustment in the one half of the jointly owned stock deemed to be owned by the surviving spouse.[76] Property transferred by the decedent within three years of death with no restrictions is generally no

---

[68]Reg. 1.1015-1(a)(3).
[69]Code: 1015(d).
[70]Code: Section 1015(d)(6) as amended by 1976 TRA: 2005(c).
[71]Reg. 1.1014-6.
[72]Code: 424(d), as amended 1981 ERTA: 424(a).

[73]Code: 1223(2).
[74]Code: 1014.
[75]*Hess, Jr.*, 537 F. 2d 457 (Ct. Cl. 1976), cert. den.; *Ford*, 276 F. 2d 17 (Ct. Cl. 1960); Rev. Rul. 54-97, C.B. 1954-1, 113.
[76]Code: 2040(b)(2); Code: 1014.

longer includible in the decedent's estate and, therefore, there will be no further adjustment of the donee's basis in the property.[77] There will also be no basis adjustment for appreciated gifts to the decedent within one year of the decedent's death and transferred after death to the donor (or spouse).[78]

The complex basis carryovers provisions, which were to apply to deaths occurring after 1979, have been repealed.[79] However, in the case of a decedent dying after December 31, 1976, and before November 7, 1978, an election can be made to use the basis carryover rules.

.07 Qualified Employee Pension Plans

The basis of employer securities or other securities distributed by qualified employee plans, including pension plans, thrift plans, and employee stock ownership plans (ESOP) will include both the aggregate amount of the employee contributions plus any gain realized on the distribution.[80] The entire net unrealized appreciation on employer securities is not taxable if a lump sum distribution in termination of the employee's interest is made to the employee; otherwise, only the net unrealized appreciation attributable to the employer securities is excluded from tax.[81] Thus, by electing a lump sum distribution, an employee can escape tax on the entire net unrealized appreciation on employer securities. Any gain realized on a lump sum distribution is either subject to long-term capital gains treatment, with respect to pre-1974 employer contributions, or may be subject to a special 10-year averaging convention.[82] A capital gains tax will be paid on the excluded net appreciation only when the employer securities are ultimately sold.

.08 Miscellaneous

The basis of securities may require adjustment due to distributions treated as a return of capital,[83] tax-free spin-off of a subsidiary corporation,[84] partial liquidation of a corporation,[85] redemption through use of related corporations,[86] deemed dividend distribution,[87] undistributed capital gains of an investment company,[88] bond premium which

---

[77]Code: 2035(d).
[78]Code: 1014(e).
[79]Code: 1023, repealed by P.L. 96-223.
[80]Reg. 1.402(a)-1(b).
[81]Code: 402(e)(4)(J).
[82]Code: 402(a)(2), 402(e)(4)(E).

[83]Code: 301(c); 1016(a)(4).
[84]Code: 355.
[85]Code: 302(e).
[86]Code: 304.
[87]Code: 305(b).
[88]Code: 852(b)(3)(D)(iii).

the investor has elected (or has been required) to amortize[89] (see ¶46.02), annual adjustment for original issue discount on bonds issued after May 27, 1969[90] (see ¶46.03) and stock rights and stock dividends received.[91] Reference to published Capital Changes services will generally provide the necessary information regarding corporate distributions.

34 HOLDING PERIOD

.01 Introduction

The determination of the holding period of securities is important in order to ascertain the nature of the gain or loss on their sale. With respect to post-1977 sales, securities held for more than the applicable holding period (6 months or 12 months) will generally result in long-term capital gain or loss, while a sale of securities held for not more than that period will generally cause the gain or loss to be treated as short-term.[92] The investor has the burden of proving the length of time he has held the securities.[93]

.02 Measurement of Holding Period

(a) Acquisition by purchase. The period of ownership is measured in terms of whole calendar months rather than in weeks or days. This period begins on the day after acquisition and ends on the day of sale. Stock acquired on the last day of a calendar month before June 23, 1984 must have been held at least until the first day of the 12th succeeding month in order to be held "long-term" for post-1977 sales.[94] A more than six-month holding period is required for long-term treatment of capital assets acquired after June 22, 1984 and before January 1, 1988.[95] For example, stock acquired on April 30, 1984 and sold on April 30, 1985 is not considered as held for more than 12 months. Similarly, stock acquired on September 30, 1984 and sold on March 31, 1985 would also not qualify for long-term treatment. However, stock acquired on February 27, 1984 and sold on February 28, 1985 is considered as held for more than one year.

The *trade dates* are the controlling dates. Therefore, dates of de-

---

[89]Code: 1016(a)(5).
[90]Code: 1272(c)(3).
[91]Code: 307.
[92]The holding period for long-term capital gain treatment was more than six months for pre-1972 sales and was increased to more than nine months for 1977 sales.
[93]*Taylor*, 76 F. 2d 904 (CA-2, 1935).
[94]*Caspe*, 82-2 USTC ¶9714 (CA-8, 1982); Rev. Rul. 66-7, C.B. 1966-1, 188.
[95]Code: 1222.

livery of stock or securities and payment (which may be delayed by holidays) generally have no effect.[96]

In an exception to the usual rule, the holding period of stock received upon the exercise of stock rights includes the day of exercise (acquisition of the stock).[97] The holding period of stock acquired through the exercise of a Call begins the day after the acquisition of the stock.[98]

The date payment is received (ordinarily the settlement date) on securities sold on a stock exchange will determine the year in which gain is to be recognized.[99] However, with the probable exception of a deferred delivery under New York Stock Exchange rule 64(3) (see ¶5.02), the holding period terminates on the trade date for purposes of determining whether the transaction is long-term or short-term.[100] The trade date determines the year in which a loss on a sale of a security is deductible.[101] (See ¶2.05 for further details.) In the case of a short sale, gain or loss is recognized in the year the transaction is closed. (See ¶37.02.)

The holding period of securities acquired as the result of the acquisition of a "when-issued" contract begins the day after the securities are actually acquired, not when the contract is purchased.[102] Where buy and sell contracts of securities trading on a when-issued basis are not sold or exchanged prior to their maturity, but are retained until settlement date, the sale and purchase of the underlying securities take place on the settlement date, resulting in short-term gain or loss.[103]

Stock scrip represents a fractional share of stock and its holding period will depend upon the manner in which it is acquired. Scrip received in payment of accrued interest or a taxable dividend is income in the year received and its holding period begins when the scrip is acquired.[104] The issuance of scrip in lieu of fractional shares as part of a stock dividend is nontaxable until sold, and it will tack on to its holding period the holding period of the underlying stock.[105]

---

[96] I.T. 3705, C.B. 1945, 174 (superseded by Rev. Rul. 70-598, C.B. 1970-2, 168); Rev. Rul. 66-97, C.B. 1966-1, 190; Rev. Rul. 70-344, C.B. 1970-2, 50.

[97] Code: 1223(6); Reg. 1.1223-1(f); Rev. Rul. 56-572, C.B. 1956-2, 182.

[98] Weir, 10 T.C.966 (1948).

[99] Rev. Rul. 72-381, C.B. 1972-2, 233. With respect to year-end sales, an election may be made to report the gain in the year of the sale rather than on the settlement date. Rev. Rul. 82-227, C.B. 1982-2, 89.

[100] Rev. Rul. 70-598, C.B. 1970-2, 168.

[101] G.C.M. 21503, C.B. 1939-2, 205 (superseded by Rev. Rul. 70-344, C.B. 1970-2, 50).

[102] I.T. 3721, C.B. 1945, 164.

[103] Shanis, 19 T.C. 641 (1953), aff'd per curiam 213 F. 2d 151 (CA-3, 1954).

[104] Andrews, 46 B.T.A. (1942) (Acq.); Patterson v. Anderson, 20 F. Supp. 799 (D.Ct. N.Y., 1937).

[105] Rev. Rul. 69-202, C.B. 1969-1, 95.

Similarly, the holding period of scrip received in other nontaxable transactions, including reorganizations and reverse stock splits whereby a shareholder exchanges his shares for a smaller number of shares, will include the holding period of the shares surrendered in the tax-free exchange. Where a shareholder purchases additional scrip in order to receive a full share of stock, the basis of the additional scrip purchased will be the purchase price of the scrip and its holding period will commence the day after purchase.[106]

Losses from worthless securities are deemed to have occurred on the last day of the taxable year of worthlessness.[107]

(b) Tax-free exchange. Stock acquired through the conversion of the issuing corporation's convertible bond will have a holding period beginning with the holding period of the bond. Where a cash payment is necessary in the exchange, the portion of each share of stock represented by such cash payment will receive a new holding period.[108]

(c) Illustration. Assume a convertible bond was purchased on February 1, 1984, for $100. On October 1, 1984, when the underlying stock is worth $200, the bond is converted into one share of stock with the payment of an additional $50. The conversion is tax-free, but the share of stock will have a split-holding period for purposes of determining long-term or short-term gain or loss. That part of the share attributable to the bond will have a basis of $100 and a holding period relating back to the purchase of the bond, whereas the portion of the share attributable to cash paid on conversion will have a basis of $50 and a holding period beginning with the day following the conversion date. However, since the stock on the conversion date had a value of $200, $150 or 3/4 of such value is attributable to the bond and $50 or 1/4 is attributable to the $50 cash payment. On any subsequent disposition of the share, 3/4 of the sales price will be attributable to the bond portion for purposes of determining the amount and the character (short- or long-term) of the gain or loss. The remaining portion will be attributed to the $50 payment as shown by the following table:

1. Sales price	200	300	160	150	60
2. Amount attributable to bond	150	225	120	112.50	45
3. Gain or loss attributable to bond	50	125	20	12.50	(55)
4. Amount attributable to $50 payment	50	75	40	37.50	15
5. Gain or loss attributable to $50 payment	0	25	(10)	(12.50)	(35)

---

[106] Rev. Rul. 62-140, C.B. 1962-2, 181.   [108] Rev. Rul. 62-140, C.B. 1962-2, 181.
[107] Code: 165(g).

In general, where the investor exchanges securities in a tax-free trans-action, and the basis of the securities received is determined in whole or in part with reference to the basis of the securities given up, there will be a tacking on of the holding period of the property exchanged.[109]

(d) Taxable exchanges. Securities received in a taxable exchange, taxable reorganization, corporate distribution or liquidation, gener-ally will have a new tax basis equal to their fair market value and, thus, will also receive a new holding period. The new holding period will commence from the time of the exchange, similar to a purchase of securities. However, in the case of a one-month liquidation under Section 333, the holding period of any securities received in the liqui-dation will include the holding period of the investor's stock in the liquidated corporation.[110]

(e) Treasury bonds and notes. The date of acquisition of U.S. Treasury bonds and notes (or bills) acquired through auction is the date the Secretary of the Treasury gives notification of acceptance in a news release to the successful competitive and noncompetitive bid-ders. The acquisition date of Treasury notes sold through an offering on a subscription basis at a specified yield is the date the subscription is submitted.[111]

(f) Gifts. A donee receiving securities as a gift may tack on to his holding period the holding period of the donor, provided that upon sale of the securities the donor's basis is required to be used, in whole or in part, in determining gain or loss on the transaction.[112] The donor's basis is always used where securities received as a gift after 1920 are sold at a gain; but if the securities are sold at a loss, the basis of the securities is the lower of the donor's basis or the fair market value at the time of the gift.[113] Where the fair market value is lower, the donee's holding period starts at the date of the gift without any tacking on of the donor's holding period.[114]

The Treasury has ruled that if stock is purchased and placed in a margin account in joint names, then there is no completed gift.[115] Un-der this questionable ruling, presumably all income is attributed to

---

[109] Code: 1223(1).
[110] Code: 334(c).
[111] Rev. Rul. 78-5, C.B. 1978-1, 263.
[112] Code: 1223(2). The donor's holding period is used even if the donee is re-quired to pay the gift taxes. *Turner,* 410 F. 2d 952 (CA-6, 1969).

[113] Code: 1015(a).
[114] I.T. 3453, C.B. 1941-1, 254 (declared obsolete by Rev. Rul. 69-43, C.B. 1969-1, 310).
[115] Rev. Rul. 69-148, C.B. 1969-1, 226.

the donor. No gift occurs until the donee withdraws the stock or other funds from the account.

If a gift of a security is made by a donor who died before 1982 and the value of the security is reported in the donor's estate tax return (value at date of death or alternate value) because the gift was considered to have been made in contemplation of death[116] or the donor retained certain rights in the security,[117] the holding period of the security would start at the date of the gift. There would be no tacking on of the donor's holding period because the donor's basis was not used in determining the donee's basis.[118] With respect to post-1981 deaths, however, gifts within three years of death are not includible in the donor's estate unless he retained certain interests in the gifted securities.[119] Accordingly, the basis and holding period of the securities in the hands of the donee would not change because of the death of the donor.[120] If the securities are included in the donor's gross estate because of the retention of certain interest or powers, then the basis and holding period would be the same as other property inherited from the decedent.

(g) Death. The holding period of securities inherited from a decedent relates back to the date of death. However, the securities are considered to have been held by the estate or heirs for more than six months even if actually held for less than six months.[121] If appreciated securities are gifted within one year of the donee's death and are returned after death to the donor, there is no basis adjustment arising from the donee's death. (See ¶33.06.) Accordingly, the original donor will retain the same holding period in the securities.[122]

With respect to securities purchased by the estate or testamentary trust, the holding period starts from the date of such purchase. In general, the date of distribution to the beneficiary is not significant in determining the beneficiary's holding period.[123]

(h) Wash sales. (See ¶36.01.)

(i) Stock rights and nontaxable stock dividends. Stock rights and stock dividends received in a nontaxable distribution take the same

---

[116] Code: 2035.
[117] Code: 2036-2038.
[118] Rev. Rul. 59-86, C.B. 1959-1, 209.
[119] Code: 2035(d), as amended by 1981 ERTA: 424(a). Gifts of insurance poli-cies would be included in the donor's estate.
[120] Code: 1014, 1223(11).
[121] Code: 1223(11).
[122] Code: 1223(2).
[123] *Brewster* v. *Gage,* 280 U.S. 327 (1930).

holding period as the "old" stock.[124] Thus, when stock rights are sold, the holding period of the "old" stock is "tacked on" in determining the holding period of the rights. However, securities acquired through exercise of the rights will not take on a "tacked on" holding period. The holding period will start on the date of exercise.[125]

(j) Short sales. (See ¶37.03.)

(k) Tax straddles. (See ¶38 and ¶39.11.)

35 IDENTIFICATION OF SECURITIES

.01 Importance of Identification

Where an investor holds various lots of securities acquired at different times or at different prices, and sells only a part of his holdings, the proper identification of which securities are sold has great significance in determining the tax effect of the sale. Because of differences in holding periods and bases, a sale may result in either short-term or long-term gain or loss, depending upon which securities are deemed sold. Adequate record-keeping on the part of the investor will enable him to control the type and amount of gain or loss to be recognized when a portion of a position is sold.

.02 Rules of the Regulations

The Treasury has provided certain guidelines, consistent with court decisions, with respect to the identification of securities sold.[126]

(a) Securities held by brokers, banks, and the like. Where securities are held by a broker in a cash or margin account or by a bank or other custodian or agent, an adequate identification of the securities sold is made if the investor specifies to the broker or other agent at the time of the sale, the particular securities to be sold and written confirmation is received from the broker or other agent within a reasonable time thereafter.[127] The designated securities are treated as sold even though the broker delivers other securities to the transferee. Identification of the securities sold from the account should be by purchase date, cost, or both.[128]

---

[124] Code: 1223(5); Rev. Rul. 72-71, C.B. 1972-1, 99.
[125] Code: 1223(6); Reg. 1.1223-1(f); Rev. Rul. 56-572, C.B. 1956-2, 182.
[126] Reg. 1.1012-1(c).
[127] Reg. 1.1012-1(c)(3)(i).
[128] Reg. 1.1012-1(c)(2).

(b) Securities held by investor. Where securities are held by the investor, the securities sold will be those represented by certificates actually delivered, even if the investor intended, or instructed the broker to sell securities from a different lot.[129] However, where a single certificate represents securities acquired at different times or at different prices, the investor will have made an adequate identification of the portion sold, if he specifies the particular lot to be sold by identifying the purchase date, cost, or both, of the securities, and written confirmation thereof is received from the broker within a reasonable time thereafter.[130] If transfer of part of the securities represented by a single certificate is made directly to the purchaser and not to a broker, adequate identification is made where the investor maintains a written record of the particular securities which he intended to sell.[131]

(c) First-in, first-out. Where the investor cannot "identify" the lots from which the securities are sold, he is required to apply the first-in, first-out (FIFO) rule, so that the securities sold are deemed to be the earliest acquired.[132] On the other hand, if delivery is made from lots held at a particular source, then the FIFO rule applies only to securities held at that source.[133] Thus, where the investor delivers stock from lots held by broker A and other lots are held by broker B, the FIFO rule will apply only to the lots held by broker A. The FIFO rule has also been applied to transactions in "when issued" securities.[134]

For purposes of the FIFO rule, the earliest acquisition date has been interpreted to mean the earliest beginning date of a holding period for purposes of determining gain or loss.[135] Thus, although there is some conflict in this area, the acquisition date for securities received as a gift should be the first day of the holding period and not necessarily the date of gift.[136] Nontaxable stock dividends are treated as having been acquired at the time of the original stock purchase. Stock acquired through the exercise of rights is deemed acquired when the rights were exercised. If a portion of such stock is sold and there is no specific identification, the stock deemed sold is that acquired through exercise of rights received from the earliest held stock (FIFO rule).[137]

---

[129] Reg. 1.1012-1 (c)(2); *Davidson,* 305 U.S. 44 (1938).

[130] Rev. Rul. 61-97, C.B. 1961-1, 394; see also TIR No. 334, 8/17/61.

[131] Reg. 1.1012-1 (c)(3)(ii).

[132] *Kluger Associates, Inc.,* 69 T.C. 925 (1978), aff'd 617 F. 2d 323 (CA-2, 1980).

[133] Reg. 1.1012-1 (c)(1).

[134] I.T. 3858, C.B. 1947-2, 71.

[135] *W. A. Forretser,* 32 B.T.A. 745 (1935); *Curtis,* 101 F. 2d 40 (CA-2, 1939); *Helvering* v. *Campbell,* 313 U.S. 15 (1941).

[136] *Richardson* v. *Smith,* (DC, Conn. 1938), rev'd on other issues 102 F. 2d 697; contra *Hanes,* 1 TCM 634 (1943).

[137] GCM 11743, C.B. XII-2, 31; *Keeler,* 86 F. 2d 265 (CA-8, 1936), cert. den. 300 U.S. 673.

(d) Securities held by trust or estate. Where the securities are held by the fiduciary of a trust or estate (and not by a broker or other custodian), adequate identification is made if the fiduciary specifies in writing in the trust's or estate's records at the time of disposition the particular security to be sold, transferred or distributed. A distributee must get written notification of the particular security distributed to him. The identified security is treated as sold, transferred, or distributed even though other securities are in fact delivered.[138]

(e) Regulated investment company stock (mutual funds). The basis of regulated investment company stock generally is computed in the same manner as stock of a regular corporation. Additional shares acquired through reinvestment of dividends, including capital gain dividends, will have a tax basis equal to the amount of the dividend income taxed to the investor. If a regulated investment company elects to treat undistributed capital gains as having been distributed to its shareholders, the shareholders should increase the tax bases of their shares by 72 percent (70 percent for pre-1979 capital gains) of the undistributed capital gains.[139] In determining the tax basis of shares sold, an investor may use FIFO or specific identification. However, if stock of a regulated investment company purchased or acquired at different prices are left with a custodian or agent appointed by the regulated investment company for that purpose, an investor may elect an average basis in lieu of the regular methods of identification.[140] Either the double-entry method (the shares are segregated into short-term and long-term capital gains stock) or single-category method (average cost of all shares in the account) may be elected.

.03 Reorganizations and Partial Liquidations

Identification is possible where securities are exchanged in a tax-free reorganization. One arbitrary method of identification that has been accepted is the assigning of the lowest numbered new certificate to the earliest lot purchased.[141] In a partial liquidation, the shareholder may specifically identify the shares to be redeemed or exchanged for newly issued shares; identification is not negated because the designations were recorded incorrectly on the corporation's record.[142] In absence of identification, the FIFO rule will be applied in determining gain or loss of the cancelled shares and the basis of the newly issued

---

[138] Reg. 1.1012-1(c)(4).
[139] Code: 852(b)(3)(D)(iii).
[140] Reg. 1.1012-1(e).

[141] *Ford*, 33 B.T.A. 1229 (1936)(A); Rev. Rul. 68-23, C.B. 1968-1, 144.
[142] *Rule*, 127 F. 2d 979 (CA-10, 1942).

or remaining shares.[143] The subsequently promulgated regulations relating to identification where a single certificate represents securities acquired at different times (see ¶35.02(b)) may also be applicable to these transactions.

Where adequate identification is not made and securities in the same corporation are received, the courts have generally held that the first-in, first-out method must be used.[144] However, where securities of another corporation are received in a tax-free reorganization and adequate identification is not made, the cost of the securities surrendered is averaged and allocated equally among the new securities received.[145]

36 WASH SALES

.01 General Rules

When an investor sells stock or securities at a loss and within a 30-day period before or after such sale acquires substantially identical securities, the loss will be disallowed as a "wash sale."[146] It is immaterial whether the securities purchased or sold were purchased on margin.[147] Similarly, under the 1984 Act, the closing of a short sale at a loss within 30 days of a sale or another short sale of substantially identical stock or securities will be a wash sale. Stock or commodity straddles may now be subject to rules similar to the wash sales rules unless all positions consist of Section 1256 contracts subject to the mark-to-market rule, the Call is a qualified covered Call, or the straddle is an identified straddle.[148] See ¶38.04 for treatment of mixed straddles. (For the definition of "substantially identical" property, see the discussion in ¶37.04 of the short sales rules, to which the term also applies.)

The entering into a contract or option to acquire substantially identical securities within the 61-day period will be treated as an actual acquisition for purposes of the wash sale rules. Thus the purchase of

---

[143] *Allington*, 31 B.T.A. 421 (1934).

[144] *Kraus*, 88 F. 2d 616 (CA-2, 1937); cf. *Fuller*, 81 F. 2d 176 (CA-1, 1936); but cf. *Big Wolf Corp.*, 2 T.C. 751 (1943)(A).

[145] *Von Gunten*, 76 F. 2d 670 (1935); cf. *Bloch*, 148 F. 2d 452 (CA-9, 1945); and Rev. Rul. 55-355, C.B. 1955-1, 418.

[146] Code: 1091(a). Note that prior to the 1984 Act, an individual trader who qualified as being in the business of buying and selling securities was exempt from the wash sales provisions, but a corporate investor was not excluded unless it was a dealer in securities. Reg. 1.1091-1(a). Both individuals and corporations will now be subject to the wash sales rules unless the taxpayer is a dealer and the loss is sustained in the ordinary course of business. Code 1091(a), effective for sales after 1984. A trader may have difficulty deducting a loss under the new provision if he trades extensively in that security.

[147] Rev. Rul. 71-316, C.B. 1971-2, 311.

[148] Code: 1092(b).

a Call (Listed or Unlisted) will bring into play the wash sale rules. Writing an "in-the-money" Put should not deny an investor a loss on the prior sale of the underlying stock unless the Put is exercised within the 30-day period. A purchase of a convertible preferred stock has also been ruled to be an acquisition of an option for wash sales purposes.[149] Apparently, the purchase of a convertible debenture would be accorded similar treatment. A loss was disallowed where the shares were sold to a close friend under an oral understanding to repurchase the same shares at the same price 33 days after the original sale.[150]

Only acquisitions by purchase or in a fully taxable exchange result in disallowance.[151] Therefore, receipt of securities as a gift or in a nontaxable exchange will not be considered an acquisition.

Employer stock received as a bonus under a work incentive plan, within 30 days from the sale of other bonus stock at a loss, is treated as an acquisition of stock for purposes of the wash sale rules.[152] Presumably a receipt of stock from a qualified employees' plan (e.g., pension plan, stock bonus plan, employee stock ownership plan (ESOP)), will also be treated as an acquisition. See below for similar treatment of employee stock options.

The basis of the substantially identical securities acquired within the 61-day period will, in effect, be increased by the amount of the disallowed loss.[153] The holding period of the securities sold at a loss will be tacked on to the newly acquired position.[154] Thus, if the old securities were held for five months and the newly acquired securities were held for more than one month, long-term gain or loss would be recognized on the sale of the new securities, under the 1984 Act.

.02 Stock Rights, Warrants, and Options

The Treasury has ruled that stock warrants come within the definition of "options" to acquire, which may cause the disallowance of a loss.[155] Thus, deduction of a loss on the sale of stock, where a warrant to buy the stock is purchased within the 61-day period, will be denied because the investor has acquired an option to buy the stock. However, it is unclear whether under Section 1091(d) a disallowed loss because of the purchase of a Call is added to the basis of the acquired Call. Similarly, with respect to the holding period of the stock sold at

---

[149] Rev. Rul. 77-201, C.B. 1977-1, 250.
[150] *Stein*, T.C. Memo 1977-241; *Est. of Estroff*, 80 T.C. Memo 1983-666.
[151] Reg. 1.1091-1(f).
[152] Rev. Rul. 73-329, C.B. 1973-2, 302.
[153] Code: 1091(d).
[154] Code: 1223(4).
[155] Rev. Rul. 56-406, C.B. 1956-2, 523.

a loss, it is also unclear whether under Section 1223 (4) such holding period is added to the holding period of the option. (See ¶39.06 for a complete discussion of the issues.)

With respect to stock rights, it is arguable that the receipt of a stock right on stock held, where a sale of the underlying stock occurs within 30 days of the receipt of the right, should not bring into play the wash sale provisions, provided the right is not exercised within the 30-day period, since the investor has not "entered into an option." However, the Treasury has ruled in a related situation, that where an employee is granted a stock option under a restricted or qualified stock option plan, for purposes of the wash sale rules, he will be deemed to have entered into an option to acquire stock on the date on which the option is granted to him.[156]

The sale of an option (stock right, warrant, Call, and the like) and the subsequent purchase of a substantially identical security must be distinguished from a sale of a stock or security followed by the purchase of an option. The wash sales rule only applies to a loss realized on a sale of a stock or security. Section 1091 and its underlying regulations are silent as to whether a warrant or other type of option constitutes a stock or security. There are conflicting rules in other tax areas as to whether these options are a stock or security. A right to subscribe to a security is considered a security in the tax provisions affecting security dealers[157] and exchanges pursuant to SEC orders,[158] but not for purposes of corporate reorganizations.[159] The Treasury has implicitly ruled that a warrant is a security[160] and it may take the same view with respect to other types of options (e.g., Listed Puts and Calls). However, it will not disallow a loss on the sale of a warrant under the wash sales rules when the underlying stock was purchased within the 30-day period unless the relative values and price changes of the stock and warrant are so similar as to make the stock warrant substantially identical to the newly acquired stock.[161] Thus, if the warrant is exercisable at a fairly minimal price (e.g., the exercise price is $1 and the stock price is $100), the stock and warrant may be considered substantially identical; however, they will not be substantially identical if there is a large exercise price because of the leverage factor and the fact that they may not have similar price movements (e.g., the warrant is selling for $5 with an exercise price of $95 and the stock is selling for $90).

---

[156] Rev. Rul. 56-452, C.B. 1956-2, 525.
[157] Reg. 1.1236-1 (c).
[158] Reg. 1.1083 (f).
[159] Reg. 1.351-1 (a) (ii) and 1.354-1 (e).
[160] Rev. Rul. 56-406, C.B. 1956-2, 523.
[161] GCM 39036. (Sept. 16, 1983), I.R.B. 1983.

The sale of a Listed option at a loss with a subsequent repurchase within 30 days of the identical Listed option will cause the wash sales rules to apply only if a Listed option is deemed to be a "security" within Section 1091. (See below about the "substantially identical" issue.) Prior to the 1984 Act, the purchase of a Listed option "to close" at a loss with a subsequent resale within 30 days of the identical Listed option was not a wash sale because you needed two purchases and one sale to come within Section 1091. However, for short sales after July 18, 1984, the purchase of a Listed option "to close" with a subsequent resale within 30 days will be a wash sale.

A granting (sale) and closing out of an option has been distinguished by the Treasury in a recent private ruling from a purchase and sale of an option. A grantor of an option does not "acquire" property within the meaning of Section 1091, and, therefore, the wash sale provisions do not apply to losses on options written by the grantor.[162] It can be inferred from the private ruling that the Treasury may consider a purchase of an option to be an acquisition of property and, accordingly, a sale of the option can come within the wash sale rules if substantially identical property was acquired within the 30-day period. Thus, if an investor sold a Call at a loss and repurchased the same Call within 30 days, the Treasury may disallow the loss under the wash sale rules.

A second consideration is whether the subsequently acquired stock or security is "substantially identical" to a stock right, warrant, Call, or other option. In general, the term has the same meaning as when used for purposes of short sales.[163] A Call has been ruled not to be substantially identical to the underlying stock for purposes of the short sale rule.[164] On the other hand, a loss on sale of a warrant was disallowed on grounds that its relative value and price changes were so similar to the later acquired stock as to make the warrant a fully convertible security and therefore substantially identical.[165] This might be the case where the stock is selling above the exercise price of the warrant so that fluctuations in the stock directly affect the market value of the warrant. The ruling did not consider other factors, such as a limited life and lack of dividend rights, in deciding that a warrant was substantially identical. Bonds issued by the same governmental agency have been ruled to be not substantially identical because of different dates of issue, dates of interest payments, maturity dates, or interest rates,[166] and similar considerations should apply to

---

[162] Private Ruling Doc. 7730002.
[163] Reg. 1.1233-1(d)(1).
[164] Rev. Rul. 58-384, C.B. 1958-2, 410.

[165] Rev. Rul. 56-406, C.B. 1956-2, 523.
[166] See footnote 215 below.

warrants and other options. Stock rights more closely resemble Calls than warrants because of the substantial difference between market price and option price and the shorter time available for exercise of the option. Generally, these different forms of options should not be considered substantially identical to the underlying stock or security, but, as stated above, under certain conditions a warrant will be treated by the Treasury as substantially identical.

If Listed options are deemed to be a security for purposes of Section 1091, then the question exists as to when Listed options are substantially identical to each other. Listed options with different striking prices and/or different expiration dates should not be substantially identical to each other.[167] However, Listed options with the same striking price and expiration date trading on different exchanges might be deemed to be substantially identical to each other.

.03   Commodity Contracts and Foreign Currency

The Treasury had resolved a dispute among the courts[168] as to whether a commodity Futures contract is a security for purposes of the wash sales rules by ruling that the wash sales provisions do not apply to commodity Futures transactions.[169] This ruling would apply to commodity straddles entered into before June 24, 1981.[170] However, the Treasury has denied a trader a loss deduction when an identical long position was repurchased on the same day on the grounds that no economic loss occurred if the entire transaction is reviewed.[171] Straddle positions after June 23, 1981, which are governed by Section 1092, will be subject to similar wash sales rules. Note that regulated Futures contracts, which are taxed under the mark-to-market rules,[172] generally are excluded from the wash sales rules. (See discussion of commodity Futures starting in ¶41.)

Losses on foreign currencies are excluded from the wash sales provisions because foreign currencies also are not securities for these purposes.[173] However, foreign currency contracts may be subject to the mark-to-market rules[174] or to the commodity straddle provisions if these contracts are part of a mixed straddle. Accordingly, rules similar to the wash sales provision would apply to these mixed straddles.[175]

---

[167] See ¶41.03 (d) dealing with commodity futures transactions and the "substantially identical" issue.

[168] *Trenton Cotton Oil,* 147 F. 2d 33 (CA-6, 1945); *Corn Products Refining Co.,* 215 F. 2d 513 (CA-4, 1954), aff'g. 16 T.C. 395 (1951), aff'd. on other issues 350 U.S. 46 (1955).

[169] Rev. Rul. 71-568, C.B. 1971-2, 312.
[170] Code: 1092 (b).
[171] Private Ruling Doc. 8241006.
[172] Code: 1256.
[173] Rev. Rul. 74-218. C.B. 1974-1, 202.
[174] Code: 1256.
[175] Code: 1092 (b).

.04 Reduction of Holdings

Losses will not be disallowed where there is a bona fide sale of securities made to reduce the investor's holdings purchased in one lot, even though the sale is made within the 30 days after the securities were purchased and even though such transaction would literally come within the statutory provisions.[176] However, the wash sale rule was held to be applicable when separate lots were purchased on the first and fifteenth day of the same month, and the last purchase was sold at a loss on the 29th day of the same month.[177] This latter ruling is inconsistent with the concept that the wash sale rule should not apply to a transaction where the taxpayer is merely reducing his holdings notwithstanding the acquisition in two separate lots.

.05 Different Lots

Where there have been multiple purchases of identical securities at different prices and the wash sale provision applies to only some of the securities sold, matching of the sales and purchases are in the order of the date of the earliest acquisition.[178] Thus, if 100 shares are purchased on February 1 for $100 and 100 shares purchased on March 1 for $50, and the 200 shares are subsequently sold on December 1 for $10, followed by a repurchase on December 15 of 100 shares, the $90 loss on the first acquisition will be disallowed, but the $40 loss on the second acquisition is deductible. However, an investor may identify which of several lots was sold, which would affect the lots that are subject to the wash sales rule. Further, if some lots are sold at a gain and one or more at a loss, no loss will be allowed for the lots sold at a loss to the extent that shares are reacquired during the 30-day period.[179]

.06 Gain Recognized

The wash sale rules are not applicable where the stock is sold at a gain and immediately repurchased. Sales of different lots at the same time are treated separately in determining gain or loss on the shares of each lot. For example, if lot A is purchased at $20 a share and lot B at $50 a share, and all the shares are sold at $45 a share, the loss on the sale of the shares of lot B may be disallowed under the wash sales rules.[180] Prior to enactment of the provision for unlimited capital loss

---

[176] Rev. Rul. 56-602, C.B. 1956-2, 527.
[177] Rev. Rul. 71-316, C.B. 1971-2, 311.
[178] Reg. 1.1091-1(c); Rev. Rul. 70-231,

C.B. 1970-1, 171.
[179] Rev. Rul. 70-231, C.B. 1970-1, 171.
[180] Rev. Rul. 70-231, C.B. 1970-1, 171.

carryover,[181] investors would accelerate gain in order to wipe out any capital loss carryover that was about to expire. Such action is now rarely advantageous except possibly to offset long-term losses against short-term gains.

.07 Sales to Related Parties

The wash sale provisions do not specifically deny a loss deduction where another member of the family or other related party purchases the same security within the 61-day period.[182] However, an attempt to circumvent these rules by having the investor's wife buy back securities sold by the investor at a loss has been frustrated by the Supreme Court under another section of the Internal Revenue Code,[183] on the ground that there was an indirect sale of the stock to the wife.[184] The wife had used her own funds, but the repurchase on the open market had occurred on the same day as the sale at substantially the same price.

Where the repurchase is at a different time and price so that there is not a "direct or indirect" sale between related parties, the loss should not be disallowed even though the repurchase by a related party is within the 61-day period.[185] If a wife is using her husband's funds and acting as his agent to repurchase the stock within the 61-day period, the transaction could be attacked as not being bona fide and the loss will probably be disallowed under the wash sale rules. Similarly, if there is an "understanding" that the securities will be repurchased the loss will be disallowed.[186]

.08 Effect of Short Sales

The regulations[187] treat a short sale as a true sale for purposes of the wash sale rules *if* on such date, the taxpayer owned (or had a contract or option to acquire) securities identical to those sold short *and* subsequently delivered them to close the short sale. When these conditions are not met, the short sale is deemed to occur when it is closed out by delivery of the securities. The regulations are intended to preclude the avoidance of the wash sale rules by use of the *Doyle* plan ("short against the box"),[188] which consisted of making a simultaneous short

---

[181] Code: 1212(b).
[182] *Norton,* 250 F. 2d 902 (CA-5, 1958).
[183] Predecessor of Code section 267; the loss would be allowed to the wife (transferee) only to the extent of the recognized gain upon subsequent sale.
[184] *J.P.McWilliams,* 331 U.S. 694 (1947).

[185] *Norton,* 250 F. 2d 902 (CA-5, 1958).
[186] *Mellon,* 36 B.T.A. 977 (1936); *E. E. Hassen,* 63 T.C. 175 (1974), aff'd 599 F. 2d 305 (CA-9, 1979).
[187] Reg. 1.1091-1(g) and 1.1233-1(a)(5).
[188] *Doyle,* 286 F. 2d 654 (CA-7, 1961).

sale and purchase of the securities, waiting for just over 30 days, and then delivering the certificates representing the original holding to close out the short sale. Under the 1984 Act, a loss on a short sale will be disallowed if within 30 days before or after the closing of the short sale, substantially identical stock or securities were sold, or the investor entered into another short sale of substantially identical stock or securities.[189] For example, if an investor realized a $1,000 loss by closing a short sale on February 28, 1985 and entered into a similar short sale on March 15, 1985, the loss would not be recognized. These special short sale rules apply only in interpreting the wash sale rules, they do not change the rules applicable to short sales generally. Therefore, the technique of going short against the box to postpone the recognition of gain would not be affected. (See ¶2.01.)

However, the expansion of the wash sales rules to short sales might cause some conflict as to the general applicability of the wash sales rules to certain transactions. For example, when a taxpayer closes out the short side of the short against the box transaction with new stock at a loss, and in the subsequent year (but within 30 days) sells out the long side at a profit, the latter sale might be viewed as a wash sale, causing the disallowance of the loss and resulting in the reduction of the subsequent gain. There appears to be no effect on holding period, i.e., no "tack on." In addition, option transactions (both Section 1256 contracts and non-1256 contracts) might be affected under rules that will be adopted which would be similar to the wash sales rules.

.09 Tax Straddles (See ¶38.02 and ¶39.11(a).)

.10 Avoidance of Wash Sale Rules

See ¶18 for discussion of ways of avoiding the wash sale rules. According to the Treasury, a contract for deferred delivery (see ¶5.02) will not be a means of circumventing the wash sale rules.[190]

37 SHORT SALES

.01 Definition

A short sale of securities may be defined as a contract for the sale and delivery of securities the seller does not own or does not intend to make available for delivery on the sale. The securities are usually

---

[189] Code: 1091(e), effective for short sales after July 18, 1984.

[190] Rev. Rul. 59-418, C.B. 1959-2, 184.

borrowed for delivery to the buyer. Such sale may be ultimately covered by the purchase of the securities in the market or by the delivery of securities already owned but not delivered to the buyer at the time of sale.[191]

.02 Taxable Event

The taxable event occurs only when the securities are delivered to close the short sale.[192] This rule is applicable whether gain or loss is realized on the sale.[193]

.03 Statutory Rules

In general, the holding period of the property delivered to close the short sale determines whether a long- or short-term gain or loss results.[194] However, statutory rules have been established with respect to "substantially identical property" in order to prevent use of short sales to convert short-term gains into long-term gains or to create artificial long-term gains and short-term losses. "Property" for this purpose includes only stock and securities including those dealt on a "when-issued" basis, and commodity Futures which are capital assets in the hands of the taxpayer.[195] A purchase of a spot commodity contract and a sale of a commodity Future ("cash and carry transaction") would not come within the short sale rules since only commodity Futures and not the actual commodity are considered property for purposes of the short sale rules. However, if the cash and carry transaction comes under the new straddle provisions,[196] then rules similar to the short sale rules will apply to any gains realized in the transaction. In addition, the applicable one-year or six-month holding period rule ordinarily will apply to the gain or loss realized on disposition of the commodity used to cover the Futures contract after appropriate adjustment for the gain or loss realized on termination of the Futures contract under the mark-to-market rules. Again, if the new straddle provision (Section 1092) applies to the Futures contract because the mixed straddle election is made, the gain may be treated as short-term under rules similar to the short sale rules.[197] Commodity Futures transactions which would ordinarily come within the short sale rules will instead be taxed under the straddle provisions, if the commodity positions are subject to the straddle rules.[198]

---

[191] *Provost,* 269 U.S. 443 (1926); Rev. Rul. 72-478, C.B. 1972-2, 288.
[192] Reg. 1.1233-1 (a).
[193] *Hendricks,* 51 T.C. 235 (1968).
[194] Reg. 1.1233-1 (a)(3).
[195] Code: 1233(e)(2)(A).
[196] Code: 1092(b). (See ¶41.03(g).)
[197] Ibid.
[198] See ¶38.03 and ¶38.04.

See a complete discussion of commodity Futures in ¶41. (See ¶34.01 for additional details on holding period.) The meaning of "substantially identical property" is discussed in ¶37.04.

The short sale rules may be summarized as follows:

(a) **Rule 1.** If property substantially identical to that sold short has been held by the taxpayer (or his spouse)[199] on the date of the short sale for not more than six months for property acquired during the period June 23, 1984 through 1987 or for not more than one year for other property, or is acquired by him after the short sale but before the closing thereof, then

A. Any *gain* on the closing of such a short sale shall be considered as a short-term gain (even if property held for more than the applicable long-term holding period is used to close the short sale).[200]

B. The *holding period* of such substantially identical property becomes "tainted" and is considered to begin on the closing of the short sale, or on the date of a sale, gift, or other disposition of the property, if earlier.[201] The "tainting" of the holding period will apply only to an equal quantity of substantially identical property in the chronological order of acquisition. This rule does not apply to any excess over the quantity sold short.

(b) **Rule 2.** If substantially identical property has been held by the taxpayer (or his spouse) for more than six months for property acquired during the period June 23, 1984 through 1987, or for more than one year for other property, at the time the short sale was made, any *loss* on closing the short sale is considered a long-term loss even if the property delivered to close the short sale was held for not more than the applicable long-term holding period.[202]

Where the taxpayer holds both short-term and long-term positions in securities substantially identical to the securities sold short, all the above rules will be applicable. Accordingly, any gain on sale would be short-term and any loss would be long-term.

Example. Investor T purchases one share of X stock on February 1, 1983, for $10 and an additional share on April 1, 1983, for $20. T

---

[199] Code: 1233(e)(2)(C); Reg. 1.1233-1. (d)(3).
[200] Code: 1233(b)(1); Reg. 1.1233-1(c)(2).
[201] Code: 1233(b)(2); Reg. 1.1233-1(c)(2).
[202] Code: 1233(d); Reg. 1.1233-1(c)(4). Note that if a security was held for less than the applicable long-term holding period at the time of the short sale but for more than that period at the time the short sale was closed, any loss realized on the sale would be short-term. Reg. 1.1233-1(c)(2).

sells short one share of X stock on March 1, 1984, at $30. On December 1, 1984, the X stock is selling at $40. If T then delivers the one share purchased February 1, 1983, in order to close out the short sale position, the $20 gain will be treated, by application of Rule 1(A), as short-term since substantially identical property (one share of stock purchased April 1, 1983) had been held "short-term" on the date of the short sale. In addition, the holding period of the one share of X stock purchased on April 1, 1983, is "tainted" and is considered, by application of Rule 1(B), to begin on December 1, 1984, the date of the closing of the short sale. However, if the April 1, 1983, position was used to close the short sale, the gain of $10 would be short-term under Rule 1(A), but the holding period of the February 1, 1983, position would not be affected since such stock was held for more than one year at the time of the short sale. If T closed his short position by purchasing one share of X stock on December 1, 1984, at $40, the loss of $10 would be a long-term capital loss by application of Rule 2 since substantially identical property had been held at the time of the short sale for more than one year. The holding period of the April 1, 1983, position would be tainted and would be considered by application of Rule 1(B) to begin on December 1, 1984, the date the short sale was closed.

An open question would appear to be whether the holding period taint rolls over to other substantially identical stock if the tainted stock is sold. Thus, where the investor purchases 100 shares of X stock on March 1 and 100 shares of X stock on March 3 and sells short 100 shares of X stock on May 15, the holding period of only the 100 shares purchased March 1 will be tainted. If the March 1 stock is sold, and the short position is left open, do the short sale rules result in the March 3 stock becoming tainted? No further affirmative act seems to have occurred so as to bring the short sale rules into operation once again. The concepts of the short sales rules are to be adopted by Treasury under the tax straddle rules.[203] It will be interesting to see whether the Treasury addresses the problem of the rollover taint.

Example. An investor enters into a calendar spread for a three-point debit in ABC stock when ABC is selling at $105 (i.e., sell October 1984 100 Calls short at $11 and purchase January 1985 100 Calls at $14). The investor thus has a net economic cost of $3 per share. This transaction should come within the tax straddle rules as being offsetting positions and, accordingly, should come within the yet-to-

---

[203] Code: 1092(b).

be-promulgated regulations under Section 1092 (b). For purposes of discussion, it is assumed that there is a substantial diminution of risk of loss in this transaction. Assume that the taxpayer also buys April 1985 100 Calls on ABC. This long position holding period should not be affected by the short October 1984 position. The October short Calls should only taint the January Calls which potentially have a more-than-six-month holding period. If the January Calls are then sold, the issue is whether the taint of the October short Calls rolls over to taint the April Calls. This issue remains unresolved.

(c) Transitional rules. The holding period of the long position at the time of the short sale will determine whether or not the short sale rules come into play. However, the normal holding period rules at the time the short sale is closed will determine whether the requisite holding period for long-term treatment was met. These transitional rules are complicated by the dual long-term holding period provisions (more than one year except for a more-than-six-month holding period for property acquired during the period June 23, 1984 through 1987). Thus, if an investor purchased 100 shares on January 2, 1984 and another 100 shares on June 28, 1984 and sold short 100 shares on December 29, 1984, the short-sale rules would be activated because the first purchase was not held for more than one year at the time of the short sale. Accordingly, any gain on the closing of the short sale could be short-term. Additionally, any loss would be long-term because the six-month holding period was met with respect to the second purchase. The tax rates in effect at the time the short sale is closed will determine the amount of tax due in the short sale because the transaction is not closed until the short sale is completed. (See ¶34.02 for further details on holding periods.)

(d) Options to sell. The acquisition of an option to sell stock at a fixed price (referred to as a "Put") is considered as a short sale for purposes of Rule 1 above and the exercise or failure to exercise such option is considered as a closing of the short sale.[204] However, the acquisition of a Put is *not* considered a short sale for purposes of Rule

---

[204] Code: 1233 (b); Reg. 1.1233-1 (c) (3); Rev. Rul. 78-182, C.B. 1978-1, 265; Special Ruling, September 7, 1973, 74-9 CCH ¶6596. This private ruling originally indicated that the sale of the previously purchased Put would retroactively reinstate the original holding period of the long stock position. A subsequent private ruling, dated April 30, 1976, retracted the IRS's original erroneous interpretation of the short sale rules. Thus, the subsequent disposition of an acquired Put will merely start the commencement of a new holding period for the stock.

2 above and the exercise or failure to exercise such option is *not* considered as a closing of the short sale.[205]

Note, that once the Put is acquired (other than on the same day— see below), the holding period of an equivalent amount of stock, which is held less than the applicable one-year or six-month period, is lost and will not start over again until the Put is disposed of. This is true even though the stock is sold later at a loss. Thus, if stock is purchased in 1983 for $21 per share and 11 months later a 9-month Put is purchased with a striking price of $20, a sale of the stock 5 months thereafter at $20 will produce a short-term capital loss because the 11-month holding period would be lost due to the purchase of the Put.

In addition, Rule 1 is not applicable if a Put and the stock intended to be used in exercising the Put are acquired on the same day, provided the stock is actually so used if the Put is exercised. Where the option does not specifically identify the property intended to be used in exercising the option, the taxpayer's records must, within 15 days after the acquisition of the stock, contain such identification. If the Put is not exercised, its cost is added to the basis of the stock with which it was identified.[206]

Where the market value of the stock has fallen so that a Put has increased in value, the Put could be sold and, if it was held for more than the applicable one-year or six-month period, the gain will be long-term.[207] This should occur since the acquisition of the Put was not considered a short sale because of the exception discussed above. The stock could be sold prior to the long-term holding period in order to have the loss sustained treated as a short-term capital loss. (See example in ¶13.01 and discussion in ¶39.04(e).) However, repeated sales of Puts under similar curcumstances could negate the taxpayer's "intention" to exercise the Put with the designated stock. Under such circumstances, it could then be argued that the exception would not apply in the case of any Puts the taxpayer acquired. If this argument prevailed and the stock appreciated in value, the holding period would be "tainted" by Rule 1, since the acquisition of the Put would be considered as a short sale. There will be some confusion until the Treasury promulgates regulations under Section 1092(b) as to whether the tax straddle rules apply to the married Put situation and as to whether there will be a loss of holding period under Section 1092(b) even though the married Put exception would ordinarily ap-

---

[205]Code: 1233(d); Reg. 1.1233-1(c)(4).
[206]Code: 1233(c); Reg. 1.1233-1(c)(3).
[207]Special Ruling, September 7, 1973, 74-9 CCH ¶6596.

ply to short sales. The authors believe that the married Put exception should also apply under the tax straddle rules.

Note that the writing of a Put does not constitute a short sale and should not be confused with the acquisition of a Put.[208] Consequently, if a Put is written at the time when the grantor held the underlying stock for less than the applicable long-term holding period, the writing of the Put will not affect the holding period of the underlying stock.[209]

.04 Substantially Identical Property

The short sale rules apply only when the investor holds other securities substantially identical to the securities sold short. The solution to the perplexing problem of what this term means is far from clear. Treasury regulations indicate that the term is to be applied according to the facts and circumstances in each case, and generally is to have the same meaning as when used in the wash sale provisions.[210] This discussion covers the meaning of the term applicable to both the wash sale and short sale rules. Based upon Treasury rulings and court decisions, certain guidelines have been established.

Stocks and securities of one corporation, although not ordinarily considered to be substantially identical to stocks and securities of a different corporation, may be so considered if the corporations are predecessor and successor in a reorganization where their securities are exchanged.[211]

Where two corporations have agreed to a merger, subject to approval by shareholders, their securities should not be considered substantially identical, in that too many contingencies exist, or may arise, which might prevent the merger. Even after approval by the stockholders, other contingencies, such as intervention by the federal government, may prevent the merger. However, if the market prices of the stocks are fluctuating proportionately to each other and stockholders' approval of the merger has been obtained, the Treasury might maintain that the stocks of the two corporations are substantially identical to each other.

When-issued securities of a successor corporation may be substantially identical to the securities to be exchanged for them in a reorganization.[212] However, the Treasury has ruled that where a taxpayer has made a short sale of the when-issued common stock of a corporation,

---

[208] Rev. Rul. 78-182, C.B. 1978-1, 265.
[209] Ibid.
[210] Reg. 1.1233-1(d)(1).

[211] Reg. 1.1233-1(d)(1).
[212] Reg. 1.1233-1(c)(6), example (6).

and at the time of the sale holds convertible preferred stock which is not substantially identical to the common, the conversion of the preferred into the common prior to the closing of the short sale does not constitute the acquisition of substantially identical stock.[213] (See ¶40.03 for further discussion of the short sale rules as applicable to when-issued transactions.)

Common stock is not considered identical to other classes of nonconvertible stock or bonds in the same corporation unless there are only minor differences between them. Convertible preferred stock, convertible bonds, or warrants are treated as substantially identical to the securities into which they are convertible only when their relative values and price changes have been generally similar to the underlying security.[214] Thus, for example, where the conversion price for the bond is greater than the market price of the underlying security, the price of the bond will be more dependent upon its yield and security than upon the value of its conversion feature. Note, however, should the value of the underlying stock rise above the conversion price, the value of the bond would more closely reflect its conversion right and its price would fluctuate more uniformly with the underlying security. If the fluctuations in the price of the convertible bond and its underlying security are not uniform, it is questionable whether the securities would be considered as substantially identical.

Bonds issued by the same governmental agency may not be substantially identical if there are different dates of issue, dates of interest payments, maturity dates, callable features, or interest rates.[215] In ruling that U.S. Treasury bonds were not substantially identical for wash sale purposes because of different annual interest rates, maturity dates, and their use in payment of federal estate taxes, the Treasury indicated that it may be sufficient if they are substantially different in any material feature.[216]

A Call is not substantially identical to the underlying security for purposes of the short sale rules.[217] Thus, the buying or writing of a Listed Call option would not come within the short sale provisions. This should be true even if the Listed Call that was written is "in the money" and is, from a practical viewpoint, expected to be exercised near the end of the option term. However, both Listed and Unlisted Calls are now subject to the special straddle provisions which contain rules similar to the short sales and wash sales rules.[218] (See ¶38.02.)

---

[213]Rev. Rul. 62-153, C.B. 1962-2, 186.
[214]Reg. 1.1233-1(d)(1); Rev. Rul. 77-201, C.B. 1977-1, 250.
[215]Rev. Rul. 58-210, C.B. 1958-1, 523; Rev. Rul. 58-211, C.B. 1958-1, 529;

Rev. Rul. 59-44, C.B. 1959-1, 205.
[216]Rev. Rul. 76-346, C.B. 1976-2, 247.
[217]Rev. Rul. 58-384, C.B. 1958-2, 410.
[218]Code: 1092(d)(2).

Certain qualified covered Calls are excepted from these straddle provisions.[219] See ¶41.03(h) for a discussion of when commodity Futures are considered to be "substantially identical."

.05 Short Sale Covered after Death

An unrealized gain or loss on a short sale that remains open at the date of the investor's death is not treated as income in respect of a decedent (Section 691 income).[220] The unrealized amount is not reportable until the short sale has been fully consummated by delivery of the underlying stock by the estate or beneficiary to close the transaction. An investor can escape gain on appreciated securities by not closing a short sale during his lifetime. Since the securities receive a new tax basis, which generally is the amount reported on the decedent's estate tax return, a potential gain could be converted into a loss by closing the short sale after death. For example, assume an investor acquired stock at $50, sold it short at a price of $100, and the value of the stock was $120 at time of death. Closing the short sale after death resulted in a loss of $20 (new tax basis of $120 less sales price of $100), whereas a $50 gain would be included in income if the short sale were closed before death. Note that for federal estate tax purposes the net asset value would be $100. The stock would be valued at $120 and the short sale contract would be shown as a liability of $120. There would also be a receivable from the broker of $100, representing the amount of the short sale.

The above rationale would also apply to a naked short sale where the investor did not own the underlying security at death. Gain or loss on the closing would depend on the cost of the stock acquired to close the short sale.

.06 Dividends and Interest Paid on Short Sales

For a discussion of the deductibility of dividends and interest paid on a short sale, see ¶51.06.

.07 Wash Sales

A loss on a short sale will be disallowed under the wash sales provisions if the investor either entered into a short sale of, or sold, substantially identical stock or securities in the 30-day period before or after the closing of the short sale.[221]

---

[219] Code: 1092(c)(4). (See ¶39.11(b).)
[220] Rev. Rul. 73-524, C.B. 1973-2, 307.

[221] Code: 1091(e), applicable to short sales after July 18, 1984. (See ¶36.08.)

.08   Tax Straddles (See ¶38.02)

.09   Tax Savings Opportunities

The short sale transaction lends itself to use in many situations where planned tax savings can be achieved. See ¶2.01, ¶8.01, ¶9.02.

38   TAX STRADDLES

.01   In General

Faced with an outpouring of new investment products with uncertain tax treatment and the penchant of some investors to use these new products and tax straddles to reduce their tax liabilities, Congress reacted by enacting new tax straddle provisions in the 1981 ERTA and has continued to make amendments, including the recent 1984 Act, to meet the changing tax environment. These changes in the 1984 Act have been incorporated in the regulated Futures contract provisions of Section 1256; in the tax straddle provisions of Section 1092, involving initially forward commodity contracts and other actively traded nonstock investments; in the capitalization of carrying charges of straddles in Section 263(g); and in Sections 1234 and 1234A involving options and Futures contracts. Below is a general discussion of Sections 1092, 1256, and 263(g). A more detailed discussion of the effects of these provisions on specific investments can be found under the sections describing each product.

.02   Straddles—Loss Deferral Rules/Offsetting Positions

Investors enter into straddles to reduce risks, as a means of making or increasing profits, or to obtain certain tax benefits. These straddles will contain offsetting positions in actively traded personal property and may take the form of a physical commodity and a commodity Futures or option, a Treasury bill and a Futures or option, stock and Listed and Unlisted options, and many other combinations of personal property, contracts, or options. An offsetting position is broader than "substantially identical" or "substantially similar" property and merely requires a substantial diminution of risk of loss of holding personal property.[222] Actively traded personal property has recently been expanded to include stock[223] and Listed options traded on an ex-

---

[222] Code: 1092(c).
[223] Code: 1092(d)(1). A straddle may also consist of stock and an offsetting posi-

tion in substantially similar or related property other than stock, such as a convertible bond.

change, other than a straddle consisting solely of one or more qualified covered Call options and the underlying stock.[224]

Since many trades involving stocks and Listed options consist not
only of stock and offsetting option positions, but also of various option positions in the same stock in lieu of owning the stock, it is
sometimes difficult to determine whether these option positions repre-
sent offsetting positions subject to the tax straddle rules. The authors
believe that the substantial diminution of risk test is a subjective test
that should be made only at the time the options are acquired. If they
are acquired solely as an investment strategy with little or no offsetting risk potential at the time they are acquired, then the options
should not be subject to the tax straddle rules. For example, if XYZ
stock is selling for $50 and an investor buys a Call with a strike price
of $50 and also a Put with a strike price of $50, these positions should
not be considered offsetting risk positions because they are literally
separate investments with little hedging potential when they are acquired. However, if either position was purchased in-the-money, the
purchase of the other position at a current market strike price will
have the effect of reducing the risk on the in-the-money position. (For
example, if the Put had a strike price of $55 in the above illustration.)
Furthermore, if certain positions, such as the purchase of stock and a
Put at the same time (married Put) are specifically excepted from the
short sales rules, the regulations should provide a similar exception to
the tax straddle rules.

The special tax straddle rules also do not apply to identified straddles, which are clearly identified on the day of the straddle, all positions are either acquired on the same day and disposed of on the same
day, or none of the positions were disposed of in the taxable year.[225]

Under these special straddle rules, losses realized on some positions in a straddle are not deductible in the current year to the extent
that there are unrecognized gains in other positions in the straddle at
year-end.[226] These disallowed losses are deductible in the year the
gains in the other positions are recognized.[227] Note that generally the
straddle provisions do not prevent an investor from recognizing a
gain on some straddle positions, although the offsetting losses are not
taken until a subsequent year. Regulations will be issued to provide
rules similar to the wash sales rules disallowing a loss under subsec-
tions (a) and (d) of Section 1091, and the short sales rules of Section

---

[224] Code: 1092(c)(4)(A). (See ¶39.11.)   [226] Code: 1092(a)(1).
[225] Code: 1092(a)(2).   [227] Code: 1092(a)(1)(B).

1233(b) and (d) converting long-term gains into short-term gains and short-term losses into long-term losses.[228] Regulations will also provide that carrying charges with respect to a straddle may have to be capitalized and added to the basis of the property under rules similar to Section 263(g).[229] The 1981 ERTA Committee Report states that the wash sales rules and the short sales rules are to be applied before the straddle loss deferral rule.[229a]

.03 Section 1256 Contracts

The scope of Section 1256 has been enlarged to include any regulated Futures contract (see ¶41), foreign currency contract (see ¶44), nonequity option (see ¶39.10 and ¶43), and dealer equity option (see ¶70.08).[230] Any Section 1256 contracts held at year-end are deemed to have been sold and any gain or loss on those contracts is reported in the current taxable year.[231] Gain or loss on final disposition of the Section 1256 contract must be appropriately adjusted for any gain or loss reported on deemed year-end sales in previous years.[232] Thus, if an economic gain of $500 is realized on final disposition in 1985 but a year-end gain of $600 was reported for that contract in 1984, a loss of $100 would be reported for 1985. At the end of each year, the actual gains and losses on dispositions of Section 1256 contracts are aggregated with the deemed gains and losses on year-end positions; 60 percent of the net gain (or loss) is treated as a long-term capital gain and 40 percent receives short-term treatment.[233] The rules of Section 1092 and 263(g) are not applicable if all the positions of a straddle consist of Section 1256 contracts.[234]

Gain or loss is realized in the current year not only on an actual or deemed sale of a Section 1256 contract but also on termination of the contract. This includes a termination or transfer of an investor's rights or obligations under the contract by taking or making delivery (short contract), by exercise or assignment, or by lapse.[235] Separate gain or loss must be computed for each component of a straddle.[236]

---

[228] Code: 1092(b).
[229] See ¶38.05.
[229]a—Senate Report on ERTA: 501.
[230] Code: 1256(b). Generally applicable to positions established after July 18, 1984. Limited partners of dealer partnerships are taxed on a mark-to-market basis but receive only short-term capital gain or loss treatment on the dealer equity option transactions. Code: 1256(f)(5).
[231] Code: 1256(a)(1). Exception applies to

business hedging transactions not entered into by a syndicate. Hedging losses allocated to limited partners are deductible to the extent of income from the same business. Code: 1256(e)(5).
[232] Code: 1256(a)(2).
[233] Code: 1256(a)(3).
[234] Code: 1256(a)(4).
[235] Code: 1256(c)(1).
[236] Code: 1256(c)(2).

Thus, if an investor is required to deliver the physical commodity specified in the contract, the current market value of the contract at the time of termination would be used in computing the gain or loss on the contract and the market value would also be used to separately compute the gain or loss on the transfer of the physical commodity.[237]

.04 Mixed Straddles

An investor holding a mixed straddle, consisting of at least one Section 1256 contract and other types of positions, may elect not to have Section 1256 apply to the contract.[238] If the election is made, the entire straddle will be governed by the loss deferral rules (including wash sales and short sales rules) of Section 1092, and no part will be governed by the 60/40 mark-to-market rules. The tax straddle rules also apply even if the election is not made.[239] Thus, any recognized losses on the Section 1256 contracts would be subject to the loss deferral rules, but any gains would be recognized as 60/40 under Section 1256, subject to netting of Section 1092 losses to be provided for in forthcoming regulations. In view of the new restrictions being imposed on mixed straddles, investors might consider electing out of Section 1256 and forsaking possible 60/40 gain treatment.

A mixed straddle consisting partly of Section 1256 contracts (e.g., regulated Futures contract or nonequity option) and other positions come under these straddle rules whether or not an election is made not to apply the mark-to-market rules to the Section 1256 contracts.[240] These rules will be greatly expanded under forthcoming regulations. Under these regulations, an investor will not be entitled to 60/40 treatment for the Section 1256 contracts and short-term losses on the other positions. In lieu of the Section 1233(d) short sales rule, an investor will be permitted to either offset gains and losses from the offsetting positions for each separately identified mixed straddle, or an active trader may set up one account for the mixed straddles with the gains or losses to be recognized and offset on a periodic basis. The 60/40 treatment for the Section 1256 contract components will apply only to the net gains or losses from the straddle. Thus, if the 60/40 total gain was $1,000 and the net gain was only $200, the

---

[237] Code: 1256(c)(3).

[238] Code: 1256(d). The straddle must be identified by the earlier of the close of the day acquired, or other time prescribed by regulations for positions established after July 18, 1984.

[239] Code: 1092(d)(5). These rules will be toughened under regulations to be issued within 6 months from July 18, 1984. Code: 1092(b)(2). (See ¶41.03(c).)

[240] Code: 1092(d)(5)(A).

60/40 treatment would apply only to the $200 net gain. With respect to the single mixed straddle account, the capital gain or loss is computed in the above manner, but the long-term capital gains cannot exceed 50 percent of the net gain and only 40 percent of any net loss will be treated as short term. If an investor at year-end has 60/40 gains in his Section 1256 contracts positions and an unrealized loss in the other positions, the regulations will limit the 60/40 gains to the net gains after deducting these unrealized losses. These and other rules will be spelled out in regulations required to be issued in the six months following the date of enactment of the 1984 Act.[241] Further, note that the mixed straddle rules and Section 1256(a)(4) do not apply if the straddle qualifies as an identified straddle and all of its positions are Section 1256 contracts.[242]

.05 Carrying Charges

Interest expense and other carrying charges (insurance, storage) are often incurred in purchasing personal property (e.g., a physical commodity, bonds, or stocks) which are components of a straddle (cash and carry). In order to prevent immediate deduction in the current year of the carrying charges and deferral until the subsequent year of the gain realized on the disposition of the straddle, the net interest and other carrying charges are disallowed.[243] The disallowed amounts are added to the cost of the personal property. Thus, instead of current deductions, the disallowed amounts will reduce possible future capital gains.

Included in the carrying charges are interest expense, insurance, storage, and transportation costs. Any charges for temporary use of the property in a short sale are included in interest expense.[244] These charges are currently deductible to the extent of any income earned on the personal property in the current year, such as original issue discount, bond market discount, or dividend income (less any dividends-received deduction for corporate shareholders). In determining the amount of carrying charges or offsetting income, other special provisions dealing with these items are to be applied before Section 263(g).[245]

---

[241] Code: 1092(b)(2), applies to mixed straddles established after 1983. The Treasury has authority to treat certain positions not described in Section 1256 (d)(4) as mixed straddles.

[242] Code: 1092(d)(5)(B).

[243] Code: 263(g)(1).

[244] Code: 263(g)(2).

[245] Code: 263(g)(4). The 1984 amendments apply to positions established after July 18, 1984.

.06 Treatment of Options in General

(a) Purchasers. Generally, gain or loss realized on the sale, exchange, or lapse of an option will have the same character as that of the underlying property.[246] Thus, if the underlying property is a capital asset or a Section 1231 asset, gain or loss on disposition of the option would receive similar treatment.[247] It was unclear prior to the 1984 Act whether the same principle would apply to the purchaser of an option on a Section 1256 contract (e.g., option on a T-bill Future or commodity Future). The 1984 Act conference report states unequivocally that the conferees "reject the assertion that the 'character' of property underlying an option on a Section 1256 contract includes the deemed holding period provided to Section 1256 contracts." Accordingly, such options issued after October 31, 1983 that do not qualify as Section 1256 contracts will receive regular capital gain or loss treatment. The tax treatment of such options granted before November 1, 1983 still remains unresolved. (See ¶41.04(b).)

Nonequity options, including options on broad-based stock indexes, now receive 60/40 capital gain treatment and are not subject to the Section 1234 general option rules unless an election was made to exclude Section 1256 contracts that are part of a mixed straddle from the operation of Section 1256.[248] Cash settlement options that are not Section 1256 contracts (e.g., options on narrow-based stock indexes) are governed by the Section 1234 option rules.[249] Ordinarily, gain or loss is not recognized on exercise of an option. However, gain or loss is now recognized on the exercise of an option on a Section 1256 contract.[250] Thus, capital gain or loss will be recognized on exercise despite the fact that 60/40 capital gain treatment will be accorded the underlying Section 1256 contract. Whether the purchaser of a cash settlement option will receive regular capital gain or loss treatment under Section 1234 or 60/40 treatment will depend upon whether the cash settlement option qualifies as a Section 1256 contract. For example, exercise of an option on a broad-based stock index will receive 60/40 treatment because it is treated as a nonequity option.

(b) Sellers. In general, a seller or grantor of an option that does not qualify as a Section 1256 contract (e.g., an equity option) will recog-

---

[246] Code: 1234(a).
[247] Reg. 1.1234-1(a).
[248] Code: 1256(d) (see ¶41.03(c)).

[249] Code: 1234(c)(2), effective for options granted after October 31, 1983.
[250] Code: 1234(c)(1), applies to options granted after October 31, 1983.

nize a short-term capital gain or loss on closing or terminating the option.[251] Exercise of a cash settlement option may be subject to Section 1234(b).[252] The character of the gain or loss will depend on whether the option qualifies as a Section 1256 contract. Ordinarily, a grantor of an option that qualifies as a Section 1256 contract will receive a 60/40 capital gain treatment. However, the grantor will receive short-term treatment if the option on a Section 1256 contract does not itself qualify as a Section 1256 contract.

39 PUTS AND CALLS—OPTIONS TO BUY AND SELL

.01 Introduction

In 1973 Call options started trading on the Chicago Board of Exchange (CBOE). Subsequently, trading of Calls commenced on the American, Philadelphia, Pacific, and Midwest Stock Exchanges, with the New York Stock Exchange considering the introduction of option trading. Trading in Puts on a pilot basis was introduced in June 1977 and has been substantially expanded in recent years. In addition, options have been introduced on stock indexes, commodity Futures, and a host of other products.

The discussion that follows will concern itself primarily with the tax implications with respect to transactions in Listed equity options. In most cases the same rules will be applicable to Unlisted equity options (i.e., those options which are not traded on the various exchanges mentioned above). Both Listed and Unlisted options are now subject to the tax straddle provisions. (See ¶39.11.) The existence of different tax rules with respect to Unlisted options will be indicated where appropriate. In addition, there is a later discussion of nonequity options (¶39.10) and qualified covered Calls (¶39.11(b)).

.02 Definitions

(a) Call. A Listed Call is an option to buy 100 shares of a particular stock at a fixed price ("striking price") within a stated period of time (i.e., prior to expiration date). The terms of the Call are fixed, with the only variable being the premium to be paid or received. Ordinary dividends will not affect the striking price of the Listed Call. The terms of an Unlisted Call are not fixed and are determined by negotiation between the buyer and seller. In addition, the rights and

---

[251] Code: 1234(b).   [252] Code: 1234(c)(2)(a).

obligations are between the buyer and seller and not between a party and the Options Clearing Corporation, as with Listed Calls. Furthermore, ordinary dividends will affect the striking price of the Unlisted Call. An "in-the-money" Call is where the Call price is less than the current market price of the underlying stock (e.g., the stock price is $40 and the Call price is $30).

(b) Put. A Listed Put is an option to sell 100 shares of a particular stock at a fixed price within a stated period of time. All other aspects discussed above with respect to a Call are applicable to Listed and/or Unlisted Puts. An "in-the-money" Put is where the exercise price of the Put is greater than the current market price of the underlying stock (e.g., the market price is $30 and the sale price is $40).

(c) Straddle—Equity options. A straddle (equity options) is a combination of a Put and Call, both exercisable at the same market price and for the same period. These Straddles should be distinguished from tax straddles that come under Section 1092.

(d) Combination. A combination, as the term is used in connection with Listed options, is similar to a straddle except that the striking price of the Put and Call elements are not the same. (The term *Spread* was previously used for Unlisted options, but such term is now used to describe two or more different Listed Calls with different striking prices and/or maturity dates—see below).

(e) Strip/Strap. A strip is a term used to describe a straddle with a second Put component, whereas a strap represents a Call plus a straddle. Both were used prior to the introduction of Listed options.[253]

(f) Time spread/Calendar spread/Horizontal spread. These terms are used for positions in options with different expiration dates and usually the same striking price (e.g., T buys one Call ABC Apr 40 at 5½ and writes (sells) one Call ABC Jan 40 at 4, or vice versa). The relationship of the market value of ABC stock to the striking price of the Calls will determine whether the spread is a Bullish or Bearish Spread.

---

[253] These combinations are referred to as "multiple options" in Reg. 1.1234-2 (b)(4). A grantor is permitted to iden- tify which two of the options constitute a straddle. Reg. 1.1234-2(c).

(g) **Vertical spread/Price spread/Strike spread.** These terms are used for positions in options with the same expiration date but different striking price (e.g., T buys one Call ABC Jan 40 at 4 and sells one Call ABC Jan 45 at 1—Bullish Vertical Spread; or T buys one Call ABC Jan 45 at 1 and sells one Call ABC Jan 40 at 4—Bearish Vertical Spread).

(h) **Butterfly spread/Sandwich spread.** These terms are given to positions which combine the Bullish and Bearish Vertical Spreads (e.g., T buys one Call ABC Jan 40, sells two Calls ABC Jan 45s, and buys one Call ABC Jan 50—1:2:1—same maturity).

(i) **Domino spread.** This term is given to positions which are similar to the butterfly spread, but have different maturity dates.

(j) **Intrinsic value.** This term is used to describe the true economic value of the option on the assumption that the option is exercised immediately (e.g., a Call ABC Jan 25 is selling for a premium of $650, and ABC is selling at $28½ per share. The intrinsic value of the option is $350 or $3½ per share).

(k) **Time value.** This term is used to describe the portion of an option's price, above its intrinsic value, which represents the value of the time left before it expires (e.g., in the example immediately above, the time value is $3 per share).

(l) **Negative parity.** This term is used to describe the occasions where the intrinsic value is greater than the total premium, which could cause an unwelcome exercise of the option (e.g., on October 1, ABC stock is selling at $45 per share and the premium on an ABC Call—Oct 35 is $975—$9¾ per share. Professional arbitrageurs might take advantage of the ¼ point spread).

(m) **Covered writing/One-for-one writing.** This terminology is given to a strategy of writing one Call for each 100 shares of stock owned, or in the alternative, writing one Put for each 100 shares of stock sold short.

(n) **Uncovered writing/Naked options/Short options.** This terminology is given to a strategy of writing Calls without owning the underlying stock, or, in the alternative, writing Puts without selling the stock short.

(o) **Ratio writing.** This terminology is given to the strategy of writing more than one Call for each 100 shares of stock owned, or, in the alternative, writing more than one Put for each 100 shares of stock sold short. In effect, the writer is naked or uncovered as to the number of options in excess of his long position or short position, respectively.

(p) **Broad-based stock index options.** These are options on a group of diversified stocks, such as the S&P 100, which are designated for contract trading by the Commodity Futures Trading Commission, or are eligible for such a designation in the view of the Treasury. (See ¶**39.10.**)

(q) **Narrow-based stock index options.** These are options on a group of stocks in the same industry, such as oil and gas.

(r) **Down and out/Up and away.** This terminology refers to options where the premium is reduced (up to 50 percent) because the option terminates if the price of the stock falls below the strike price (usually 5 percent). Thus, "down and out" refers to a Call and "up and away" refers to a Put with these special provisions.

Warrants and purchased stock rights are generally subject to the same tax rules as Calls. For treatment of stock rights received by a shareholder as a distribution. (See ¶**55.03.**)

.03 Functions of Equity Options

The most important economic functions of Puts, Calls, and so on, are either:

1. To provide a means of reducing the risk of loss where an investment or speculation in stock is concerned, or
2. To increase the leverage that can be employed.

They may be used as a vehicle for trading the underlying stock against the option or to protect a profit in a position. Certain tax considerations may favor the purchase and/or sale of each option (see ¶**2.02,** ¶**2.03,** ¶**3.05,** ¶**3.06,** ¶**3.07,** ¶**3.08,** ¶**4,** ¶**5.01,** ¶**10,** ¶**11,** ¶**12,** ¶**13,** ¶**15**). It is important that the cost of the option and all brokerage commissions be considered in any economic or tax planning.

.04 Tax Effect on the Investor Who Purchases an Equity Option

(a) **Capital asset.** These options are considered to be capital assets in the hands of the investor[254] and tax treatment depends upon their dispositon.[255] The Tax Reform Act of 1976 did not affect the tax treatment to purchasers of options, but only to writers of options (discussed below). The premium paid to acquire an option is carried as a capitalized expenditure made in an incomplete transaction.[256] The ultimate tax treatment will depend upon whether the option is sold, allowed to lapse or exercised. Special 60/40 long-term/short-term rules now apply to broad-based stock index options. (See ¶39.10.) The rules set forth below apply to equity options other than broad-based stock index options.

(b) **Sale of equity option.** If the option is sold, the difference between the cost of the option and the proceeds from the sale is treated as a capital gain or loss. The period for which the investor has held the option determines whether the capital gain or loss is short-term or long-term.[257] Inasmuch as Listed options have expiration periods of less than one year, they did not qualify for long-term capital gain treatment on sales of options acquired prior to the 1984 Act. With the six-month holding period rule in effect for options acquired after June 22, 1984 and before January 1, 1988, these options can qualify for long-term capital gain treatment.[258] This may affect the premium for these long-term options. Unlisted options can have terms of more than one year and, accordingly, long-term treatment was available even before the holding period requirement was reduced to more than six months.

(c) **Failure to exercise equity option.** If an option is not exercised, it is treated as having been sold on the expiration date.[259] Therefore, under the 1984 Act, the expiration of the option can result in a long-term or short-term capital loss depending upon the period the option was held before expiration.

Consideration should be given to the sale of a more-than-six-month option before the expiration of the six-month holding period if it is

---

[254] Code: 1234(a). Special rules apply to dealers in options. (See ¶70.08.)

[255] See Rev. Rul. 78-182, C.B. 1978-1, 265 for detailed discussion of tax treatment of holders and writers of Puts, Calls, and straddle options.

[256] Rev. Rul. 71-521, C.B. 1971-2, 313.

[257] Reg. 1.1234-1(a).

[258] Code: 1222.

[259] Code: 1234(a)(2).

expected that the option will not be exercised. This should create a short-term (rather than a long-term) capital loss. Where a Put has been acquired on the same date as the stock which is identified to be used if the Put is exercised so as to come within the exception to the short sale rules ("marriage" of the Put to the stock), then upon expiration of the Put, the cost thereof is not treated as a capital loss, but must be added to the basis of the stock with which it has been identified.[260] (See ¶37.03(d).)

(d) Exercise of equity option. If a Put or Call is exercised, the investor will treat the cost thereof as follows: the amount paid for the Call will increase the cost of the stock acquired, while the amount paid for the Put will decrease the proceeds of sale of the stock sold.[261] Upon the exercise of a Call, the holding period of the stock so acquired does not include the holding period of the Call, but starts the day after the Call is exercised.

(e) Short sale rules. The acquisition of a Put is treated as a short sale for purposes of the short sale rules so as to affect the holding period of stock held for less than the applicable long-term holding period, and the exercise or failure to exercise such Put is considered as a closing of the short sale.[262] (See ¶37.03(d).) Note, the holding period is lost and will not start over again until the Put is disposed of. This is true even though the stock is sold later at a loss. However, if a Put and the stock intended to be used in exercising the Put are acquired on the same day, the short sale rules mentioned above are not applicable, provided the stock is actually so used if the Put is exercised (marriage of the Put to the stock) (see ¶37.03(d)).[263] Where an Unlisted Put which has been held for the applicable long-term holding period has increased in value because the market value of the stock has fallen, a sale of the Put would produce long-term capital gain (see Example in ¶13.01). However, a question has been raised as to the tax consequences of a sale of the identified or married Put (e.g., at a gain or even to recoup a portion of the investment in the Put). Does such a disposition dissolve the identification or marriage such that the

---

[260] Code: 1233(c).
[261] Rev. Rul. 58-234, C.B. 1958-1, 279.
[262] Code: 1233(b); Reg. 1.1233-1(c)(3); Special ruling September 7, 1973, 74-9 CCH ¶6596. This private ruling originally indicated that the sale of the previously purchased Put, would retroactively reinstate the original holding period of the long position. A subsequent private ruling dated April 30, 1976, retracted the IRS's original erroneous interpretation of the short sale rules. Thus, the subsequent disposition of an acquired Put will merely start the commencement of the new holding period of the stock.
[263] Rev. Rul. 78-182, C.B. 1978-1, 265.

Put, from the beginning, would be treated as a short sale causing the holding period of the stock held less than the applicable long-term holding period to be lost? The stronger position appears to be that these short sale rules are not activated. Certainly, if the Put is not exercised because the stock has increased in value, the holding period of the married stock is not tainted retroactively and such holding period would continue. A sale of the Put has the same effect as the failure to exercise the Put[264] and accordingly, the married stock should not be tainted retroactively. Only if the Put is exercised does the identified or married stock have to be delivered. If other stock is delivered, then the short sale rules would activate from the beginning and, if applicable, the holding period of the original identified stock would be lost. The tax treatment of married Puts may also be affected by the tax straddle rules. (See ¶38.02.)

Before passage of the 1984 Act, whether or not options were securities for purposes of the short sales rules was important in planning transactions. (A similar question existed for purposes of the wash sales rules.) If an option was not a security under the short sales rules, it might have been possible to effectuate a short-against-the-box position similar to stock positions. (See ¶2.01.) Thus, for example, if T purchases on October 15, 1983, an Unlisted one-year 10-day Call on ABC for $700 and two months later the value of the Call was $2,000, T could write an Unlisted Call to expire on the same date as the Call he purchased for $700. He thus would have created a short-against-the-box position and by keeping the position open for more than one year, would have matured the $1,300 locked-in gain into long-term capital gain. If an option is a security, then this conversion could not occur under the short sales rules. This strategy can no longer be applied with the inclusion of all stock options under the tax straddle rules. (See ¶38.02.)

.05　Tax Effect on the Investor Who Grants an Equity Option

(a) In general. Income is not recognized on the receipt of the premium for writing an option, nor will any gain or loss be recognized until the option is exercised, expires, or is terminated by the grantor.[265]

---

[264] In interpreting Code: 1233(b), the April 30, 1976 private ruling, referred to in the above footnote 262, stated "For purposes of Section 1233(b), the failure to exercise a Put includes, for example, the lapse of the Put or the sale of the Put." The same conclusion should be reached with respect to the "marriage" provisions of Code: 1233 (c).

[265] See Rev. Rul. 78-182, C.B. 1978-1, 265 for detailed discussion of tax treatment of holders and writers of Puts, Calls, and straddle options.

(b) Nonexercise of equity option. Expiration of options will result in short-term capital gain.[266] The premium received for options granted prior to September 2, 1976, is treated as ordinary income at the time the option expires unexercised.[267] Recognition of short-term gain under the current rules will enable the writer of the option to offset the gain by capital losses realized in the same taxable year or carried over from prior years. This was not possible under the prior provisions.

(c) Exercise of equity option. The stock purchased by the investor upon the exercise of a Put he granted will acquire as a basis the option price paid by him, less the premium received on the writing of the Put.[268] The holding period of such acquired stock begins on the day after the date of the exercise of the option.[269]

For purposes of determining gain or loss, the proceeds from the sale of stock pursuant to the exercise of a Call granted by the investor will be increased by the amount of premium received upon the granting of the Call. If the stock was held by the investor for the applicable long-term holding period, any gain or loss, after including the premium on the granting of the option as part of the proceeds of sale, will be long-term.[270]

(d) Equity options repurchased. With the advent of Listed options, it became common practice for owners of stock to write Listed Call options on such stock. If the price of the stock rose, he could terminate the outstanding Call by repurchasing in the open market the identical Call option in a closing transaction. Any gain or loss realized on a closing transaction will be treated as short-term capital gain or loss.[271] (See special rules for qualified covered Calls in ¶39.11.) Gains and losses realized on terminations of options granted prior to September 1, 1976, were accorded ordinary gain or loss treatment.[272]

The potential tax advantage of option writing (long-term capital gain and ordinary loss), that was closed by the Tax Reform Act of 1976, was available primarily when stock prices rose. Many times it resulted in a tax disadvantage in declining markets (i.e., long or short-term capital loss and ordinary income). Thus, many writers of options on a "one-to-one basis" realized a pretax reasonable rate of return on invested dollars and mitigated their loss in declining markets, but suffered adverse tax consequences in such declining mar-

---

[266] Code: 1234(b)(1).
[267] Rev. Rul. 58-234, C.B. 1958-1, 279.
[268] Ibid.
[269] Cf. *Weir*, 10 T.C. 996 (1948).

[270] Rev. Rul. 58-234, C.B. 1958-1, 279.
[271] Code: 1234(b)(1).
[272] Special Ruling, April 8, 1974, 74-9 CCH §6597.

kets. The current rules eliminate the adverse tax consequences in declining markets and allow a portion of the advantages in rising markets. Now that stock and Listed and Unlisted options come under the tax straddle rules, an investor generally can no longer create a long-term capital gain on the stock purchased and a short-term capital loss on the option written. (See ¶39.11.)

A loss incurred on the reacquisition of a Call is currently deductible as a short-term capital loss and is not added to the basis of the underlying stock.[273] This is consistent with the proposition that, on lapse of an option, the premium received by the writer is taxable and is not relevant in determining the amount of gain or loss on the disposition of any particular stock.[274] A prior ruling requiring the loss on reacquisition of the Call to be added to the basis of the underlying stock has been repealed except for taxpayers who relied on the prior ruling.[275]

Where the premium attributable to the time value of a short Call is very low, or where negative parity exists, there might be an unwelcome exercise of the Call. The writer of the Call should take care to repurchase, in a closing transaction, such short Call with the possible view of rewriting another Call option with a higher striking price and further maturity date. Unwelcome exercises of Calls can occur substantially prior to maturity date, such as when the underlying stock is about to go ex-dividend a significant amount or buyers of the underlying stock are interested in large acquisitions without significantly affecting the price, or for other reasons. The investor may not have owned the underlying stock for more than the applicable long-term holding period and unwelcome exercise and delivery of the underlying stock would cause any gain to be short-term capital gain. This problem may be cured by purchasing additional shares for cash and use the new shares to satisfy the exercised Calls. If newly purchased stock is used to satisfy the exercised Call, it could be argued that stock is borrowed temporarily by the broker on behalf of the investor for delivery in satisfaction of the exercised Call and that, in effect, the equivalent of a short sale for tax purposes has occurred, with the resulting loss of holding period on the long position that was held for less than the applicable long-term holding period. Such an argument appears to be far-fetched inasmuch as a conscious short sale should be required in order to activate the short sale rules and not merely a temporary borrowing in the satisfaction of an exercised Call until the newly purchased stock can be used to satisfy the exercised

---

[273] Rev. Rul. 78-181, C.B. 1978-1, 261.
[274] Rev. Rul. 63-183, C.B. 1963-2, 285.
[275] Rev. Rul. 70-205, C.B. 1970-1, 174.

Call. Stock purchased "for cash" to satisfy the exercised Call prior to settlement date would solve this potential problem.

.06 Wash Sales

Where an investor sells stock or securities at a loss and within a 30-day period before or after such sale, acquires (or enters into an option to acquire) substantially identical securities, the loss will be disallowed as a wash sale.[276] Thus, the acquisition of a Call within 30 days before or after the sale of stock or securities at a loss will cause the loss to be disallowed. The authors believe that the loss and the holding period of the stock sold should be added to the basis and holding period of the option acquired (see **¶36.01**).[277] If the Call is subsequently exercised, the basis of the new stock would effectively include the total basis of the Call (i.e., the cost of the Call plus the disallowed loss on the original stock position). The holding period of the new stock should not include the holding period of the option nor the holding period of the original stock position because of the general rule that the total holding period of the option upon exercise is lost.[278]

If the Call expires unexercised, the loss should be equal to the tax basis of the Call (i.e., the cost of the Call plus the disallowed loss attributable to the original stock and the nature of the gain should depend upon the total holding period of the Call).

As indicated previously, it is not clear whether an option is deemed to be a security for purposes of the wash sale rules. Thus, the sale of a Listed option at a loss with a subsequent repurchase within 30 days of the identical Listed option will cause the wash sale rules to apply only if such option is deemed to be a "security" within Section 1091. Options with different maturity dates and/or different striking prices should not be substantially identical to each other so as to come within the wash sale rules.

Prior to the 1984 Act, the purchase of a Listed option "to close" at a loss with a subsequent resale within 30 days of the identical Listed

---

[276] Code: 1091(a).

[277] Reg. 1.1091-1(a).

[278] Code: 1223(4). A literal reading of Section 1091(d) (basis provision) and Section 1223(4) (holding period provision) could lead to the conclusion that the disallowed loss and the holding period of the stock sold are not added to the basis and holding period of the option. In addition, if the option is exercised, the disallowed loss is then effectively added to the basis of the new stock, and the holding period of the old stock, but not the holding period of the option, is tacked onto the holding period of the new stock. These literal interpretations appear to be strained and contrary to legislative intent, especially where the options are not exercised.

option was not a wash sale, because you generally needed two purchases and one sale to come within Section 1091, and under these circumstances, there are two sales and only one purchase. In addition, under the 1984 Act, two sales and one purchase could produce a wash sale. (See ¶36.01.) However, if the options were part of a tax straddle, then rules similar to the wash sales rules would be in effect. (See ¶39.11.)

A sale of a Call at a loss with a purchase of the stock within the 30-day period is not a wash sale. (See ¶36.02.) If these transactions involved a straddle position, however, rules similar to the wash sales rules may apply. (See ¶39.11.)

Traders in options are now subject to the wash sales rules.[279] In the past, if the individual investor was very active so as to be considered a trader, an exemption from the wash sales rules was provided. This exemption is no longer effective for trades after December 31, 1984.

.07 Dividends and Other Rights Paid during Period of Unlisted Options

Both Unlisted Calls and Puts usually provide that the option price will be reduced by the value of any distributions (cash dividends, stock dividends, warrants, and the like) received on the stock during the life of the option. In such cases, all dividends, to the extent taxable, are includible in the gross income of the owner of the stock when its holder receives the dividend.[280] The adjustment to the sales price affects only the tax basis of the stock acquired on the exercise of the option and has no other tax effect.[281] The option price of Listed Puts and Calls is not affected by ordinary dividends.

.08 Straddles—Equity Options

(a) Listed Straddles—Equity options. Transactions on Listed Puts and Calls with the same striking price and expiration date may be considered as a transaction in straddles. The separate identifiable premiums paid for the Put and Call components of a Listed Straddle must be used in determining the respective gain or loss on disposition of each option rather than an allocation of the total premium received for the straddle.[282] However, if a single premium is received for the

---

[279] Code: 1091 (a), applicable to post-1984 sales.
[280] Rev. Rul. 58-234, C.B. 1958-1, 279; see generally I.T. 4007, C.B. 1950-1, 11 (superseded by Rev. Rul. 74-562,

C.B. 1974-2, 28); Rev. Rul. 56-153, C.B. 1956-1, 166; and Rev. Rul. 56-211, C.B. 1956-1, 155.
[281] Rev. Rul. 58-234, C.B. 1958-1, 279.
[282] Rev. Rul. 78-182, C.B. 1978-1, 265.

entire Listed Straddle and the amount attributable to the Put and Call
components cannot be determined, then an allocation of the total premium should be made.[283] The allocation can be based either upon the
relative market value of each component option, or 55 percent of the
premium can be allocated to the Call and 45 percent to the Put. The
writing of such Listed Straddles should not create an allocation problem that existed and probably still exists with respect to Unlisted
Straddles, inasmuch as the separate components of the Listed Straddles will be known (i.e., the Listed Call and Listed Put are traded
separately on the exchange). Losses realized from closing only the
loss positions in stock option spreads (tax straddles under current
rules) were held by the Treasury not to be deductible until the year
the taxpayer liquidated all of the option spread positions.[284] The new
tax straddle provision limiting losses realized on tax straddles has
been amended and now applies to both Listed and Unlisted options.
(See ¶39.11.)

(b) Unlisted Straddles—Equity options. It is expected that the
Treasury will apply similar allocation rules with respect to premiums
received for Unlisted Straddles. Where separate identifiable premiums have been paid for the Put and Call components, then these
identified amounts must be used if the options are exercised or in
determining gain or loss on disposition of the options. When a single
premium is received for Put and Call options and the amount attributable to each component is not readily identifiable, the premium can
be allocated under either of the two following methods. The premium
received by an investor for writing a straddle must be allocated based
upon the market values (at the time the straddle was written) of the
Unlisted Put and Unlisted Call options contained therein.[285] In lieu of
determining the market values of the two options, the taxpayer may
elect by a statement attached to his income tax return to allocate 55
percent of the premium to the Call option and 45 percent to the Put
option, provided that these ratios (or subsequently announced ratios)
are used in allocating all future premiums received in writing straddles.[286] The premium applicable to the unexpired option will be

[283] Rev. Rul. 78-182, C.B. 1978-1, 265; Rev. Rul. 65-31 (obsolete), C.B. 1965-1, 365.
[284] Priv. Rul. Doc. 8313003. The basis and rationale for the ruling appears to be deficient and wrong. A similar argument that a straddle transaction becomes closed and complete only when all positions of the straddle are termi-nated was rejected by the Tax Court in *Smith*, 78 T.C. 350 (1982). However, the straddle losses were denied because of a lack of a nontax economic motive for the transaction. (See ¶41.03(f).)
[285] See footnote 283, supra. Similar rules are contained in Reg. 1.1234-2(d).
[286] Rev. Proc. 65-29, C.B. 1965-2, 1023.

treated as short-term capital gain upon its expiration.[287] The premium allocated to the exercised portion of the straddle will reduce the cost of stock acquired or increase the proceeds of sale of the stock sold, depending upon whether the Call or the Put option was exercised. If both options lapse, the premiums would be taxed as a short-term gain.[288] Since the new provision limiting the use of losses realized on tax straddles applies to both Listed and Unlisted options (see ¶39.11), it is immaterial whether the option qualifies for the more-than-6-month or 12-month long-term capital gain holding period.

With respect to straddles or other combinations of Unlisted Puts and Calls acquired by the investor, theoretically the exercise of one side of the contract should not affect the status of the unexercised portion. The part of the cost of the straddle applicable to the unexercised option should be treated as a sale of that option on the expiration date. Thus, if the Call is exercised, the cost of the straddle applicable to such buy option would be added to the basis of the stock acquired, while the cost attributable to the Put would result in a capital loss upon its expiration. Many investors have in the past taken the position that the entire cost of the straddle should be allocated to the portion exercised. However, in light of the Treasury's position with respect to the writing of a straddle, a separate allocation will be required.[289] The tax treatment of straddles in Unlisted options has been changed for straddles entered into after June 23, 1981. These straddles will come under the new straddle provisions which can limit the amount of loss recognized when only one position in the straddle is closed in the taxable year and can also apply the wash and short sales rules to the straddle. (See discussion of the new straddle rules starting in ¶39.11.)

If the Unlisted Call portion of an Unlisted Straddle is exercised, the stock so acquired will not receive a holding period until the Un-

---

[287] Code: 1234(c) (applicable to straddles written after January 25, 1965, and before September 2, 1976). Section 1234(c) was deleted from the Code by the 1976 TRA because grantors of options now realize short-term capital gain on lapse of options and therefore it is no longer necessary to have a special short-term capital gain provision for writers of straddles. Under the pre-1976 TRA rules the premium applicable to the unexercised portion of a spread written before September 2, 1976, or to any unexercised part of a strip or strap not identified as part of a straddle, was treated as ordinary income to the writer when the option expires. Reg. 1.1234-2(f), Example (7). Again, these gains will be short-term for multiple options written on or after September 1, 1976.

[288] Reg. 1.1234-2(f), Example (3). The Treasury reversed its prior position in Prop. Reg. 1.1234-2(a) that the lapse would be taxed as ordinary income. The final regulation corresponds more closely with the literal language of old Section 1234(c) and is the same treatment accorded under the 1976 TRA.

[289] Reg. 1.1234-2(f), Example 1.

listed Put portion either is sold or expires, since the Put will be considered an open short sale and thus taint the holding period of the newly acquired long position. The holding period thus commences when the short sale is considered closed. It is therefore recommended that if the Put portion of a straddle has any time remaining before its expiration date and is of no immediate value to the investor, the Put should be disposed of in order to allow the holding period of the newly acquired stock to commence.

.09 Options on Commodity Futures (Double Options)

Trading in options on commodity Futures has been prevalent in Europe for many years and is now available in the United States. These include Futures options in gold and sugar. Futures options are also traded in West German marks. It is expected that ultimately such options trading will become as important to commodity Futures trading as Listed options are to stock trading today. (See ¶41.04 for further discussion of commodity Futures options.)

.10 Nonequity Options

The regular short- and long-term capital gain rules do not apply to Section 1256 contracts. Instead, under the mark-to-market rules, all of these contracts on hand at the end of the year are deemed to have been sold. In addition, regardless of holding period, 60 percent of the gain recognized on actual or deemed sale of these contracts is long-term and 40 percent is short-term.[290] Nonequity options have been added to the list of investments that qualify for this special treatment.[291] These include broad-based Listed stock index options, such as Standard & Poor's 100 and 500 and New York Stock Exchange Options.[292] Both Call and Put options will qualify for special tax treatment. Other equity options, including narrow-based Listed stock index options, such as options in specialized industries (computer technology, oil and gas, telephone), and Listed and Unlisted regular stock options will continue to be subject to their normal tax treatment. (See ¶39.04 and ¶39.05.) Several currently traded stock index options which have not yet received designation by the Commodities Futures Trading Commission (CFTC) will not be treated as a nonequity option until the Treasury determines that they meet the requirements of

---

[290] Code: 1256(a). (See ¶38.03.)   [292] Code: 1256(g)(6).
[291] Code: 1256(b).

law for such a CFTC designation.[293] Options trading on a market other than a board of trade or exchange may qualify for special treatment after a determination is made by the Treasury.

On the following pages is a chart that summarizes the tax treatment of various types of options.

.11 Tax Straddles

(a) **In general.** In order to prevent deferral of income and conversion of ordinary income or short-term capital gains into long-term capital gains, tax straddle rules were initially imposed to apply to all actively traded personal property and offsetting positions in a straddle, other than stock and Listed options.[294] These tax straddle rules will defer losses to the extent of unrecognized offsetting gains, apply rules similar to the wash and short sales rules, and require capitalization of certain straddle carrying charges. The revised straddle rules will apply to actively traded stock investments if there is an offsetting position consisting of a Listed or Unlisted option with respect to such stock or substantially identical stock or securities.[295] Forthcoming regulations will apply the straddle rules to stock if the offsetting position consists of substantially similar or related property (other than stock), such as convertible bonds, or if a shareholder uses his corporation to take offsetting risk positions. Stock in an investment company and a short position in a stock index option or Futures, or where a portfolio of stocks whose performance mimics that of a stock index or Futures are examples of straddles that will come under the tax straddle rules. Merely buying stock on margin or borrowing from other sources will not bring the tax straddle rules into play. An exception to these rules will also apply if the entire straddle consists of one stock and the offsetting positions are only qualified covered Call options.[296] Writing a Put, or purchasing a Call or Put as part of a straddle would disqualify the straddle from meeting the qualified covered Call exception.

(b) **Qualified covered Calls.** Detailed rules have been established with respect to qualified covered Calls. To qualify, the Call must be with respect to stock held or will be acquired in connection with the Call, but only if the Call:[297]

---

[293] Code: 1256 (g) (6) (B).

[294] Code: 1092, before amendment by 1984 Act.

[295] Code: 1092 (d) (3) (B), generally effective for positions established after 1983.

[296] Code: 1092 (c) (4).

[297] Code: 1092 (c) (4) (B).

Tax treatment of options under the Tax Reform Act of 1984

| | | Prior law | | | Current law | | | |
| | | Investors | | Option dealers/ | Investors | | Option dealers/ | Effective |
Type of option	Exchange	Long	Short	Market makers	Long	Short	Market makers	dates(5)
Stock Options								
Options on stock		A	B	E	A	B	G(3)	H
Stock underlying the option (dealers only)		—	—	E	—	—	A(4)	H
Options on RFCs								
Treasury bonds	CBT	C	D	F	G	G	G	I
Gold	CMX	C	D	F	G	G	G	I
S&P 500	CME	C	D	F	G	G	G	I
West German mark	CME	C	D	F	G	G	G	I
NYSE composite	NYFE	C	D	F	G	G	G	I
Value Line	KC	C	D	F	G	G	G	I
Sugar	CSC	C	D	F	G	G	G	I
Index Options								
S&P 100, S&P 500	CBOE	A(1)	B(1)	E	G(2)	G(2)	G	H
Major Mkt Index	AMX	A(1)	B(1)	E	G(2)	G(2)	G	H
Amex Mkt Value Index	AMX	A(1)	B(1)	E	G(2)	G(2)	G	H
NYSE Options	NYSE	A(1)	B(1)	E	G(2)	G(2)	G	H
Computer Tech; Oil & Gas	AMX	A(1)	B(1)	E	A(2)	B(2)	G(3)	H
Gaming/Hotel; Gold/Silver	PHI	A(1)	B(1)	E	A(2)	B(2)	G(3)	H
Transportation	AMX, CBOE	A(1)	B(1)	E	A(2)	B(2)	G(3)	H
Telephone	CBOE, NYSE	A(1)	B(1)	E	A(2)	B(2)	G(3)	H
Technology	PCSE	A(1)	B(1)	E	A(2)	B(2)	G(3)	H
Interest Rate Options								
Treasury Notes; Bills	AMX	A	B	E	G	G	G	H
Treasury Bonds	CBOE	A	B	E	G	G	G	H
Foreign Currency Options								
Pound, Swiss Franc, Yen, Mark, Can.$	PHI	A	B	E	G	G	G	H

(A) Capital gain or loss when closed. IRC 1234(a).

(B) Short-term gain or loss when closed. IRC 1234(b).

(C) Options on regulated Futures contracts (RFCs)—the current state of the law is unclear. One school of thought looks at the character of the underlying property to determine whether the gain is capital or ordinary. The other school of thought treats the "character of the underlying property" as either 60/40 or ordinary gain or loss.

(D) Options on regulated futures contracts (RFCs)—the current state of the law is unclear. A short position in and of itself may be treated as a regulated Futures contract (§1256, mark-to-market 60/40) or §1234(b) may be applicable, yielding short-term gain or loss upon closing or expiration of the option.

(E) Ordinary gain or loss.

(F) Tax treatment is unclear.

(G) Marked-to-market, 60% long-term, 40% short-term, except for hedging transactions.

(H) Positions established after date of enactment, July 18, 1984.

(I) Positions established after October 31, 1983.

(1) There is uncertainty as to whether §1234 applied to cash settlement options, such as indexes, which may not be options on "property." Potential ordinary treatment might be accorded certain transactions.

(2) It appears that the S&P 100, S&P 500, and the NYSE Options would qualify as "broad-based" index options (and therefore be "nonequity" options) qualifying for 60/40 treatment. It appears that the Major Market Index and the Amex Market Value Index options should also qualify based on the recent approval by the CFTC for similar futures contracts. The remaining index options appear to be subindex options ("equity" options), and therefore not eligible for 60/40 treatment.

(3) Gain or loss on equity options that is allocable to limited partners will be marked-to-market, but will not be eligible for 60/40 treatment. Instead, all gains and losses will be short-term.

(4) An options dealer will recognize a capital gain or loss on transactions in the underlying stock unless he is also a dealer in the underlying stock.

(5) Two alternative elections are available to apply the 60/40 mark-to-market rules either to positions held on July 18, 1984 or to positions held at any time during the year of enactment, 1984.

1. Is traded in a national securities exchange registered with the SEC or other market approved by the Treasury.
2. Is granted more than 30 days before it expires.
3. Is not "deep-in-the-money" (option strike price less than stock price).
4. Is not granted by an options dealer in connection with his options business.
5. Is a capital asset resulting in capital gain treatment.

These rules are complicated by the necessity of determining whether the qualified covered Call is deep-in-the-money; i.e., its strike (exercise) price is lower than the lowest qualified benchmark. Generally, the lowest qualified benchmark is the highest available strike price that is less than the applicable stock price (last closing stock price the day before the Call was granted, or if more than 10 percent greater, the opening price on the option day).[298] Thus, if the stock is selling at $49, a qualified covered Call with a strike price of $45 or more and a term exceeding 30 days would qualify for the exception. With respect to a Call with a term exceeding 90 days and a strike price of more than $50, the lowest qualified benchmark is the second highest available strike price which is less than the applicable stock price.[299] For example, for a stock selling for $63, a 120-day Call with a call price of $55 (two benchmarks) would qualify for the exception. If the lowest qualifying benchmark for a stock selling at up to $25 would be less than 85 percent of the applicable selling price, the lowest qualifying benchmark will be limited to the 85 percent requirement. Thus, if the stock is selling at $25, a benchmark price of $20 will not qualify because it is less than 85 percent of the applicable selling price. For stocks selling at no more than $150, the lowest qualified benchmark will qualify even if it is $10 less than the applicable stock price.[300] These lowest qualified benchmark rules are illustrated in the schedule on the following page.

Failure to meet these qualified covered Call exceptions may convert a long-term gain on the sale of the stock into a short-term gain under rules similar to the short sales rules. The qualified covered Call exceptions will not apply to year-end transactions when the Call is closed before year-end and the stock is sold at a gain in a subsequent year but within 30 days of the closing of the Call.[301] A short-term loss

[298] Code: 1092(c)(4)(D). An investor can purchase listed options at $5 intervals (benchmarks) for stock trading at prices under $100 and $10 benchmarks for higher priced stocks. The lowest available strike price is $10 with no maximum strike price.

[299] Code: 1092(c)(4)(D)(ii).
[300] Code: 1092(c)(4)(D)(iv).
[301] Code: 1092(c)(4)(E). The holding period rules of Section 246(c) generally apply in determining whether the stock was held for at least 30 days.

Tax Reform Act of 1984: Qualified covered Call options

Applicable stock price*	Call is not deep-in-the-money if strike price† is at least:		Applicable stock price*	Call is not deep-in-the-money if strike price† is at least:	
	31–90 day Call	More than 90-day Call‡		31–90 day Call	More than 90-day Call‡
5⅛–5⅞	5	5	75⅛–80	75	70
6 –10	None§	None§	80⅛–85	80	75
10⅛–11¾	10	10	85⅛–90	85	80
11⅞–15	None§	None§	90⅛–95	90	85
15⅛–17⅝	15	15	95⅛–100	95	90
17¾–20	None§	None§	100⅛–105	100	95
20⅛–23½	20	20	105⅛–110	100	100
23⅝–25	None§	None§	110⅛–120	110	110
25⅛–30	25	25	120⅛–130	120	120
30⅛–35	30	30	130⅛–140	130	130
35⅛–40	35	35	140⅛–150	140	140
40⅛–45	40	40	150⅛–160	150	140
45⅛–50	45	45	160⅛–170	160	150
50⅛–55	50	50	170⅛–180	170	160
55⅛–60	55	55	180⅛–190	180	170
60⅛–65	60	55	190⅛–200	190	180
65⅛–70	65	60	200⅛–210	200	190
70⅛–75	70	65	210⅛–220	210	200

*Applicable stock price is either the closing price of the stock on the day preceding the date the option was granted or the opening price on the day the option is granted if such price is greater than 110 percent of the preceding day's closing price.

†Assumption is that strike prices are only at $5 intervals up to $100 and $10 intervals over $100. Note: If the stock splits, option strike prices will have smaller intervals for a period of time.

‡Summary of special rules for over 90-day Calls:

Stock price	Rule
5⅛–60	1 benchmark
60⅛–150	$10 rule
150⅛ or more	2 benchmarks

§No in-the-money Calls will be qualified.

on disposition of an in-the-money qualified Call will be converted into a long-term loss if long-term gain would be realized on sale of the stock.[302] In addition, the holding period of the stock is suspended while the in-the-money qualified Call sold by the investor remains in effect.[303] If the qualified covered Call is not in-the-money, holding period continues to run.

---

[302] Code: 1092(f)(1), applies to positions entered into after June 30, 1984.

[303] Code: 1092(f)(2), applies to positions entered into after June 30, 1984. It is not clear whether one or both positions have to be established after that date for this provision to be effective. If both positions have to be established after June 30, 1984, then for offsetting positions acquired before July 1, 1984, the Call will be eligible for the qualified covered Call exception to the loss deferral rule, while the stock will not be subject to the suspension of holding period requirement. Nor will any loss on the option have to be long-term solely because the stock had been held for the applicable long-term holding period.

> **Example.** T owns XYZ stock less than the applicable long-term holding period. On the day after the stock closed at $75, T writes:
>   a. A call with a strike price of $80.
> *Result:* holding period of the stock continues.
>   b. A call with a strike price of $75.
> *Result:* holding period of the stock continues.
>   c. A call with a strike price of $70.
> *Result:* holding period of the stock is suspended during the period the call is open.
>   d. A call with a strike price of $60.
> *Result:* holding period of the stock is terminated. New holding period begins when the Call position is closed.

The schedule on the next page summarizes the above rules.

40   WHEN–ISSUED TRANSACTIONS

.01   Nature of Transactions

When an investor buys or sells securities when-issued, he actually contracts to purchase or sell the securities "when, as, and if issued," and for tax purposes there is no purchase or sale until the securities are issued.[304] An investor who buys and subsequently sells securities on a when-issued basis is technically acquiring two contracts. When these contracts are cleared on the settlement date, the sale and exchange of the securities is deemed to take place on such date. Thus all gains or losses realized in such matching transactions are short-term.[305] When the investor who holds several blocks of "old" securities, has sold at various times the "new" securities on a when-issued basis and cannot identify sales with specific acquisitions (see ¶**35.02(c)**), the gains or losses on the transactions are measured by matching the earliest when-issued sales with the securities sold in order of their dates of acquisition.[306] Options written on when-issued securities are treated the same as options written on issued securities. (See ¶**39.04** through ¶**39.05** for tax treatment of purchasers and writers of options.)[307]

.02   Wash Sale Rules

A loss sustained as of the settlement date of the when-issued contracts will be disallowed if substantially identical securities are ac-

---

[304] *Walker,* 35 B.T.A. 640 (1937).
[305] *Shanis,* 19 T.C. 641 (1953), aff'd per curiam 213 F. 2d 151 (CA-3, 1954): IT 3721, C.B. 1945, 164.
[306] *Haynes,* 17 T.C. 772 (1952) (Acq.).
[307] Code: 1234(b)(2)(B).

Covered Call writing tax summary

	Out-of-the-money Qualified Call*	At-the-money Qualified Call†	In-the-money Qualified Call‡	Non-Qualified Call
Positions established prior to January 1, 1984:				
Loss deferral rules	N/A	N/A	N/A	N/A
Year-end 30-day loss deferral rule	N/A	N/A	N/A	N/A
Loss characterized as long-term	N/A	N/A	N/A	N/A
Holding period for capital gains/losses	Unaffected, continues to accrue	Unaffected, continues to accrue	Unaffected, continues to accrue	Unaffected, continues to accrue
Holding period for dividend received deduction	Unaffected, continues to accrue	Unaffected, continues to accrue	Unaffected, continues to accrue (see note below)	Unaffected, continues to accrue (see note below)
Positions established prior to July 1, 1984 and after December 31, 1983:				
Loss deferral rules	N/A	N/A	N/A	X
Year-end 30-day loss deferral rule	X	X	X	N/A
Loss characterized as long-term	N/A	N/A	N/A	X
Holding period for capital gains/losses	Unaffected, continues to accrue	Unaffected, continues to accrue	Unaffected, continues to accrue	Terminated
Holding period for dividend received deduction	Unaffected, continues to accrue	Unaffected, continues to accrue	Unaffected, continues to accrue	Suspended
Positions established after June 30, 1984:				
Loss deferral rules	N/A	N/A	N/A	X
Year-end 30-day loss deferral rule	X	X	X	N/A
Loss characterized as long-term	N/A	N/A	X	X
Holding period for capital gains/losses	Unaffected, continues to accrue	Unaffected, continues to accrue	Suspended	Terminated
Holding period for dividend received deduction	Unaffected, continues to accrue	Unaffected, continues to accrue	Unaffected, continues to accrue	Suspended

Note: In Rev. Rul. 80-238, the IRS concluded that granting out-of-the-money Calls does not affect the holding period for purposes of the dividend received deduction. They implied a different result with in-the-money Calls.

* "Out-of-the-money": strike price of Call greater than applicable stock price.
† "At-the-money": strike price of Call equals applicable stock price.
‡ "In-the-money": strike price of Call less than applicable stock price.
X—Provision applicable.
N/A—Provision not applicable.

quired within 30 days of that settlement date.[308] For this purpose, securities acquired under when-issued contracts are deemed to be acquired on the settlement date. (See ¶36.04 for further discussion of the wash sale rules and their inapplicability where sales are made in a bona fide reduction of holdings acquired within 30 days.)

.03 Short Sales

A when-issued security is considered property for purposes of the short sale rules.[309] Therefore the acquisition of a when-issued security and the short sale of the "old" security or vice versa, where both are substantially identical, will cause the short sale rules to apply. (See ¶37.03 for further discussion of the short sale rules.)

.04 Holding Period of Securities Originally Purchased When Issued

If the actual securities are received pursuant to the when-issued contract, the investor's holding period for the "new" securities will start from the settlement date and not when the when-issued contract was acquired.[310] Thus, a sale of the "new" securities at a gain immediately after the receipt thereof would result in short-term gain even if the when-issued contract had been held for more than the applicable long-term holding period.

.05 Sale of Contract

The Treasury has ruled that a sale or exchange of a when-issued contract itself is the sale or exchange of a capital asset resulting in gain or loss.[311] Thus, it is theoretically possible to sell a contract to buy when-issued stock which has been held for more than the applicable period and have the gain treated as long-term.[312] According to the same ruling, an identical result could be achieved by selling a contract to sell securities when-issued.[313] Although the Treasury ruling apparently remains in effect, there is a possibility that the Treasury would contend that the subsequently enacted short sales rules (see ¶37.03) prevent the long-term capital gain treatment.[314]

---

[308] IT 3858, C.B. 1947-2, 71; however, cf. Rev. Rul. 56-602, C.B. 1956-2, 527.

[309] Reg. 1.1233-1(c)(1).

[310] IT 3721, C.B. 1945, 164; question (e) at page 173.

[311] IT 3721, C.B. 1945, 164; Rev. Rul. 57-29, C.B. 1957-1, 519.

[312] Ibid.

[313] Ibid.; see also Stavisky, 34 T.C. 140 (1960), aff'd 291 F. 2d 48 (CA-2, 1961).

[314] See Sen. Rep. No. 2375, 81st Con.,

(a) Practical limitations. An attempt to sell a contract to buy or a contract to sell securities when-issued through a stockbroker may be frustrated in that the stockbroker, applying the stock exchange rules, will consider the sale of a contract to buy when issued as an open sale of the when-issued securities. Similarly, an attempted sale of the contract to sell securities when-issued will be considered a purchase of the when-issued securities. Thus two positions, one long, the other short, will remain open until the settlement date. It is possible that the transaction will never be consummated, thus causing all trades to be canceled.[315] Perhaps the only solution therefore is a private assignment of the contracts.[316]

.06 Payment for Release from When-issued Contract

In lieu of transferring all the rights under a when-issued contract, if the investor could obtain a release from and cancellation of the contract itself by a payment to the other party, it could have been contended prior to enactment of Section 1234A that ordinary loss would result instead of capital loss. However, a payment to a third party to assume a when-issued contract to sell has been held to result in capital loss.[317]

.07 Worthlessness of When-issued Contracts

If the transaction contemplated in a when-issued contract, such as a reorganization, does not take place so that the when-issued contract becomes worthless, it is believed that the cost of the contract, such as commissions, may be taken as an ordinary deduction.

2nd Sess. p. 87, C.B. 1950-2, 483, 545. The Treasury's failure to reflect in the regulations this committee report indicating that the assignment of a "when-issued" contract is equivalent to the closing of a short sale, together with its virtual reaffirmation of I.T. 3721, Rev. Rul. 57-29, C.B. 1957-1, 519, would make it very difficult for the Treasury to deny long-term capital gain treatment. In *Stavisky*, 34. T.C. 140, aff'd 291 F. 2d 48, the Tax Court had an opportunity to discuss whether or not the short sale rules apply in this situation, but avoided the issue because the transaction took place prior to the

effective date of the short sale rules. Under the facts of the case, the Court ruled a loss on the transfer of a short position in the "when-issued" securities to be long-term capital loss. Subsequent cases dealing with the sale of "short" forward contracts have also treated the gain on sale as long-term. *American Home Products Corp.*, 601 F. 2d 540 (Ct. Cl., 1979); *Hoover Co.*, 72 T.C. 206 (1979); *Carborundum Co.*, 74 T.C., 730 (1980) (Acq.).

[315] See *Stavisky*, 291 F. 2d 48 (CA-2, 1961).

[316] Ibid.

[317] Ibid.

41 COMMODITY FUTURES AND OPTIONS

.01 Definition

A commodity Future is a contract to purchase or sell a fixed amount of a commodity at a future date for a fixed price.[318] The exchange on which the Futures are traded specifies certain essential terms of the contract. There are two types of commodity Futures contracts. A regulated Futures contract (Futures) which is subject to the rules of a board of trade or a commodity exchange (including a designated foreign exchange) and is valued daily and a Forward contract (Forward), which is not regulated by an exchange or a board of trade.[319]

.02 Types of Commodity Futures Transactions

Transactions in commodity Futures generally fall into four classifications:

1. Hedge transactions used to insure against losses caused by fluctuations in price of a commodity, included in inventory or contracted for future delivery, to be used or sold in the course of business. Such transactions will invariably give rise to ordinary income or loss treatment and therefore are not further considered here. (See ¶70.04.)
2. Nonhedge transactions entered into for speculation or investment purposes with a view towards making a profit. Such transactions will generally generate capital gain or loss.
3. Straddle transactions, whereby a simultaneous purchase and sale of two commodity Futures contracts on the same exchange but requiring delivery in different months, with the expectation of realizing gain through the variation of the prices of the Futures contracts as a result of market conditions. Capital gain or loss will generally result from these transactions, but the new straddle provisions will prevent taking a loss on one position in the current year and a gain on the offsetting position in the following year.
4. A "cash and carry" transaction, whereby there is a simultaneous purchase of a "spot" commodity contract requiring present delivery of the commodity (or purchase of the nearest month Futures contract with the expectation of taking delivery of the contract) and a sale of a Futures contract with the expectation of

---

[318] *Corn Products Refining Co.*, 350 U.S. 46 (1955), fn. 1.   [319] Code: 1092(d) and 1256(b).

realizing an overall gain due to a change in interest rates and other economic factors on the subsequent delivery of the commodity upon the closing of the Futures contract. The expenses incurred while the commodity is stored in a warehouse are now required to be capitalized and will offset any capital gain realized upon the closing of the Futures contract.

.03 Tax Consequences

(a) In general. Commodity Futures contracts which are not hedges are generally treated as capital assets; gain or loss therefrom will generally be accorded capital gain or loss treatment. The tax treatment of unregulated Forward contracts has not been disturbed by the 1981 ERTA except where the Forward contract is part of a straddle transaction. Major changes have been made to regulated Futures contracts whether or not part of a straddle transaction. Because of the importance of these new provisions, a discussion of the general commodity rules has been placed at the end of this section.

Prior to the 1976 TRA, an investor could realize an ordinary loss on commodity transactions by buying and selling a Call and Put in a commodity. An ordinary loss was allowed when he closed the option he had written at a loss. Before the enactment of the new straddle provisions, a similar transaction would result in a short-term loss in the year the loss leg was closed. [320]

Under the 1981 ERTA, the tax results would depend on whether the straddle consisted entirely of Futures contracts (regulated by a domestic board of trade or an exchange or similar designated foreign exchange and is valued at the end of each day), Forward contracts (unregulated contracts), options, or mixed straddles (a combination of Futures contracts, and Forward contracts, options, or physical commodities). Initially, these rules related to actively traded personal property, including metals, other commodities, currency, Treasury bills, other debt instruments, and Unlisted stock options, but have since been expanded to include stock and Listed stock options. (See ¶38.02.) [321] Positions held by an investor's spouse, partnership, trust, or similar flow-through entity are aggregated for these purposes. [322]

Business hedging contracts are excepted from these provisions. [323]

---

[320] Code: 1234(b).
[321] Code: 1092(d).
[322] Code: 1092(d)(4). With respect to partnership positions, the better rule should be an allocation of the partner's

pro rata share and not the total position.
[323] Code: 1256(e). Neither the commodity straddle rules, mark-to-market rules nor capitalization of carrying charges apply to hedging transactions.

These rules cannot be avoided by investing in a syndicate (i.e., more than 35 percent of the losses are allocable to limited partners).[324]

(b) Futures contracts. With respect to Futures contracts acquired after June 23, 1981, gain or loss must be reported on an annual basis under a mark-to-market rule. These Futures contracts held at the end of the year are marked-to-market as if sold at year-end. Any gain or loss on each contract held at year-end are included with the gains and losses on such contracts closed out during the taxable year. A termination of a Futures contract by offsetting, taking or making delivery, by transferring the Futures contract to and from partnerships or other flow-through entities, or by other means, will be treated as a sale of the Futures contract, using the fair market value at the time of the termination.[325] If a straddle contains two or more Futures contracts, taking delivery under any one of the contracts will terminate the other Futures contracts on the same day.[326] A cancellation, lapse, or other termination of a Futures contract will be treated as gain or loss from the sale of a capital asset.[327] With respect to such gains or losses, 40 percent is treated as short-term and 60 percent as long-term (the effective tax rate in 1984 on Futures gains cannot exceed 32 percent).[328] However, if the Futures contract is not part of an identified hedging transaction and a disposition would result in ordinary income, then ordinary income would be reported under the mark-to-market rules.[329] In determining gains or losses on the Futures contracts in subsequent years, proper adjustment must be made for gains or losses recognized in prior years under the mark-to-market rule.

Example. On October 1, 1983, T purchases a December 1984 gold Futures contract at $370. On December 31, 1983, the value of the gold Futures contract was $420. In 1983 under the mark-to-market rule, T reported a long-term gain of $30 (60 percent × $50 unrealized gain) and a short-term gain of $20 (40 percent × $50). In December 1984, gold rises to $500 and T takes delivery of the gold. In 1984, T will report a long-term gain of $48 (60 percent × $80 gain) and short-term gain of $32 (40 percent × $80 gain), computed as follows:

---

[324] Code: 1256(e)(3).
[325] Code: 1256(c).
[326] Code: 1256(c)(2).

[327] Code: 1234A.
[328] Code: 1256(a).
[329] Code: 1256(f).

Value of gold Futures contract in December 1984	$500
Contract price	370
Gain	130
Less gain reported in 1983	50
1984 gain	$ 80

Note that the tax basis of the gold received will be $500, consisting of the cost of $370 plus $130 total gain realized on the Futures contract.

An investor can elect to have Futures contracts, which are part of an identified mixed straddle (includes Futures contracts and Forward contracts or spot commodities), taxed under the general straddle provision rather than the mark-to-market rule.[330]

An investor with a net commodity Futures loss for a taxable year can elect to carry-back the net loss (60 percent is long-term and 40 percent is short-term) to the three preceding taxable years (the first preceding year is 1981) and offset the loss against the net commodity Futures gains in these years.[331] The 60/40 ratio is retained although the Futures' losses may have offset only long-term gains or short-term gains in the loss year or in prior carry-back years. However, a carry-back would not be allowed to the extent it increases or creates a net operating loss in the carry-back year. The carry-back also cannot exceed the capital gain net income for the carry-back year. For example, assume T incurred a Futures loss of $50,000 in 1983. During 1983, T also had other net short-term capital gains of $10,000. The $50,000 loss is first offset against the $10,000 short-term gain and T elects to carry-back the balance of $40,000 (assuming no other taxable income) to 1981. In 1981, T had Futures gains of $20,000 and a short-term capital loss of $5,000, or net gains of $15,000. The carry-back can offset only the net gains of $15,000 and the balance of $25,000 is carried to 1982. In 1982, T had other net capital gains of $60,000. Because there were no Futures gains in 1982, the $25,000 Futures carry-back cannot be used in 1982. Instead, it can be carried over to 1984 and be offset against any capital gains realized in that year, but $10,000 of the carry-over will be short-term ($25,000 × 40 percent) and $15,000 ($25,000 × 60 percent) will be long-term.

---

[330] Code: 1256(d)(4) and 1092(d)(5).
[331] Code: 1212; under the 1984 Act, these Futures losses would have to be combined with other Section 1256 contract gains or losses in determining the net amount of the gains or losses and the amount that can be carried back to a previous year.

(c) Mixed straddles. Those investors with mixed straddles— combination of Futures contracts, Forward contracts, options, or physical (spot) commodities—which are clearly identified before the earlier of the close of the day the first Futures contract is acquired or such time prescribed by regulations, must treat the entire mixed straddle under the general straddle rules described below in subparagraph **(d)** if an election was made to exclude all Futures contracts in mixed straddles from the mark-to-market rule.[332] The Technical Corrections Act of 1982 clarified the tax treatment of mixed straddles where the Futures contracts components are taxed under the mark-to-market rule.[333] Thus, an investor with a Futures gain would report the gain as if the contract was sold at year-end under the mark-to-market rule, but would not be able to deduct the offsetting loss position unless the position was sold by year-end. On the other hand, if the loss was in the Futures contract, despite the mark-to-market rule, the loss would be recognized only to the extent it does not exceed the unrecognized gain from the offsetting position. An unwary investor can be the victim of detrimental tax treatment under these rules unless proper action is taken before year-end. (See ¶**38.02** for additional 1984 changes.)

The following examples will illustrate the intricacies of the mixed straddle rules.

Example. Assume that T does not elect out of Section 1256 with respect to Futures contracts that are part of mixed straddles. In October 1982, T buys spot gold for cash at $370 and sells a December 1983 gold contract at $430. The economic gain of $60 is primarily attributable to the interest factor in pricing gold for future delivery. On December 31, 1983, the value of the spot gold is $400 and the gold Futures value is $470. The $40 unrealized loss in the Futures contract will be recognized in 1982 under the mark-to-market rule to the extent of $10 due to the existence of an unrealized gain of $30 in the spot gold.

On December 1, 1983, spot gold is trading at $500 and T delivers the spot gold in fulfillment of his Futures contract. This would result in a loss of $60 on termination of the Futures contract after adjustment for the $10 loss taken in 1982, of which $24 is a short-term loss and $36 is a long-term loss, computed as follows:

---

[332] Code: 1256(d). The Committee Reports indicate that the election to be excluded from the mark-to-market rule may be required before the close of the day the first Futures contract is acquired. The election is binding for current and future years until revoked with the consent of the Treasury.

[333] Code: 1092(d)(5).

Value of gold Futures contract on termination	$500
Delivery price	430
Loss	70
Less: Mark-to-market loss in 1982 ($40 less unrealized gain of $30)	10
1983 loss (40% short term, 60% long term)	$ 60

On delivery of the spot gold, T would recognize a short-term capital gain of $130 (delivery price of $500 less cost of $370).[334]

The 1984 Act Conference Report indicates that the ability to obtain 60/40 treatment on the Futures contract and a short-term loss on the physical commodity component of a mixed straddle will be changed by regulations. These regulations may provide that the capital loss on the physical commodity will be netted against the Section 1256 gains for straddles created after 1983.

Example. Assume in the above example that the market value of the spot gold drops to $300 at the time of delivery in December 1983. In this event, T would recognize a short-term gain of $56 and a long-term gain of $84 on termination of the Futures contract as follows:

Delivery price	$430
Value of the gold Futures contract on termination	300
Gain	130
Plus: Mark-to-market loss 1982 ($40 less unrealized gain of $30)	10
1983 gain (40% short term, 60% long term)	$140

On delivery of the spot gold, T would recognize a short-term loss of $70 ($370 cost of spot gold less deemed delivery price of $300).[335] Note that the short-term capital loss may be netted against the 60/40 gains under regulations to be released by the Treasury. These regulations would apply to post-1983 mixed straddles.

(d) Forward contracts. These unregulated contracts acquired or straddle positions established after June 23, 1981, will be governed by the new straddle provisions.[336] An election may be made to include all Futures and other positions held on June 23, 1981, under the straddle provisions. Straddles consisting only of regulated Futures contracts are subject to the mark-to-market rules.[337]

---

[334] Even though the spot gold was held for more than one year, the gain would be short-term under rules similar to the short sales rules.

[335] The rules discussed in footnote 334 apply.
[336] Code: 1092.
[337] Code: 1256(a)(4). (See ¶38.03.)

As stated previously in subparagraph **(c)**, mixed straddles are governed by the general straddle provisions even if the offsetting position is a Futures contract taxed under the mark-to-market rule.[338] Thus, if an investor was long a Forward contract or held the spot commodity, and short a Futures contract subject to the mark-to-market provisions, the Section 1256 rules would still apply to the Futures contract but it would be subject to the loss deferral and other provisions of the general straddle rule which governs the entire straddle position. If there were multiple straddle positions, some of which did not include Futures contracts, then these nonoffsetting positions would be subject to the general straddle provisions. Furthermore, if an election is made to apply the general straddle provisions to the entire mixed straddle, the Section 1256 rules would not apply to the Futures components even if the offsetting positions were terminated.[339]

Under the general straddle provisions, a loss recognized in one or more positions during a tax year will be deductible in the current year only to the extent it exceeds the unrecognized gains with respect to offsetting positions of the same straddle.[340] For this purpose, unrecognized gains include the amount of gain that would be realized if these offsetting positions were sold at market value at the end of the year, as well as gains on sales made before year-end but recognized for tax purposes in the following year.[341] Included under the general straddle rules are offsetting positions with respect to which the loss arose or positions acquired before the loss was realized.[342] However, gains from an identified straddle[343] are ignored in determining the amount of deductible loss for the year.[344] Gains or losses on identified straddles are not recognized until the entire position is closed.[345] Any losses that are not deductible as a result of the straddle provisions are carried over and treated as sustained in the succeeding taxable year, subject to the straddle limitations for that year.[346]

To insure compliance with these new straddle provisions, an investor with a commodity loss during the taxable year will have to dis-

---

[338] Code: 1092(d)(5).
[339] Code: 1256(d). An election is binding for the year it is made and all future years unless the Treasury consents to a revocation of the election.
[340] Code: 1092(a)(1). (See ¶38.02.)
[341] Code: 1092(a)(3).
[342] Code: 1092(a)(1). The actual language was deleted from the provision as being redundant. One of the unresolved issues is which realized loss is deferred when there are multiple losses in the same straddle, some of which are long

term and others of which are short term.
[343] Positions acquired on the same day and not part of a larger straddle must be clearly identified on the investor's records as an identified straddle on the day of acquisition, and either all of the positions are closed on the same day or remain open during the taxable year. Code: 1092(a)(2)(B).
[344] Code: 1092(a)(2)(A)(i).
[345] Code: 1092(a)(2)(A).
[346] Code: 1092(a)(1)(B).

close any unrealized gains with respect to any position (whether or not a straddle) held at year end, except for inventory, hedging transactions, or identified straddles, in accordance with regulations to be issued by the Treasury.[347] A 5 percent penalty may be imposed for failure to report the unrealized year-end gains if a tax deficiency is imposed because a loss is disallowed under the straddle provisions.[348]

The wash sale rules (see ¶36.01)[349] and the short sale rules (see ¶37.03)[350] are to apply to gains or losses realized with respect to any position of a straddle. These provisions will be contained in regulations to be issued by the Treasury.[351] It appears that, in general, the test would be "offsetting positions" rather than "substantially identical" property. These rules are to be applied before the year-end deferral of loss provision. Thus, if a Forward contract is sold at a loss and a substantially identical position was acquired within 30 days of the sale, the loss would be disallowed under the wash sale rule and added to the basis of the new position.[352] Similarly, if an investor had an offsetting position before the commodity or contract was held for the applicable long-term holding period, any gain or loss on the sale would be short-term. Presumably a long-term loss would arise if an offsetting position was held for more than the applicable long-term holding period at the time the investor entered into the straddle position. There will also be a loss of holding period when one of the offsetting positions is terminated.

(e) Other rules. Futures contracts entered into before June 24, 1981, or post-June 23, 1981 Regulated Futures Contracts which are part of a mixed straddle but which are excluded from the mark-to-market rule, retain the six-month holding period requirement in determining the character of the gain or loss on disposition. Thus, a sale of a "long" Futures contract held for more than six months results in long-term capital gain or loss. Similarly, a sale of a "short" commodity Futures contract can result in long-term capital gains or losses.[353] The mark-to-market rules may supersede these discussions with respect to regulated Futures contracts.[354]

The applicable long-term holding period (six months for assets ac-

---

[347] Code: 1092(a)(3)(B).
[348] Code: 6653(g).
[349] Code: 1091(a) and (d).
[350] Code: 1233(b) and (d).
[351] Code: 1092(b).
[352] The regulations to be issued by the Treasury may use a shorter period than 30 days, which might be considered too long a period than is appropriate for commodities.
[353] *American Home Products Corp.*, 601 F. 2d 540 (Ct. Cl., 1979); *Hoover Co.*, 72 T.C. 206 (1979) (acq.); *Carborundum Co.*, 74 T.C. 730 (1980) (acq.).
[354] Code: 1256(a).

quired between June 24, 1983 and 1987) applies to the sale of unregulated Forward contracts or to a sale of a commodity, as distinguished
from a commodity Futures contract. For positions or property acquired before June 24, 1981, the one-year rule applies even if the
commodity is used to close a Futures transaction. For example, if in
January 1981 an investor buys a spot commodity contract and sells a
Futures contract which requires delivery after the seventh month, the
closing of the Futures contract with the spot commodity will result in
a short-term gain because the one-year holding rule applies to the sale
of the commodity. Note that if the above transaction occurred after
June 23, 1981, the termination of the Futures contract would be
treated as sale of the Futures contract using the market value at the
time of termination.[355] Thus, 60 percent of the gain or loss on termination of the Futures contract would be long-term and 40 percent
would be short-term. Any gain or loss on disposition of the commodity would be short-term in this example because it was held less than
one year.[356]

Offsetting trades through the same broker in the same agricultural
commodity Future (e.g., wheat, eggs, corn, and the like) in the *same
market* for delivery in the *same contract period* are closed as of the
moment the offsetting trade is made, pursuant to the rules of the Commodity Exchange Authority[357] and gain or loss is recognized at that time.
Where the offsetting trade is made through a different broker, the transaction is not closed. Therefore, "long" and "short" positions are established and gain or loss is recognized only when the positions are covered.[358] Offsetting trades in nonagricultural commodity Futures (e.g.,
copper, zinc, and so on) may not be required to be closed by the exchange on which they are traded. Here also, long and short positions are

---

[355] Code: 1256(c).
[356] Code: 1222. The retention of the more-than-six-month holding period with respect to commodity Futures was intended to be limited to agricultural commodity
Futures contracts. Conference Commit-tee Report TRA 1402; Joint Committee
explanation, page 508. However, the House language was adopted covering all
commodity Futures. The IRS announced that all commodity Futures are covered
by the six-month rule. News Release IR 1787 (3/30/77).
[357] Commodity Exchange Authority Rules, Section 1.46(a).
[358] Reg. 1.1233-1 (d)(2)(iii). The Trea-sury had ruled, prior to the enactment

of the short sale rules (Section 1233), that gain or loss must be recognized at
the moment an offsetting trade is made in the same commodity Future on the
same market for delivery in the same contract period, even if the offsetting
trade is made through a different bro-ker. Mim 6243, C.B. 1948-1, 44 (obsolete); Mim 6789, C.B. 1952-1, 38 (obsolete); however cf. *Joseph Maloney,* 25 T.C. 1219 (1956). These rul-ings apparently have no current effect
in light of the applicability of the short sale rules to commodity Futures and
the example given in Reg. 1.1233-1 (d)(2)(iii).

established and gain or loss is recognized only when the positions are covered unless the mark-to-market rules apply.[359]

Prior to the 1982 Technical Corrections Act, in determining the holding period of a commodity received in satisfaction of a commodity Futures contract (whether a Futures or Forward contract), the holding period of the Futures contract was tacked on.[360] Since taking delivery under a Futures contract is now a taxable event, the holding period for Futures contracts taxed under Section 1256 can no longer be added to the holding period of the physical commodity. However, the tacking rule still applies to Forward contracts and Futures contracts which are part of a mixed straddle when an election was made not to be taxed under Section 1256.

(f) Pre-6/24/81 straddles. As indicated above, prior to the 1981 ERTA, a purchase of a commodity Future requiring delivery in one calendar month and a simultaneous sale of a commodity Future requiring delivery in another calendar month did not fall within the short sale rules. Therefore, an investor could have availed himself of this statutory exception when entering into this transaction for profit, to realize a short-term capital loss in the current taxable year and possible long-term capital gain in the succeeding year.

However, the Treasury has ruled that the short-term capital loss generated in a silver straddle transaction is not an economic loss and is not deductible.[361] The ruling further indicates that the net economic loss, after merging two years' transactions, is not deductible. This revenue ruling has far-reaching effects. The Treasury's utilization of a broad "substance over form" concept and a "lack of real economic loss" concept could cause many transactions, in addition to commodity straddles, to be challenged. There is no effective date to this ruling and accordingly, it could be applied to any commodity straddle or similar transaction as long as the tax year is still open.

In the first court decision on a commodity tax straddle case, the taxpayer won the battle but lost the war.[362] The Tax Court rejected the Treasury's contentions that the long and short positions of the straddle (a "Butterfly" in this case) should be treated as one economic unit and that the separate gains and losses should be integrated and not separately recognized on closing the short or long positions. It also

---

[359] Idem.
[360] Code: 1223(8). The Futures contract exception is effective as of June 24, 1981.

[361] Rev. Rul. 77-185, C.B. 1977-1, 22.
[362] *Smith*, 78 T.C. 350 (1982).

rejected the argument that a commodity straddle is a sham and the losses automatically should be disallowed. On the other hand, the court scored the practice of artificially valuing these contracts to produce greater tax losses rather than using true market prices. Applying a subjective test, the court further held that the taxpayer entered into the straddle for tax avoidance motives and disallowed the losses under Section 165(c) for lack of economic profit motive. The enactment of the 1981 ERTA did not affect the outcome of this case.

The *Smith* case discussed above placed the burden on the taxpayer to demonstrate that the straddle transactions were entered into with an expectation of realizing a profit. The econonics and profit potential of the taxpayer's commodity straddle must be fully explored.

In an attempt to resolve the uncertainty concerning commodity straddles acquired before 1982, Congress has instituted new rules.[363] Any loss on a position is deductible if the straddle was entered into for profit. An investor regularly engaged in investing in Futures is presumed, unless the Treasury proves otherwise, to have entered into the straddle for profit. Even where an investor cannot establish that there was a profit motive for the straddle, the loss positions can be deducted in determining the investor's net gain or loss from the entire straddle. This would prevent the benefit of earlier use of the losses and could complicate matters if the investor incurred other tax losses to offset the later profit positions. The amount and timing of the gain or loss for each position is determined without regard to whether the position constitutes part of the straddle. Sections 1233 and 1234 will apply in determining whether the gains or losses are short-term or long-term. Many investors who have purchased one or two straddles solely for tax motives, will obtain limited tax benefits from these provisions. Investors in straddles other than commodity straddles will also not benefit from these provisions.

An investor, for example, in a silver straddle, who is long the near-month Futures and short the far-month Futures will realize a significant pretax profit if interest rates drop, causing the spread between the contracts to narrow. An inversion (i.e., the further-out silver Futures falling in price below the nearer-term silver Futures) will result in a substantial pretax profit in relationship to the amount of invested capital. The ability to defer income by means of commodity straddles will no longer be available under the 1981 ERTA to traders in commodities or those entering into straddles primarily for tax purposes.

[363] 1984 Act: 108. These provisions do not apply to syndicates.

(g) Pre-6/24/81 cash and carry. A cash and carry transaction is similar to a commodity straddle except that the investor purchases a "spot" commodity contract in lieu of a Futures contract and takes delivery of the commodity, ordinarily through a warehouse receipt. (The investor could also purchase the nearest-month Futures contract and take delivery of the commodity.) He simultaneously sells a commodity Futures requiring delivery, preferably more than one year out. The investor hopes to make money in this transaction due to expectations of changes in interest rates and other costs of carrying the spot commodity, when compared to the "locked in" spread between the cost of the spot and the selling amount of the Futures contract. Silver, gold, and other metals lend themselves to the cash and carry transactions. However, care must be taken to be sure that the proper spread exists and other economic conditions are favorable before entering into the transaction. Prior to the 1981 ERTA, the expenses for storage, insurance, transportation, and interest on borrowed funds to purchase and carry the commodity would be deductible against ordinary income.[364] A deduction for interest and other expenses, however, was disallowed with respect to purchases of London spot silver and sale of Futures contracts where the taxpayer failed to establish that purchases of silver had actually occurred and that there was a valid indebtedness. Similar deductions were disallowed in later commodity transactions for failure to establish a profit motive for the transactions other than to obtain tax advantages.[365] While this decision is damaging to taxpayers in similar circumstances, it should not be controlling in cases where the investor can show that actual cash and carry transactions were entered into for economic purposes as well as for possible tax benefits.

With respect to a spot commodity purchased or positions taken after June 23, 1981, the above-mentioned carrying charges are no longer deductible but, instead, must be capitalized and added to the cost of the commodity.[366] The list of nondeductible expenses has been expanded to also include charges for temporary use of the spot commodity in a short sale to the extent that the expenses are in excess of the current income from the position.[367] This will either reduce the

---

[364] *C. A. Higgins,* 75 F. Supp. 252 (Ct. Cl. 1948), *Heaven Hill Distilleries, Inc.,* 476 F. 2d 1327 (Ct Cl. 1973); not followed where storage improved whiskey, *George L. Schultz,* 50 T.C. 688 (1968), aff'd. per curiam 420 F. 2d 490 (CA-3, 1970); Rev. Rul. 70-356, C.B. 1970-2, 68.

[365] *Julien,* 82 T.C. No. 37 (1984).
[366] Code: 263(g).
[367] Code: 263(g)(2)(A)(ii). Effective for property acquired and positions established after September 22, 1982. (See ¶38.05 for further discussion.)

amount of capital gains or create a capital loss on the sale of the commodity. Furthermore, under the old rules, the closing of the short position with the commodity held in storage was not a short sale,[368] and, therefore, would result in long-term capital gains if held for more than one year (the six-month holding period rule applied only to regulated Futures).[369]

If the investor now purchases a spot commodity and sells a Futures contract that is regulated by a board of trade or exchange and marked-to-market, the transaction will constitute a mixed straddle.[370] In this event, an investor will be subject to the mark-to-market rule with respect to the regulated Futures contract unless he elects otherwise.[371] The general straddle provisions apply to the offsetting positions in the cash and carry transactions if the investor chooses to apply the mark-to-market rule to the Futures contract. Even if an election is not made, the deferral rules and short sale rules will still apply to all mixed straddles. (See ¶41.03(c) for further discussion of mixed straddes.) Under these rules, a loss would not be recognized on the closing of one position and the establishment of a new offsetting position, and any gain on the subsequent closing of the transaction will be short-term pursuant to the short sale rules.[372] Note that no capitalization is required if the investor owns only the physical commodity and has not entered into a straddle or the transaction qualifies as a business hedging transaction.

(h) **Short sales.** Under the short sale rules (see ¶37.03) a commodity Futures requiring delivery in one calendar month is not substantially identical to another Futures in the same commodity requiring delivery in a different calendar month.[373] Thus, the regulations indicate that commodity Futures in May and July wheat are not substantially identical and, therefore, the short sale rules are not applicable.[374] The short sale rules also do not apply to Futures which trade in different markets even though they are substantially identical if offsetting transactions are entered into on the same day and both are closed on the same day.[375] Whether Futures in the same commodity traded in different markets are substantially identical will depend upon the facts and circumstances. According to the regulations, historical similarity in price movements in the two markets is the pri-

---

[368] Code: 1233(e).
[369] Code: 1222.
[370] See ¶41.03(c).
[371] Code: 1256(d).

[372] Code: 1092(b).
[373] Code: 1233(e)(2)(B).
[374] Reg. 1.1233-1(d)(2)(i).
[375] Code: 1233(e)(3).

mary factor to be considered.[376] An investor who has sold a commodity Futures short is precluded by the short sale rules from enjoying any long-term capital gain upon closing the short sale by buying in the commodity Futures.[377] Note that for purposes of the short sale rule, property includes only commodity Futures, and therefore the use of a commodity to close the commodity Futures would not fall within the province of the short sale provisions.[378] However, the mark-to-market rules will apply to the Futures contract so that only 60 percent of the gain or loss will be long-term and 40 percent will be short-term.[379] A Futures contract that is a component of a mixed straddle will be subject to rules similar to the short sales provisions whether or not an election is made to exclude the Futures contract from the mark-to-market rules.[380] (See ¶**41.03(c).**) Forward contracts were subject to short sales rules prior to the 1981 ERTA[381] and may also be subject to the new short sale rules for commodity straddles.[382]

(i) Wash sale rules. The courts are in conflict both as to whether the wash sale provisions apply to commodity Futures transactions and, if so, whether Futures contracts with different delivery dates are "substantially identical" for purposes of the wash sale rules.[383] However, the Treasury has ruled that the wash sale rules do not apply to commodity Futures.[384] As mentioned previously, for purposes of the short sale rules, the latter type of contracts are not "substantially identical."[385]

Rules similar to the wash sale and short sale rules will now be applicable to straddle positions in commodities taken after June 23, 1981.[386] (See ¶**36.01** for a discussion of wash sale rules.)

.04 Commodity Options

(a) Introduction. While options on physical commodities ("Actuals") have been offered by a limited number of Commodities Fu-

---

[376] Reg. 1.1233-1(d)(2)(i).
[377] Code: 1233(a); Sen. Rep. No. 2375, 81st Cong. 2nd Sess. p. 87 C.B. 1950-2, 483, p. 545; cf. *Joseph Maloney*, 25 T.C. 1219 (1956).
[378] Code: 1233(e)(2)(A).
[379] Code: 1256(c).
[380] Code: 1092(b) and (d)(5) and 1256 (d)(4).
[381] Code: 1233(e).
[382] Code: 1092(b).

[383] *Trenton Cotton Oil Co.*, 147 F. 2d 33 (CA-6, 1945), *Corn Products Refining Co.*, 16 T.C. 395, aff'd on other issues 350 U.S. 46; *Sicanoff Vegetable Oil Corp.*, 27 T.C. 1056 (1957) rev'd on other issues 251 F. 2d 764 (CA-7, 1958).
[384] Rev. Rul. 71-568, C.B. 1971-2, C.B. 312.
[385] Code: 1233(e)(2)(B).
[386] Code: 1092(b).

tures Trading Commission (CFTC) approved dealers for a number of years now, exchange (contract market) listed options on regulated commodity Futures have been approved for trading covering a broad range of commodities (e.g., sugar, gold, Treasury bonds, etc.) (See chart on page 110.) These options may have a life of more than one year (up to 15 or 16 months in some cases). Exchange listed options on Futures as well as on Actuals will be attractive to speculators and hedgers who wish to limit risk of loss to the premium cost of Put and Call options acquired.

(b) Tax effect on purchasers of options on Futures. Congress decided to give investors in options on Futures the same tax treatment as investors in Futures receive. These long or short options qualify as nonequity options[387] and are accorded mark-to-market, 60/40 capital gains treatment.[388] Due to the retroactive change in treatment of these Futures options, some investors may obtain refunds by filing amended returns for 1983.

The treatment for options on Futures acquired before November 1, 1983 is unclear. Section 1234(a) provides that the gain or loss attributable to the sale of an option to buy or sell property has the same character as the underlying property.[389] The rules have been extended to include cash settlement options.[390] Neither the 1984 Act Committee Reports nor any cases or rulings specifically deal with the pre-November 1983 treatment of options on Futures. (See ¶38.06.)

Prior to the 1981 ERTA, sale or termination of an option resulted in long-term or short-term gain or loss depending upon the period the options were held before disposition.[391] Since the underlying Futures would have been treated as a capital asset in the hands of a trader or investor, gain or loss on the disposition of the option owned would be characterized as capital in nature. In order for gain or loss to have been treated as long-term in nature (notwithstanding the pre-ERTA more-than-six-month holding period requirement for Futures) a more-than-12-month statutory holding period requirement would have to have been satisfied in order for the gain or loss on disposition of an option to have been considered long-term in nature.

Alternative treatments of the pre-November 1, 1983 options on Fu-

---

[387] Code: 1256(g)(3), effective for positions established after October 31, 1983.
[388] Code: 1256(a). (See ¶38.03.)
[389] See ¶38.06 for a more detailed discussion.
[390] Code: 1234(c)(2), applies to options granted after October 31, 1983.
[391] Code: 1234(a).

tures have been suggested. Based on the literal language of Section 1234(a), gain or loss on disposition of the option should receive the same treatment as the underlying property. If the underlying property qualifies for 60/40 capital gain treatment, the options should be accorded similar treatment.[392] A second interpretation is that the term "the same character" refers solely to the nature of capital gain versus ordinary income and has no application to the special 60/40 capital gain treatment under Section 1256. This latter position would be in accordance with the Conferees' statement that under current law it objects to the assertion that the "character" of property includes the deemed holding period provided to Section 1256 contracts. Despite contrary statements made by Treasury representatives, the Treasury has not reached any final decision on the proper treatment for pre-November 1, 1983 options on Futures.

(c) Tax effect on purchasers of options on physical commodities (Actuals). Options on physical commodities, whether long or short positions, now constitute nonequity options[393] and qualify for mark-to-market, 60/40 capital gain treatment.[394] Even prior to the 1984 Act, the tax treatment of options on Actuals was clear. The general rule of Section 1234 would characterize the options as capital in nature and gain or loss would be treated as long-term or short-term depending upon the applicable holding period requirement. Should the option be exercised, no gain or loss would be realized upon exercise, but the premium paid would be added to the basis of the actual commodity acquired. However, there would not be a tacked-on holding period. (See general rules with respect to options on stock—¶**39.04(d)**.) The tax treatment of options on Forward contracts (Futures contracts on commodities which do not meet the definiton of regulated Futures contracts) will be the same as options on Actuals.

(d) Tax effect on sellers of options on Futures or physical commodities (Actuals). Sellers of listed options on Futures or Actuals will now receive mark-to-market and 60/40 capital gain treatment on their option positions established after October 31, 1983.[395] For pre-November 1, 1983 positions, the same rules dealing with options on stock were also applicable to these options. (See ¶**39.05.**) Thus, under the previous rules, gain or loss on repurchase of either a Put or Call

---

[392] Code: 1256(a).
[393] Code: 1256(g)(3), effective for positions established after October 31, 1983.
[394] Code: 1256(a). (See ¶**38.03.**)
[395] Code: 1256(a)(1). (See ¶**38.03.**)

option on a Futures or Actual was treated as a short-term gain or loss regardless of the length of time the option was outstanding prior to its termination. In case of a lapse of an option, the gain was always a short-term capital gain.[396]

(e) Other rules. If an investor takes a straddle position solely in Futures or commodity options or takes offsetting positions in the commodity, Forward options, or commodity contracts, then the commodity straddle provisions as to loss deferral and rules similar to the short sales or wash sales rules may be applicable. (See the discussion of mixed straddles in **¶41.03(c)** if the offsetting position is a Futures contract or an option on a Futures or Forward contract.) If an investor held a commodity or Forward contract for less than the required period for long-term gains and acquired an option to sell the commodity or Forward contract (Put), any gain on the ultimate sale of the commodity or Forward would be a short-term capital gain.[397] With respect to a Futures contract, the gain would be 60/40 subject to special mixed straddle rules.[398] For purposes of the commodity straddle rules, an investor will be considered to have invested in a straddle if he owns offsetting positions in a commodity or a contract or option interest in the commodity.[399] Thus, if the investor has entered into a straddle with part or all of the offsetting positions consisting of Futures options, then any gain or loss with respect to any position of the straddle that is subject to the commodity straddle rules will also be subject to rules similar to the wash sales and short sales provisions. Accordingly, not only will a loss realized on disposition of one of the offsetting positions be allowed only to the extent it exceeds the unrealized (unrecognized) gain on the offsetting position,[400] the excess loss would be disallowed under the wash sales rules if the investor entered into another option or contract to reduce the risk of loss on the open position.[401] Prior to the 1984 Act, any gain realized on disposition of the option on Futures, Actuals, or Forwards should have been similarly treated as short-term under the short sales rules for commodity straddles held for less than 12 months at the time the investor entered into an offsetting position.[402] Since these options now qualify for 60/40 treatment as nonequity options,[403] the short sales rules would no longer be applicable.

---

[396] Code: 1234(b).
[397] Code: 1233.
[398] Code: 1256(a). (See also ¶41.03(c).)
[399] Code: 1092(d)(2).

[400] Code: 1092(a)(1).
[401] Code: 1092(b).
[402] Ibid.
[403] Code: 1256(b). (See ¶38.03.)

42 TREASURY BILLS, FUTURES, AND OPTIONS

.01 Description

Treasury bills are obligations of the United States which are issued on a discount basis and payable without interest at a fixed maturity date not exceeding one year from the date of issue. The price of these bills is determined by weekly auctions conducted by the Federal Reserve Bank. In 1976 the Chicago Board of Trade began trading Futures contracts on Treasury bills in a manner similar to commodity Futures. The Futures market is intended to provide a hedge against the volatility in interest rates for owners of substantial amount of Treasury bills or similar indebtedness. Many investors have taken simultaneous "long" and "short" positions in Treasury bill Futures (different months) in the expectation of deriving economic profit from the transaction and, for tax purposes, ordinary losses similar to the sale of Treasury bills. As discussed below, an investor can no longer obtain ordinary loss treatment by investing in Treasury bills, Treasury bill options, or Treasury bill Futures.[404]

.02 Definition

A Treasury bill Future, like a commodity Future, is a contract to purchase or sell a fixed amount of Treasury bills at a future date for a fixed amount. The basic trading unit is $1 million of face value of 90-day Treasury bills maturing in up to 24 months.

.03 Tax Consequences

The tax treatment of Treasury bills, Treasury bill Futures, and Treasury bill options has undergone extensive changes since 1980. Prior to the 1981 ERTA, sale of a Treasury bill resulted in ordinary income or loss because it was excluded from the definition of a capital asset.[405] Sale of a Treasury bill option also resulted in ordinary income or loss.[406] After some vacillation, the Treasury ultimately ruled that a Treasury bill Futures contract is a capital asset, resulting in capital gain or loss on its sale.[407] Despite the Treasury's capital gain

---

[404] Code: 1234(a). Since Treasury bills acquired after June 23, 1981, will be considered a capital asset, gain or loss on an option on Treasury bills will no longer be considered ordinary in nature. See 1981 ERTA: 505.

[405] Code: 1221(5), repealed by 1981 ERTA: 505(a).

[406] Code: 1234(a).

[407] Rev. Rul. 78-414, C.B. 1978-2, 313. The principles of Rev. Rul. 77-185 were held to be also applicable to Treasury bill straddles. (See ¶41.03(f).)

or loss determination, an investor with a short Futures position could still obtain an ordinary loss by delivering a Treasury bill in closing the contract. An investor with a long position could also obtain an ordinary loss on the Futures contract by taking delivery of the Treasury bill in satisfaction of the Futures contracts and selling the bill at a loss.

To rectify this situation, Treasury bills acquired after June 23, 1981 are no longer excluded from the definition of a capital asset.[408] As a consequence, losses realized on sale of Treasury bills, Treasury bill options, or Treasury bill contracts result in capital rather than ordinary losses.[409] Any gain realized on disposition of Treasury bills is treated as ordinary income to the extent of the investor's ratable share of the acquisition discount (excess of redemption price over investor's cost).[410] Gains in excess of the discount amount are taxed as capital gains. Unless an election is made to currently include in income the acquisition discount, the discount income on Treasury bills acquired after the enactment date of the 1984 Act will continue to be taxed only on the sale or redemption of the Treasury bills.[411] If an election is made, the basis of the Treasury bill will be increased by the acquisition discount that is currently includable in income. Since Treasury bill Futures contracts are treated in a manner similar to the treatment of commodity Futures contracts, gain or loss is determined under rules applicable to regulated Futures contracts.[412] These include application of the mark-to-market rule and 60/40 capital gain treatment. (See ¶41.03(b).) Treasury bills and Treasury bill options are subject to the tax straddle provisions.[413] Treasury bill options acquired after July 18, 1984 are also covered under the mark-to-market rule and receive 60/40 capital gain treatment.[414]

43 CASH SETTLEMENT CONTRACTS

Subsequent to the enactment of 1981 ERTA, the Commodity Futures Trading Commission (CFTC) has allowed trading in several mark-to-market Futures contracts that provide for cash settlement rather than delivery of personal property. One of the first cash settlement contracts was the Eurodollar Futures contract traded on the Chicago Mercantile Exchange. Stock index Futures such as the Value

---

[408] Code: 1221(5), repealed by 1981 ERTA: 505(a).
[409] Code: 1234(a) and (b).
[410] Code: 1271(a)(3).

[411] Code: 1282(b)(2). See ¶46.09(b) for additional discussion.
[412] Code: 1256.
[413] Code: 1092. (See ¶38.02.)
[414] Code: 1256(g)(3).

Line Average Stock Index and the Standard & Poor's 500 Stock Price Index have also emerged since 1981. These cash settlement contracts did not qualify for the maximum tax of 32 percent and mark-to-market treatment under the original Section 1256 because these contracts did not require "delivery of personal property or an interest in such property."[415]

To rectify this situation, the delivery of personal property requirement was retroactively stricken from the Code. Thus, these contracts now qualify provided they are traded under a system using variation margin and are regulated by the CFTC or traded on an exchange approved by the Treasury.

There is some question as to whether writers of options subject to variation margin qualify for mark-to-market treatment under the pre-1984 rules. The authors believe that Congress did not intend to qualify options, which are not truly Futures contracts, for special treatment when it eliminated the "delivery of property" requirement. This question was resolved by the inclusion of nonequity options in the list of investments that qualify for mark-to-market treatment.[416]

Taxpayers who may benefit from the retroactive change in the law can file amended returns for 1981 and 1982.[417]

44 FOREIGN CURRENCY CONTRACTS

Trading in foreign currency for future delivery may be done through regulated Futures contracts or by use of Forward contracts traded through a number of commercial banks comprising an informal market for such trading (the interbank market). Because these contracts either settle in dollars or were Forward contracts, they did not qualify for mark-to-market treatment under the original Section 1256. To rectify this situation, the Code was amended retroactively to allow any foreign currency contract to qualify as a regulated Futures contract.[418] To be eligible, the contract:

1. Requires trading of a foreign currency which is also traded through regulated Futures contracts,
2. Is traded in the interbank market, and
3. Involves prices at arm's length, as determined by reference to the prices in the interbank market.[419]

---

[415] Code: 1256(b)(1) before amendment by the Technical Corrections Act of 1982.
[416] Code: 1256(b). (See ¶38.03.)
[417] Announcement 83-62, I.R.B. 1983-14, 42.
[418] Code: 1256(b). (See also ¶38.03.)
[419] Code: 1256(g)(2)(A).

The Treasury is empowered to issue regulations that may exclude any contract that would be inconsistent with these purposes.[420]

A taxpayer holding a foreign currency contract in 1981 was permitted to make certain elections with respect to the currency contract and other regulated Futures contracts.[421] Amended returns may be required for 1981 and 1982 due to the retroactive change in the law.[422]

45 OTHER FUTURES CONTRACTS

In order to prevent a purchaser or seller of an option to buy or sell property from obtaining ordinary loss treatment, any gain or loss on sale or failure to exercise the option is treated the same as the sale of the underlying property.[423] One obvious flaw with respect to Treasury bills was corrected by including Treasury bills in the definition of capital assets.[424] Another technique for obtaining ordinary loss treatment was to take a straddle position with regard to Forward contracts in commodities or government obligations, such as a GNMA, close out the loss position, and claim ordinary loss treatment because there was no sale or exchange of the contract.[425] This possible flaw was also corrected by treating any cancellation, lapse, or other termination by an investor of a contract right or obligation with respect to personal property (other than stock or Listed options) as a sale or exchange of a capital asset.[426]

46 BONDS

.01 General Rules

A bond, like stock, is generally considered to be a capital asset in the hands of an investor. Capital gain treatment may be denied, however, on disposition of certain long-term unregistered bonds issued after 1982. (See ¶46.09 (h).) The rules for stock are also applicable to bonds: such as basis, holding period requirements, wash sale rules, and the like. Purchase commissions and similar expenses of acquiring bonds are included as part of the cost of acquisition; however, the amount paid on account of accrued interest is not included in the basis

---

[420] Code: 1256(g)(2)(B).

[421] Technical Corrections Act of 1982: 105 (c)(5)(B).

[422] Announcement 83-62, I.R.B. 1983-14, 42.

[423] Code: 1234.

[424] 1981 ERTA: 505(a).

[425] The Treasury has ruled privately that the loss on a GNMA straddle would not be recognized until all related positions are closed. Priv. Rul. Doc. 8117016.

[426] Code: 1234A, effective for contracts acquired after June 23, 1981.

of the bond, but must be offset against the first payment of interest income.

Some hybrid securities have features that closely resemble those of stock and other features that are normally found in debt instruments. Due to the many conflicting decisions as to whether a hybrid security is debt or equity, certain criteria were established by Congress to resolve this issue.[427] Among the factors to be considered are:

1. Whether there is an unconditional promise to pay a fixed sum on demand or on a specified date, and also pay a fixed rate of interest.
2. Whether the debt is subordinated.
3. The debt-to-equity ratio.
4. Whether the security is convertible.
5. The relationship between the stockholders and the holders of the hybrid security.

Recently, some corporations have issued adjustable (floating) rate convertible notes (ARCNs). The ARCN is subordinated, convertible into stock, callable after two years, and has an interest rate tied to the amount of dividends paid on the common stock. Typically, the issue price is $1,000, but the holder receives only $600 if he decides not to exercise the conversion rights. The ARCN was held to be stock rather than a debt instrument.[428]

.02 Amortization of Bond Premiums

(a) Wholly tax-exempt bonds. The investor is required to amortize the premium on wholly tax-exempt bonds for the purposes of computing basis;[429] however, no deduction for such amortization is allowable.[430] The premium is amortized on a straight-line basis over the life of the bond. If the annual amortization based on an earlier call-date price would be greater, then the bond premium is reduced by the larger amount.[431] For example, if a 10-year, $1,000, tax-exempt bond purchased on January 1, 1983 for $1,100 is callable on January 1, 1985 for $1,060, a nondeductible amortizable bond premium of $40 must be taken for the two-year period in lieu of a $20 amortization based on the maturity price and period ($100 over 10 years). If the bond was not called on January 1, 1985, the balance of the premium

---

[427] Code: 385. The Treasury was authorized to issue regulations, but after several attempts it has withdrawn all of its proposed and final regulations.

[428] Rev. Rul. 83-98, C.B. 1983-2, 40.
[429] Reg. 1.1016-5(b).
[430] Code: 171(a)(2).
[431] Rev. Rul. 60-17, C.B. 1960-1, 124.

of $60 would be amortized over the remaining eight years on a straight-line basis ($7.50 a year) unless there is another intervening call date which would also accelerate the amount of annual amortization. Note that no gain or loss would be realized if in the above example, the bond were called on January 1, 1985. Sale of the bond prior to the call date could result in gain or loss to the extent of the difference between the proceeds of sale and the unamortized basis of the bond. For state income tax purposes many states do not require the bond premium to be amortized if the interest income is subject to state tax. Front load fees charged for the purchase of shares of municipal bond funds or Massachusetts trusts, taxed as corporations, should not be amortized since they are incurred in the purchase of a stock interest and not in the purchase of a direct interest in a tax-exempt bond. Therefore, the unamortized amount should be taken into account in reporting gain or loss on a subsequent disposition. A similar treatment may not be applicable to front load fees charged in acquiring municipal bond trust interests. The purchaser is treated for tax purposes as the owner of the property and must report income and deductions as if the grantor owned the property directly. Accordingly, fees incurred in acquiring tax exempts would have to be amortized over the life of the bonds, and the amortization would not be deductible since attributable to tax-exempt income. Any unamortized fees would be taken into account in determining gain or loss on a premature disposition of the trust interest.

(b) Other bonds. Investors who elect to amortize bond premiums paid in acquiring fully taxable bonds will be allowed an amortization deduction in computing taxable income (and must make a corresponding negative basis adjustment to the tax basis of the bonds).[432] However, an amortization deduction will be deemed to have been taken in the standard deduction year for purposes of computing the adjusted tax basis of the bonds.[433] The binding election applies to all such bonds owned in the year of the election and to such bonds acquired in subsequent years. It is made by claiming the deduction in the return for the taxable year in question.[434] A separate election may be made by the estate or donee if the investor desires to make a lifetime gift.[435] If the decedent dies before the accrued interest is received, the decedent may still take an amortization deduction on the

---

[432] Code: 171(a)(1).
[433] Reg. 1.171-1(b)(5).
[434] Reg. 1.171-3.
[435] Code: 171(c).

final tax return, although the interest income will be reported by his estate or beneficiaries.[436] An investor who has not received any interest in the taxable year is permitted but not required to deduct the amortization.[437]

The total premium to be amortized with respect to any fully taxable bond acquired after 1957 is the excess of the basis of the bond for determining loss on a sale or exchange over the amount payable at maturity or any earlier call date, whichever produces the lower tax deduction.[438] (See ¶33.02 for determination of basis.) Special rules apply to premiums on bonds acquired before 1958.[439] The amortizable premium on a bond does not include that part of the premium which is attributable to the conversion features of the bond, determined as of the time of acquisition.[440] Thus, if an investor purchased $100 Eurodollar bonds which were either convertible into stock of the issuer or callable at $115 at the end of five years, there would be no amortizable bond premium before the call at $115 is exercised assuming the value of the conversion privilege is at least $115 at the time the bond is issued.[441] The premium attributable to the period prior to the beginning of amortization may not be amortized, but remains part of the basis of the bond to be taken into account in determining gain or loss on disposition.[442] Where the bond is called before maturity and a portion of the premium has not been amortized, the remaining premium may be deducted in the year the bond is called.[443] Note, however, on a sale of the bond, the unamortized premium remains part of the adjusted tax basis in computing gain or loss on the disposition. In the case where the bonds are not called on the call date and the premium has not been fully amortized, the remaining premium is adjusted over the period to the next call date or maturity date.[444]

.03 Amortization of Original Issue Discount

Investors owning noninterest-bearing obligations issued at a discount and redeemable for fixed amounts increasing at stated intervals,

---

[436] Reg. 1.171–1(c).
[437] Reg. 1.171–2(e).
[438] Code: 171(b)(1)(B)—The premium on callable tax-exempt bonds must be amortized to the "earlier" call date determined under Reg. 1.171–2(b).

[439] Code: 171(b)(1)(B); Reg. 1.171–2(a) (2).
[440] Code: 171(b)(1); Reg. 1.171–2(c).
[441] Reg. 1.61–12(c)(5), Example.
[442] Reg. 1.171–2(a)(5), Example (1).
[443] Reg. 1.171–2(a)(2)(iii).
[444] Reg. 1.171–2(b)(2).

such as Series E U.S. savings bonds, may elect to report each year the annual increment in value as income received.[445] Without the election, the investor would report the bunched amount of income when the bond is redeemed. The election is binding as to all such obligations owned or thereafter acquired and for all subsequent years. In the year of election, all increases in redemption value as of the beginning of the year must also be included in income. An executor may elect to include all of the unrealized interest on the U.S. savings bonds in the final return of the deceased investor.[446] In the case of most types of obligations other than long-term corporate obligations issued after May 27, 1969, original issue discount is not given any tax effect until the obligation is redeemed or otherwise disposed of.[447] However, under the new market discount bond rules, an election may be made to report the market discount income annually.[448] A similar election can be made to currently report the accrued acquisition discount income on short-term obligations.[449]

For corporate obligations with a term of more than one year issued after May 27, 1969 and before July 2, 1982, the original issue discount must be included in the investor's income on a ratable monthly basis over the life of the obligation.[450] With the extensive use of zero-coupon bonds, i.e., noninterest-bearing long-term bonds with a large lump sum payment at maturity, the Treasury realized that the use of a ratable or straight-line method of computing the annual amortization of original issue discount resulted in substantial deductions to the issuers of these bonds. Accordingly, with respect to long-term bonds issued after July 1, 1982, an investor will determine the amount of the annual discount income using a constant interest rate (a compound interest method), resulting in less income in the early years and greater income in the later years.[451]

The first step in computing the original issue discount for obligations issued after July 1, 1982, is to determine the yield to maturity of

---

[445] Code: 454(a). This election is not available with respect to savings certificates issued by banks, savings and loans associations, and similar organizations. Interest (or "dividends") on such certificates is held to be taxable when there is a right to withdraw it even if the principal must be withdrawn at the same time. (Rev. Rul. 66-44, C.B. 1966-1, 94; Rev. Rul. 66-45, C.B. 1966-1, 95).

[446] Priv. Rul. Doc. 7907120.

[447] Code: 1271(c).

[448] Code: 1278(b). See ¶46.09(c).

[449] Code: 1282(b)(2). See ¶46.09(b).

[450] Code: 1272(b). This rule does not apply to noncorporate and governmental issuers, tax-exempt bonds, or to investors who purchase the bonds at a premium.

[451] Code: 1272(a). Exceptions are provided for obligations issued by a natural person, tax-exempt obligations, and short-term obligations, such as T-Bills. (See ¶46.09(b) for further discussion.)

the discount obligation, employing semiannual compounding.[452] Both the original issue discount (stated redemption price at maturity[453] less adjusted issue price) and the interest income payable on the obligation during its life are taken into account in determining the yield to maturity. The yield is then applied to the issue price of the obligation (or the adjusted price at the beginning of a subsequent accrual period) to compute the discount for the first year after deducting any interest income received during the year.[454] The amount of original issue discount is then added to the adjusted basis of the obligation in computing the discount income for the second year.[455] For example, an investor purchases for $121,700 a 30-year, zero-coupon bond with a face value of $10 million on January 1, 1983. The yield to maturity is assumed to be 15.83 percent. The interest income for the first period will be $19,265 ($121,700 cost of obligation at issuance × 15.83%). Thus, the value at the end of the first bond period is $140,965 ($121,700 cost + $19,265 discount). For the second bond period, the discount income will be $22,315 (15.83% × $140,965). Similar computations are made for the succeeding years until the bond is sold or redeemed. If, in the above example, the bond were acquired on July 1, 1983, the amount of discount for 1983 would be $9,712 ($19,265 × 184/365).

A subsequent purchaser of the bond is required to amortize the remaining discount, less any amount paid for the obligation over the adjusted issue price (issue price of obligation plus the amount of the accrued original discount before the date of purchase).[456] The basis of the obligation is increased by the bond discount included in income.[457] If the obligation is redeemed prior to maturity and there was no plan or agreement for the premature redemption, any unearned original issue discount or premium paid in the redemption will be treated as gain from the sale of the bond.[458] The earned portion of the original issue discount (whether pro rata or calculated using compound interest) will be taxed as ordinary income. When the bond is issued as part of an economic unit (includes a warrant or other option, other security, or property), the cost of the economic unit must be allocated

---

[452] Code: 1272 (a) (5). Annual compounding was in effect for obligations acquired before July 19, 1984.

[453] This stated redemption price at maturity includes interest and other payments required at maturity other than fixed interest payments made at least annually over the life of the obligation. Code: 1273 (a) (2).

[454] Code: 1272 (a) (3).

[455] Treasury Department News Release, June 9, 1982.

[456] Code: 1272 (a) (6).

[457] Code: 1272 (d) (2).

[458] Code: 1271 (a) (2) (A); *Bolnick*, 44 T.C. 245 (1965) (acq.).

among each component of the economic unit based on their respective values at the time the bond is acquired in order to determine the amount of original issue discount with respect to the bond.[459]

If there is a series of obligations that mature serially, or there is a single obligation with sinking fund provisions, each series or installment payment is treated as a separate obligation for purposes of allocating the total original issue discount.[460] Special rules apply in determining the issue price of obligations issued for property,[461] or when deferred payments are made for services rendered or the use of property.[462] (See **¶46.09 (b)** for further discussion of bonds originally issued at a discount.)

Assuming the investor exercises the warrant and receives stock of the debtor corporation in exchange for the bond, the tax basis of the stock will be equal to the basis of the economic unit, consisting of the bond and warrant, plus any original issue discount income earned by the investor during the interim period before the conversion into stock. Thus, if the investor paid $1,000 for the economic unit and realized $20 of original issue discount income before the conversion, the basis of the stock would be $1,020.

The lack of any specific rules as to the proper manner of amortizing the discount on tax-exempt bonds and as to whether the amortization added to the basis of the tax-exempt bond created uncertainty as to the proper tax treatment. This problem was particularly acute with the increased use of zero-coupon tax-exempt bonds. Based on old rulings,[463] investors were creating artificial tax losses by increasing the basis of the bonds using the straight-line or ratable method. To rectify this situation, the lower compound interest method of computing original issue discount for taxable bonds was extended to tax exempts.[464] The basis of the tax-exempt bond is also increased by the amount of amortization.[465]

.04 Accrued Interest on Purchase or Sale

The amount paid for a bond purchased between interest payment dates will generally include the interest earned to the date of purchase. The investor will reduce his first interest payment received by

---

[459] Code: 1273(c)(2); Reg. 1.1232-3(b)(2)(ii)(a). In the case of a private placement, the issuer and the purchaser may agree on an assumed price for the obligation. Reg. 1.1232-3(b)(2)(ii)(b).

[460] Reg. 1.1232-3(b)(2)(iv).

[461] Code: 1274.

[462] Code: 1275(b).

[463] GCM 10452, C.B. 1-1, 18 (1932); Rev. Rul. 73-112, C.B. 1973-1, 47.

[464] Code: 1288(a)(1), applies to obligations issued after September 3, 1982 and acquired after March 1, 1984.

[465] Code: 1288(a)(2).

this amount.[466] When the bonds are sold, the portion of the proceeds attributable to interest earned to the date of the sale will be reported as interest income.[467] In practice, settlement dates are used in determining the amount of accrued interest.

.05 Interest Income

Interest income may be classified in two types: fully taxable and fully tax exempt (partially tax-exempt bonds are no longer in existence). Most interest income from corporate bonds and federal bonds falls within the first classification. Interest on obligations of a state or other local authority, the District of Columbia, or a territory or possession of the United States generally is fully exempt from federal tax.[468] An investor who simultaneously purchases a tax-exempt obligation and a Put on the obligation will not affect the tax-free status of the obligation.[469] Tax-exempt interest may also be received from partnerships, trusts and municipal bond funds.[470] If tax-exempt mutual fund shares are held for less than 31 days, then any loss on the sale of the shares will be disallowed to the extent of the exempt interest dividend.[471] An investor who lends his tax-exempts to a broker for delivery to a purchaser under a short sale arrangement will not be permitted to treat the amounts received from the broker as tax-exempt income.[472] In determining which type of obligation gives the largest return, the comparison should be based on the after-tax yield.

.06 Tax-Exempt Savings Certificates

Investors were permitted to purchase tax-exempt savings certificates (all-saver's certificates) from qualified institutions that participate in real estate or agricultural loans.[473] These one-year certificates were available during the period October 1, 1981 through December 31, 1982. A lifetime exclusion of $1,000 of interest ($2,000 for joint returns) was allowed, but the entire interest (after penalty) became taxable if the certificates were redeemed before maturity. Investment in the certificates could result in a disallowance of investment expense, including interest expense. The excluded interest income was also

---

[466] *Thompson Scenic Railway,* 9 BTA 1203 (1928); Sol. Op. 46, 3 C.B. 90 (obsolete).
[467] Reg. 1.61-7(d).
[468] Code: 103. Certain "industrial development" bonds issued after May 1, 1968, and "arbitrage" bonds issued after October 9, 1969, are no longer tax-

exempt. Code: 103(c) and (d).
[469] Rev. Rul. 82-144, C.B. 1982-2, 34.
[470] Code: 852(b)(5).
[471] Code: 852(b)(4)(B).
[472] Rev. Rul. 80-135, C.B. 1980-1, 18.
[473] Code: 128. Applicable in 1982 and 1983.

treated as a tax preference item for purposes of the alternative mini-mum tax.[474] (See ¶61 for discussion of alternative minimum tax rules.)

As a substitute for the all-saver's certificates, commencing in 1985, an investor would have been permitted to exclude from tax 15 percent of the first $3,000 of net interest income (15 percent of $6,000 for joint returns) after reduction for consumer interest ex-pense.[475] This provision was repealed by the 1984 Tax Reform Act.

.07 GNMA Bonds

Investors have discovered that the interest yields from bonds issued or guaranteed by the Government National Mortgage Association (GNMA), the Federal National Mortgage Association (FNMA), or similar pooling arrangements are comparable to, if not greater than, yields from other types of investment obligations. These bonds repre-sent individual interests in a pool of residential mortgage loans, and each investor will have a proportionate interest in the mortgage pool. Unlike other bonds on which the interest is paid currently and the principal is paid at maturity, with these pool bonds, each payment received by an investor will include interest and principal, as well as late payment charges, prepayment penalties, assumption fees, and discount income if the bonds are purchased at a price below the re-maining amounts due on the mortgages. Consequently, while the re-payment of principal is tax-free, representing a recovery of the cost of the bond, the balance of the income less any fees paid for servicing the mortgages generally is taxed as ordinary income.[476] The discount income is taxed as ordinary income, but a proportionate share of the discount attributable to any mortgages in the pool that are obligations of corporations or governmental units is taxed as capital gains under Section 1271.[477] The bonds will not be treated as U.S. obligations for state income tax purposes despite the involvement of governmental agencies in the issuance of those obligations, because the income pay-ments are deemed to have been received from the mortgages and not from the government agencies.

.08 Flat Bonds

Many bonds which are in default of interest or principal are traded "flat." The quoted price covers not only the principal, but gives the

---

[474] Code: 58(a)(1).
[475] Code: 128 repealed.
[476] Rev. Rul. 70-544, C.B. 1970-2, 6; Rev. Rul. 74-169, C.B. 1974-1, 147; Rev. Rul. 84-10, I.R.B. 1984-3, 9.

[477] For obligations issued after July 1, 1982, the retirement of all obligations issued by persons other than a natural person will qualify for capital gain treatment. Code: 1271.

purchaser the right to unpaid accrued interest without any additional or separate charge. Payments of interest accrued prior to the date of purchase are treated as recovery of cost,[478] while payments attributable to interest earned after such date constitute interest income. If the payment of pre-purchase-date interest exceeds the basis of the bonds to the investor, the excess is taxed as proceeds of redemption usually capital gain.[479] Where bonds are sold flat, the portion of the proceeds attributable to the interest accrued after the date of purchase to the date of sale will be treated as interest income, not as giving rise to capital gain or loss.[480]

Where bonds, which are trading flat, are sold short, a question is raised about the treatment to the short seller of the payments in lieu of interest that are subsequently made by him. The rule should be similar to payments in lieu of dividends on short sales (see ¶51.06) (i.e., deductible as a nonbusiness expense).[481] However, a profit motive must exist in order for the deduction to be sustained.[482] The repurchase of the short position immediately subsequent to the payment of the "flat" interest will result generally in a short-term capital gain equal to the reduction in value of the flat bond.

.09 Retirement, Redemption, and Disposition of Bonds

(a) **General rule.** The retirement of a bond will be considered as the sale or exchange of that bond resulting generally in capital gain or loss treatment. Bonds issued prior to 1955 must be with interest coupons or in registered form in order to qualify for this treatment.[483]

(b) **Bonds originally issued at a discount.** Gain on the sale or retirement of bonds held by an investor, which were originally issued after 1954 at a discount of more than .25 percent a year, is given special treatment.[484] That portion of the gain representing the original discount element which was not previously taxed is treated as ordinary income, with the excess gain, if any, given capital gain treatment.[485] Brokerage commissions are disregarded in computing original issue

---

[478] Reg. 1.61-7(c).
[479] *Rickaby*, 27 T.C. 886 (Acq.) (1958); Rev. Rul. 60-284, C.B. 1960-2, 464.
[480] *Jaglom*, 303 F. 2d 847 (CA-2, 1962); *Langston*, 308 F. 2d 729 (CA-5, 1962).
[481] Rev. Rul. 72-521, C.B. 1972-2, 178 (replacing I.T. 3989, C.B. 1950-1, 34). The earlier ruling, specifically dealing with dividends paid on short sales, has been cited as applicable to

interest paid on borrowing of securities, although the interest was disallowed on grounds of sham. *J. G. Gold*, 41 T.C. 419, 426, (1963).
[482] *Hart*, 41 T.C. 131 (1963), aff'd. 338 F. 2d 410 (CA-2, 1964). (See footnote 658.)
[483] Code: 1271(c).
[484] Code: 1271(c)(2)(A) and 1273(a)(3).
[485] Rev. Rul. 75-117, C.B. 1975-1, 273.

discount.[486] (See ¶46.03 for additional discussion of original issue bond discount.) Under previous law, a tax-free exchange of bonds for other bonds or preferred stock of the issuer, with no additional cost to the issuer, would not give rise to original issue discount.[487] However, with the repeal of the reorganization exception,[488] an exchange of bonds, stock, or other property can result in original issue discount if either the exchanged bond, or the bond or stock received in the exchange, is publicly traded.[489] In the case of convertible bonds, the issue price is not reduced by the value of the conversion feature in determining original issue discount.[490] Where bonds are issued with detachable warrants, however, a portion of the issue price must be allocated to the warrants, and thus original issue discount may result.[491] Allocation of each element of the investment unit is made on the basis of relative market values. A failure to exercise warrants issued as part of the investment unit will not affect the amount of original issue discount determined at the time the bonds were issued.[492] If a loss is realized on disposition of the bond, it is treated as a capital loss. The original discount rule generally does not apply to tax-exempt bonds or bonds purchased at a premium. However, gain on sale of tax-exempt bonds attributable to original issue discount is treated as tax-exempt interest, while the gain attributable to market discount is taxed as capital gain.[493] Similarly accrued interest income and original issue discount received on redemption of tax-exempt bonds prior to maturity represent tax-exempt income.[494] Any unearned original issue discount or premiums received on an early redemption will be taxed as gain from exchange of the bonds.[495] Because of the reversal of its prior position the Treasury will treat unearned original issue discount received on redemption of tax exempts issued before June 9, 1980, as tax-exempt income. Where dealers acquire a series of bonds from a governmental unit at par and sell some of the bonds to the public at a discount, the Treasury has ruled that the discount is not tax-exempt.[496]

The discount on unfinanced noninterest-bearing federal or munici-

---

[486] *National Can Corp.*, 520 F. Supp. 567 (DC Ill., 1981).

[487] *National Alfalfa Dehydrating and Milling Co.*, 417 U.S. 134 (S. Ct. 1974); Rev. Rul. 77-415, C.B. 1977-2, 311.

[488] Code: 1232(b)(2), as amended by the 1982 Technical Corrections Act, applicable to bonds issued after 1982.

[489] Code: 1273(b)(3) and (c).

[490] Reg. 1.1232-3(b)(2).

[491] Ibid.

[492] Rev. Rul. 72-46, C.B. 1972-1, 50.

[493] Rev. Rul. 60-210, C.B. 1960-1, 38.

[494] Rev. Rul. 72-587, C.B. 1972-2, 74.

[495] Rev. Rul. 80-143, C.B. 1980-1, 19, modifying Rev. Rul. 72-587, C.B. 1972-2, 74.

[496] Rev. Rul. 57-49, C.B. 1957-1, 62; Rev. Rul. 60-210, C.B. 1960-1, 38, modified by Rev. Rul. 60-376, C.B. 1960-2, 38.

pal obligations, which are payable within one year of the date of issue, is generally not to be taxed until the obligation is disposed of or redeemed.[497] There is also no accrual of original issue discount on certain nonleveraged, short-term nongovernment obligations, such as certificates of deposit held by cash-basis investors.[498] In the case of federal obligations and certain nongovernment obligations, the original issue discount is taxed as ordinary income.[499] With respect to municipal bonds, the gain attributable to earned original issue discount is tax exempt, while gain attributable to market discount is taxable as capital gains.[500] If the investor acquired the short-term obligation (other than a tax-exempt obligation) by means of a financing, including a short sale, the net interest expense is not deductible to the extent of the ratable portion of the bond discount attributable to the current year.[501] However, the interest will be deductible if an election is made to include the discount earned in the current year in taxable income.[502] An irrevocable election can be made to compute the amount of acquisition discount to be included currently in income under the constant interest rate (compound interest) method rather than the ratable method.[503] This should result in a lesser amount of discount income being reported in the current year. Note that if the election applies to a nongovernment obligation, the discount will be treated as original issue discount (see ¶46.03) rather than as acquisition discount in determining the portion of the discount income that is taxed in the current year.[504] The basis of the short-term obligation will be increased by the amount of discount income taxed in the current year.[505] (For a discussion of Treasury bills, see ¶42.03.)

(c) Market discount bonds. A bond may decrease in value after issuance due to adverse market conditions, such as an increase in interest rates. Prior to the 1984 Act, any gain resulting from this mar-

---

[497] Code: 454(b). Accrual basis taxpayers, banks, securities dealers, mutual funds, certain partnerships and other pass-through entities, and taxpayers involved in special hedging transactions will have to accrue and include in taxable income for the current year a ratable portion of the acquisition discount on short-term obligations acquired after July 18, 1984. Code: 1281(a) and (b).

[498] Reg. 1.1232-3(b)(1)(iii).

[499] Code: 1271(c)(2) and 1272.

[500] Rev. Rul. 60-210, C.B. 1960-1, 38; Code: 1271(a)(3).

[501] Code: 1282(a). The disallowed interest is deductible when the bond is disposed of. (See ¶46.09(c) for treatment of disallowed interest expense in tax-free transactions.)

[502] Code: 1282(b)(2). The election applies to short-term obligations acquired in the election year or subsequent years until the Treasury consents to a revocation of the election. If the election is made, Sections 454(b) and 1271(a)(3) will not apply to the short-term obligation. Code: 1283(d)(3).

[503] Code: 1283(b)(2).

[504] Code: 1283(c).

[505] Code: 1283(d)(1).

ket discount would be taxed as a capital gain. Capital gain treatment is still available for bonds issued before July 19, 1984.[506] However, the gain will be taxed as ordinary income, if the market discount bond was purchased after July 18, 1984 and directly financed, to the extent that the disallowed interest expense is later allowed under Section 1277(b)(1).[507] The tax treatment of market discount bonds (or other evidence of indebtedness) issued after July 18, 1984 will more closely resemble the ordinary income treatment of original issue discount, except that the market discount generally will not be taxed until disposition. Any gain realized on the sale or taxable exchange of the market discount bond will generally be taxed as interest income to the extent of the amount of market discount that accrued during the period the bond is held by the investor.[508] A gift of the market discount bond will be treated as a sale at market value, but no income will be recognized by the investor in other tax-free transfers under regulations to be issued by the Treasury.[509] If the investor exchanges the bonds for other property in a tax-free transaction, the exchanged property is deemed to be a market discount bond to the extent of the accrued market discount that is untaxed, and the accrued amount will be taxed as ordinary income upon subsequent disposition of the property.[510] For example, if a convertible bond with $1,000 of accrued market discount is converted into stock in a tax-free exchange, any gain up to $1,000 realized on the disposition of the stock will be taxed as ordinary income. When the market discount bond is transferred to another person, such as a corporation or a partnership, in a tax-free transaction, the transferee is substituted for the investor in computing the amount and character of the gain or loss on the subsequent taxable disposition of the bond.[511]

The amount of accrued market discount is determined by using the straight-line (ratable) method. In arriving at the accrued amount, the market discount (stated redemption amount less total cost of the bond) is multiplied by the days the investor held the bond over the remaining maturity period from the date of acquisition.[512] Thus, if an investor purchased a $10,000, five-year-to-maturity bond for $9,000 and sold the bond for $9,500 after one year, $200 of the gain would be

---

[506] Code: 1276(e).
[507] Code: 1277(d).
[508] Code: 1276(a). The interest income is includable in computing the investment interest expense limitations. (See ¶51.05.) However, the accrued market discount will be treated as income for purposes of withholding at source for certain bonds held by nonresident aliens or for information reporting under Section 871(a), 881, 1441, 1442 and 6049, or as specified in regulations.
[509] Code: 1276(a)(2) and (c).
[510] Code: 1276(c)(2).
[511] Code: 1276(c)(1).
[512] Code: 1276(b)(1).

ordinary income ($1,000 market discount × ¹/₅), and $300 would be capital gain. In lieu of computing the deferred market discount under the ratable method, an election may be made to calculate the market discount annually using the constant interest rate (compound interest) method as if the bond were originally issued to the investor for the price paid by the investor.[513]

The amount of market discount will be much lower in the early years under the compound interest method, especially for bonds with long remaining times to maturity which yield more capital gain on disposition. If the election is made, the basis of the bond should be increased by the amount of market discount included in income. Regulations will be issued concerning the amount of original issue discount when an election is made with respect to a bond originally issued at a discount.[514]

The following bonds are excepted from the market discount bond rules:[515]

1. Short-term obligations with a life of not more than one year.
2. Tax-exempt obligations.
3. United States savings bonds.

The market discount rules also do not apply under a *de minimis* rule if the discount is less than .25 percent of the stated redemption price of the bond at maturity multiplied by the number of complete years remaining to maturity after the bond was acquired by the investor.[516] Ordinarily, the market discount rules do not apply to installment obligations taxed under Section 453 except when the obligations are exchanged for a market discount bond in a tax-free exchange.[517] The Treasury is also empowered to issue regulations as necessary to carry out the purposes of these provisions.[518]

Prior to passage of the 1984 Act, investors could not only enjoy the benefit of deferred capital gain treatment by purchasing market discount bonds, but could also obtain current interest deductions by borrowing funds to purchase the bonds. The interest expense directly attributable to the purchase or carrying of market discount bonds acquired after July 18, 1984, including those financed through short

---

[513] Code: 1276(b)(2); 1278(b). The election applies with respect to all bonds acquired on or after the first day of the election year and all subsequent years until the Treasury consents to a revocation of the election. While in effect, the deferral rules with respect to accrued market discount and interest expense incurred in acquiring the bond are not applicable.
[514] Code: 1276(b)(2)(B); 1278(a)(2)(B).
[515] Code: 1278(a)(1)(B).
[516] Code: 1278(a)(2)(C).
[517] Code: 1278(a)(1)(B)(iv).
[518] Code: 1278(c).

sales, is deductible only to the extent of the interest income and any original issue discount income includable on the bond in the current taxable year.[519] However, any excess interest expense must be deferred to the extent of any accrued market discount on the bond for the period the bond is held during the taxable year.[520] Only the balance of the net interest expense is deductible in the current year. The deferral rules apply separately to each market discount bond, and the net direct interest expense for all market discount bonds cannot be aggregated in determining the amount of disallowed interest expense. To avoid this limitation on the current deductibility of interest expense, the investor can elect to report the accrued market discount currently (under either the ratable or constant rate method). Once made, this election can not be revoked without the permission of the Commissioner. However, if the investor intends to finance most of his purchases, this may be a useful election, since the deduction of financing costs will not be deferred. The trade-off is more income up front.

Any disallowed interest expense will be deducted in the year the market discount bond is sold or otherwise disposed of in a taxable transaction.[521] If the bond is transferred in a tax-free transaction, the disallowed interest will be deductible to the extent of any gain recognized in the transaction.[522] Any remaining disallowed interest will be deductible by (1) the person who received the bond and is required to report any accrued market discount income under Section 1276(c) (1), or (2) the investor who received other securities in exchange and is still liable for the accrued market discount under Section 1276(c)(2).[523]

(d) Bonds convertible into commodities. When there was a surge in the value of many commodities, corporations found that they could obtain better financial terms and defer paying tax on commodities by issuing bonds at a low interest rate with the bondholder receiving cash or a stated amount of commodities at maturity. Such commodities as silver or oil have been used, with the investor being entitled to either a stated quantity of the commodity or its cash equivalent at maturity. There should be neither an original issue discount nor a bond premium at issuance since the investor may receive the face value of the bond at maturity, and it is impossible at this time to reasonably compute the value of the commodity at the time the bond

---

[519] Code: 1277(c).
[520] Code: 1277(a).
[521] Code: 1277(b)(2)(A).

[522] Code: 1277(b)(2)(B).
[523] Code: 1277(b)(2)(B). See above discussion of Section 1276(c)(1) and (2).

matures. Accordingly, the bondholder should be entitled to capital gain treatment if the commodity or cash received upon redemption of the bond exceeds his cost of acquiring the bond. If the investor is entitled to a stated amount of a commodity, a subsequent sale will result in capital gain or loss treatment depending upon the amount received for the commodity, as compared with its value when received by the investor and the period the commodity was held before sale.

(e) **Sale and repurchase.** A common practice for owners of tax-exempt or other securities is to agree to sell the securities to a broker or bank at a fixed price and then repurchase the same amount of securities at the same price plus interest (a "Repo"). This type of transaction is treated as a secured loan, with the investor entitled to the tax-exempt interest income.[524] Any interest deduction would probably be disallowed if the loan was secured by tax-exempts. (See ¶51.05.) It is understood that the Treasury may be reconsidering a new approach whereby the sale would be treated as a taxable sale unless identical securities are returned to the seller. While gain would be taxable on the sale, any loss would be disallowed under the wash sale provision. Future private rulings will not be issued on this point until the matter is resolved. Rev. Rul. 74–27 has been distinguished by the Treasury on the grounds that identical securities were returned. A change of position may open up new avenues for tax planning, including artificially recognizing gain on the transaction where advisable or enabling the broker or bank to receive tax-exempt income and in exchange the investor may obtain better terms for the loan.

Holding that the transaction is taxable merely because the identical securities are not returned to the investor is inconsistent with other rules dealing with securities held by brokers on behalf of investors. In the latter situation, no taxable exchange results merely because the original certificates are not returned to the investor. In a sale and repurchase transaction, the securities are merely collateral for a loan and economic ownership does not pass. A sale does *not* take place (the terminology "sale and repurchase" is misleading). It should not

---

[524] Rev. Rul. 74-27, C.B. 1974-1, 24; *First National Bank in Wichita,* 57 F. 2d 7 (CA-10, 1932), Cert. den. 287 U.S. 636; *American National Bank of Austin,* 421 F. 2d 442 (CA-5, 1970), Cert. den. 400 U.S. 819; but see *Bank of California, National Ass'n.* 80 F. 2d 389 (CA-9, 1935); *Citizens National Bank of Waco,* 551 F. 2d 832 (Ct. Cl., 1977); and *American National Bank of Austin,* 573 F. 2d 120 (Ct. Cl., 1978); to the contrary where the securities were not always repurchased.

matter that the same securities are not returned or whether or not tax-exempt securities are involved.

A variation of the sale and repurchase is where an investor purchases Treasury bonds due in the succeeding year and borrows funds from the brokerage firm to finance the purchase. The purchase may be financed by the purchaser selling the obligations back to the broker and repurchasing them at a higher amount equivalent to an interest charge.[525] In this manner an investor can defer the payment of taxes by obtaining interest deductions in the current year (subject to investment interest limitations) and receiving interest income (or capital gains if a sale of discounted bonds) in the succeeding year. The 1984 Act has restricted the use of Repos for purposes of deferring income and obtaining long-term capital gains in the case of market discount bonds.[526] Deferred income may still be possible by financing the purchase of coupon bonds, but the investor may incur an economic loss if the price of the bond were to fall before receipt of the bond coupon at the beginning of the succeeding year. These transactions can also be questioned by the Treasury unless the investor can prove that he entered into the transaction for profit (e.g., the investor anticipated a drop in the interest rates, which would lower his interest expense while his interest income is fixed). With the current fluctuations in interest rates, an investor can readily establish that he entered into the transaction to make a profit. Note: an investor can sustain a substantial economic loss if the interest rates were to rise.

(f) Stripped taxable bonds. Prior to the 1982 tax changes, the owner of a bond could obtain a capital loss by selling the stripped bond and retaining the coupons or could accelerate income by selling only the coupons.[527] This practice has been stopped for sales of stripped bonds or coupons after July 1, 1982 by requiring the seller to apportion the basis of the bond between the bond and coupons based on their respective fair market values on the date of the sale.[528] The seller will also be required to include in income any accrued and unreported interest income on the stripped bonds. The accrued interest will be included in the bond's tax basis to be apportioned between the

---

[525] In Priv. Rul. Doc, 8011067, the Treasury inexplicably refused to rule that the "Repo financing," which was incurred for valid business reasons, would result in interest deductions and long-term capital gains on sale of the bonds.

[526] Code: 1276, 1277, 1281, and 1282.

[527] Priv. Rul. Doc. 8108108; *R. H. Shafer,* 204 F. Supp. 473 (DC Ohio, 1962), aff'd per curiam 312 F. 2d 747 (CA-6, 1963).

[528] Code: 1286(b).

bond and the coupons. In addition, the seller is treated as having purchased the retained bond or coupons and must amortize as original issue discount over the remaining life of the bond or coupons the difference between the amount payable at maturity and the allocated basis.

Those who purchased stripped bonds or coupons after July 1, 1982 will also be required to amortize the difference between the amount payable on maturity of the bond or coupons and the allocated cost over the remaining life of the bond or coupons.[529] Thus, the purchaser is required to currently report income instead of deferring the income until disposition of the property and can no longer convert ordinary income into capital gains by selling the detached coupons before their maturity date.[530]

Gain realized on the sale of stripped bonds purchased after 1957 and before July 2, 1982 will be taxed as ordinary income to the extent of the market value of the detached coupons at the time of purchase.[531] Thus, if the bond with the coupons attached had a value of $900 but was sold for $800 without the coupons, the first $100 on the subsequent sale of the bond would be ordinary income. Note that this provision does not affect the original seller of the stripped bond. As explained above, the original seller normally realized a capital loss on the sale of the stripped bond and would not include the interest on the detached coupons in gross income at the time the interest is received.

(g) **Stripped tax-exempt bonds.** The original issue discount treatment of sellers or purchasers of stripped bonds or detached coupons is generally not applicable to stripped tax exempts.[532] Since any original issue discount income would also be tax-free, retention of this rule for stripped bonds would only permit the purchasers or sellers to increase their tax basis in the stripped bonds and detached coupons. However, the seller of a stripped bond or detached coupons is required to allocate the cost of the bonds between the stripped bond and detached coupons based on their respective values, thereby depriving the seller of an artificial loss on the sale of the stripped bond. In addition, a purchaser of a stripped tax-exempt bond or a seller of the detached coupons may realize taxable gain on the subsequent sale or redemption of the stripped bond to the extent of the portion of the cost of the tax-exempt bond allocated to the detached coupons.

---

[529] Code: 1286(a).
[530] Sol. Op. 46, C.B. 3, 90, declared obsolete by Rev. Rul. 68-575, C.B. 1968-

2, 603.
[531] Code: 1286(c).
[532] Code: 1286(d).

(h) Registered bonds. Most corporate and government bonds with a maturity of more than one year must be in registered form if they were issued after 1982.[533] Holders of any unregistered bonds will be denied capital gain treatment on disposition of these bonds[534] or any deduction if the unregistered bonds are sold at a loss.[535]

.10 Exchange of Bonds—Deferral of Gain or Loss

Ordinarily an exchange of bonds for other securities, stock or property is a taxable exchange.[536] An exchange of bonds of the same debtor will also be taxable when there are material changes in the terms of the securities. Differences in the fair market value of the bonds is not a controlling factor.[537] Capital gain or loss results from an exchange of a note, secured by a real estate mortgage, for a corporate bond of the same par value but with a different market value. Unpaid interest on the note is not taxed to the noteholder because the value of the property received in exchange is less than the face value of the note.[538] Similarly, an exchange of New York City bonds for "Big MAC" bonds constitutes a taxable exchange since the bonds are not considered substantially identical. The difference between par value and the market value of the Big MAC bonds represents original issue discount and is exempt from tax on a subsequent sale or redemption.[539]

Special rules, however, permit tax-free exchanges of bonds for other bonds, securities or stock, bonds in the same or a lesser principal amount (interest rates may vary), or stock in connection with a tax-free reorganization.[540] Conversion of bonds by their terms into stock of the debtor corporation also constitutes a tax-free exchange,[541] but not a conversion into stock of another corporation.[542] In the case of tax-free exchanges of market discount bonds, the accrued untaxed market discount income may be attached to the security received by the investor in exchange for the market discount bond.[543] For corporate acquisitions contracted after May 27, 1969, marketable bonds or

---

[533] The date was extended to June 30, 1983 for most tax exempts. The issuer of the bond may be subject to excise tax under Section 4701, as well as loss of interest expense deductions under Section 163(f) for failure to issue the obligations in registered form.

[534] Code: 1287(a).

[535] Code: 165(j).

[536] Code: 1031(a).

[537] Rev. Rul. 81-169, C.B. 1981–1, 429. Differences in the interest rates, matur-

ity dates, and sinking fund provisions were sufficient to cause the exchange to be taxable.

[538] Rev. Rul. 73-328, C.B. 1973-2, 296.

[539] Priv. Rul. Doc. 7902002.

[540] Code: 354, 368, 371.

[541] Rev. Rul. 72-265, C.B. 1972-1, 222.

[542] *Timken*, 47 B.T.A. 494 (1942); Rev. Rul. 72-265, C.B. 1972-1, 222; Rev. Rul. 69-135, C.B. 1969-1, 198.

[543] Code: 1276(c)(2). (See ¶46.09(c) for additional discussion.)

bonds payable on demand will be treated as cash for purposes of computing the amount of deferred gain under the installment method. Prior to the change in the installment sale rules, marketable or demand obligations could disqualify a seller from meeting the 30 percent of sale price test.[544] The receipt of nonmarketable convertible debentures on sale of property could qualify for installment treatment since the conversion feature is considered part of the debenture and is not valued separately.[545] Where convertible debentures are received as part of the sales proceeds, the Treasury has questionably ruled that the amount of gain taxed at the time the convertible bonds are converted into stock would be based upon the value of the stock received in the exchange and would not be limited to the deferred gain. An identical position was taken that a gift of the convertible debenture would also result in tax to the grantor to the extent that the fair market value of the convertible debentures exceeded basis.[546] Certain exchanges of U.S. obligations are also nontaxable.[547] The most common types of exchanges are the exchange of Series E bonds for other government obligations, resulting in deferment of accrued interest until ultimate redemption, and exchanges of one type of long-term government obligation for another pursuant to a special announcement. Owners of Series E bonds held for more than 40 years should either exchange the bonds for other government bonds or cash them and report all of the deferred interest income because the bonds cease paying interest after 40 years. The transfer of converted Series E bonds to a trust of which the investor is treated as the owner for tax purposes will not be treated as a disposition causing the deferred interest income to be taxed.[548] Published Capital Changes services generally provide the necessary information regarding exchanges of publicly held securities.

.11 Flower Bonds

Certain U.S. Treasury bonds ("flower bonds") may be used after death in payment of the investor's estate tax liability at their par

---

[544] Code: 453(f); Rev. Rul. 75-117, C.B. 1975-1, 273.

[545] Rev. Rul. 71-420, C.B. 1971-2, 220.

[546] Rev. Rul. 72-264, C.B. 1972-1, 131. This harsh interpretation of Section 453(d) would result in an investor realizing a greater amount of income by electing the installment method than if he reported the full amount of gain at the time of the exchange. The intent of the installment sale provision was to alleviate a hardship caused by requiring a taxpayer to pay a tax on the entire gain realized on the sale although he received little or no cash in the year of sale, and not to impose a penalty for making the election. This point has not yet been litigated.

[547] Code: 1037.

[548] Priv. Rul. Doc. 7729003.

value. Due to the low interest yields on these bonds, they generally sell at a discount and therefore in the past a benefit could be obtained by acquiring these bonds at a discount and redeeming them at face value in payment of estate taxes. However, because the bonds are redeemable at face value, this value must be used in valuing the assets of the deceased investor's estate in computing both federal and state estate or inheritance taxes. Excess flower bonds that were sold at market value after the estate tax return was filed, and accordingly were unavailable to pay a subsequent estate tax deficiency, must also be included in the estate at par value.[549] Inclusion at face value would therefore reduce the benefits of these flower bonds to the extent of the estate tax rates. Thus, if the estate tax rate were 70 percent, the benefit of utilizing flower bonds would be reduced to 30 percent of the discount. Naturally, the lower the estate tax rate, the greater the benefits from flower bonds. The recent changes made by the 1981 ERTA, including the gradual reduction of the maximum tax rate to 50 percent, should increase the benefits derived from flower bonds. No gain will be recognized on redemption of these bonds because the basis to the estate would be their face value reported in the estate tax return. Note that the number of these bonds is diminishing since the Treasury has not been authorized to issue these bonds after March 3, 1971.[550]

47 WORTHLESS SECURITIES

If a security becomes completely worthless during the taxable year, its cost (tax basis) is deductible as a loss from the sale or exchange of a capital asset taking place on the last day of the taxable year.[551] No deduction is allowed for partial worthlessness or decline in market value until the security is sold or exchanged in a closed transaction. Mere bankruptcy is not sufficient to claim worthless stock loss if a shareholder may receive shares of the reorganized corporation.[552] Nor can a shareholder claim a theft loss where the bankruptcy was caused by the corporate management's fraudulent actions and statements if the shares were purchased in the open market.[553] However, an ordinary theft loss deduction may be claimed when the shareholders were induced to vote for merger because of misleading financial statements unless there is a reasonable prospect of recovery of the investment through the bankruptcy reorganization.[554] If a shareholder sells his

---

[549] *Estate of Simmie*, 69 T.C. 877 (1978), aff'd 632 F. 2d 93 (CA-9 1980).
[550] Code: 6312, repealed by P.L. 92-5.
[551] Code: 165(g).

[552] Rev. Rul. 77-17, C.B. 1977-1, 44.
[553] Ibid.
[554] Rev. Rul. 77-18, C.B. 1977-1, 46.

stock before the recovery prospects materialize, it is understood that the Treasury will permit the unrecovered cost to be deductible as an ordinary theft loss rather than a capital loss.

Usually the deduction for a worthless stock loss is allowed in the year in which there is an identifiable event demonstrating worthlessness, such as bankruptcy of the corporation, reorganization with no provision for stockholders, cessation of business, and so on. Merely showing that the corporation had no liquidation value and was incurring losses each year was not sufficient reason for claiming a worthless stock deduction before the year it ceased doing business.[555] The Treasury frequently will insist that the loss was sustained in a later or earlier year than the one in which the loss was claimed on the return. A special seven-year statute of limitations for refund claims accords some additional protection to the taxpayer who reported the loss in the wrong year.[556] However, as one court has suggested, the only safe practice is to claim a loss for worthlessness in the earliest year possible and to renew the claim in subsequent years if there is any chance of its being applicable to the income for those later years.[557]

48 LOSS ON FAILURE TO DELIVER

A loss suffered by an investor arising from the failure of his broker to deliver stock which was fully paid was held to be an ordinary loss and not a nonbusiness bad debt (a short-term loss).[558] The investor had rescinded the purchase agreement, but because of the insolvent condition of his broker he agreed to settle for an amount less than the original purchase price. An ordinary loss was allowed because there was no sale or exchange and a creditor-debtor relationship did not exist between the investor and his broker. However, a loss realized on the sale of an investor's margin stock by the trustee of an insolvent brokerage firm in the course of liquidating its business resulted in a capital loss to the investor.[559]

Losses realized on subordination agreements with stock brokerage firms were originally held to be ordinary losses.[560] Subsequent court decisions have found the losses to be capital losses unless the loss arose from a bailment arrangement with the brokerage firm.[561]

---

[555] *Thun*, T.C. Memo 1977-372.
[556] Code: 6511(d).
[557] *Young*, 123 F. 2d 597 (CA-2, 1941).
[558] *Meyer*, T.C. Memo 1975-349, aff'd per curiam 547 F. 2d 943 (CA-5, 1977).
[559] Rev. Rul. 74-293, C.B. 1974-1, 54.
[560] *Stahl*, 441 F. 2d 999 (CA-DC, 1970); *Michtom*, 573 F. 2d 58 (Ct. Cl., 1978).

[561] *Michtom*, 626 F. 2d 815 (Ct. Cl., 1980), vacating its prior decision; *Lorch*, 70 T.C. 674 (1978), aff'd 605 F. 2d 657 (CA-2, 1979), cert. den. 100 S. Ct. 1024 (1980); *Meisels*, 83-2 USTC ¶9390 (Ct. Cl., 1983), aff'd. 84-1 USTC ¶9376 (CA-F, 1984).

49 ASSIGNMENT OF INCOME

Ordinarily, a shareholder or bondholder cannot validly assign part or all of the dividends or interest payable on the security and still retain ownership of the security.[562] The assigned income will be taxed to the assignor when paid. (See statutory exception for short-term trust in ¶67.) However, an assignment of future income for consideration in a bona fide commercial transaction generally will result in ordinary income in the year of receipt.[563] A trust beneficiary who assigned his trust interest to a charity was held taxable on dividend income payable to the trust because the assignment was after the dividend declaration date.[564] In this ruling the date of declaration was the same as the record date, but the record date is usually controlling with respect to which shareholders are entitled to the dividend. On the other hand, an assignment of future dividend income to the shareholder's son for adequate consideration to enable the shareholder to utilize large interest deductions in the current year was upheld on the grounds that the transaction was not a sham.[565] The payment of adequate consideration, the dividend was from a publicly held corporation not controlled by the assignor, and the fact that the assignor was not required to perform future services in order to fulfill his obligations are important factors in determining whether the assignment will be recognized for tax purposes. This type of assignment is distinguishable from a sale of future rents, future manufacturing profits or future pipeline revenues where the purchasers had to look solely to the sellers to produce the future income.[566] Amounts received on a sale of detached bond coupons before July 2, 1982 were also included in income in the year the amounts were received.[567] A seller of stripped bonds or coupons after July, 1982 is now required to apportion the basis of the bonds between the bond and the coupons, thereby reducing the amount of gain on sale of the stripped coupons. (See ¶46.09(f).)

The assignment of income doctrine is not limited to gifts of income, such as interest and dividends, but applies equally to gains which have fully ripened and are unconditionally payable in due course. A gift of appreciated securities generally will not fall under this doctrine unless the stock is sold immediately after the gift is

---

[562] *Lucas* v. *Earl,* 281 U.S. 111 (1930); *Helvering* v. *Horst,* 311 U.S. 112 (1948).
[563] *P. G. Lake, Inc.* 356 U.S. 260 (1958).
[564] Rev. Rul. 74-562, C.B. 1974-2, 28.

[565] *Stranahan Est.* 472 F. 2d 867 (CA-6, 1973), rev'g. T.C. Memo 1971-250.
[566] *Mapco Inc.,* 556 F. 2d 1107 (Ct. Cl., 1977).
[567] Priv. Rul. Doc. 8108108.

made.[568] However, a gift of stock made shortly before the effective date of a merger of the issuing corporation will result in the unrealized gains being taxed to the original owner and not to the donee.[569] Attempts to avoid tax by a gift of securities under similar circumstances (e.g., adoption of plan of liquidation) to a charitable organization have also been unsuccessful.[570] Tax on gains can also not be avoided by transferring the stock to family members after entering into a binding agreement to sell the stock to a third party.[571] A donor was successful in escaping tax when the stock was given before there was a final agreement to sell it.[572] These assignment of income cases must be distinguished from a valid installment sale of stock to a family trust after the shareholders voted to merge or liquidate the corporation.[573] Note, however, a tax on the gain will be imposed on the transferor if there is a bargain sale to the family member rather than a sale at full market value, as in the Rushing case.[574]

Note that a sale of a production payment (i.e., a right to a specified amount of future receipts from mineral property), by the owner of the property to an investor or financial institution is treated as a loan rather than a sale of property.[575]

50 INSTALLMENT SALES

An investor will recognize a gain when the amount of cash and the value of other property received exceeds the adjusted tax basis of the stock, securities, or other property given in the exchange.[576] Part or all of the gain recognized on sale, but not any losses, may be deferred if the transaction qualifies for installment sale treatment.[577] A deferral of part or all of the gain can be obtained by receiving cash in the following years or by accepting notes, with one or more payments due after the year of sale.[578] Thus, if an investor receives a note with equal payments over five years, the gain on the sale will be reported proportionately as the payments are received. Receipt of a purchaser's obligation that is payable on demand or is readily marketable (traded on an established exchange or market) will be treated as the

---

[568] *Court Holding Co.*, 324 U.S. 331 (1945).
[569] *Estate of Applestein*, 80 TC 331 (1983).
[570] *Jones*, 531 F. 2d 1343 (CA-6, 1976); *Kinsey*, 477 F. 2d 1058 (CA-2, 1973).
[571] *Salvatore*, 434 F. 2d 600 (CA-2, 1970); *Usher*, 45 TC 205 (1965).
[572] *Bassett*, 33 B.T.A. 182 (1935), aff'd. per curiam 90 F. 2d 1004 (CA-2, 1937).

[573] *Rushing*, 441 F. 2d 593 (CA-5, 1971). (See also ¶50.)
[574] *Friedman*, 346 F. 2d 506 (CA-6, 1965), aff'g. 41 T.C. 428 (1963).
[575] Code: 636.
[576] Code: 1001.
[577] Code: 453.
[578] Code: 453(b).

receipt of cash.[579] The installment sales rules apply even if more than 30 percent of the sales price is received in the year of sale or the total sales price is less than $1,000.[580] Installment notes received on sales of property after adoption of a plan of liquidation under Section 337 (one-year liquidation) can now qualify for the installment method.[581]

Under a recent ruling, a cash-basis taxpayer, making a year-end sale with the settlement date in the following year, may elect out of the installment sale method and report the entire gain in the year of the sale.[582] In certain cases an investor will want to report the full gain on sale (e.g., expiring net operating losses or investment credits), or the investor will want to offset the short-term gains realized on sale against long-term losses. In this event he can timely elect not to apply the installment method to this particular sale.[583] (See ¶53 for discussion of sales to related persons.) An installment note will qualify even if the note is guaranteed by a third party,[584] but not if the installment sale is secured by placing all the funds in escrow.[585]

51 EXPENSES OF THE INVESTOR

.01 In General

Ordinary and necessary expenses paid or incurred by an investor for the production or collection of income or for the management or conservation of his investments are deductible.[586]

.02 Types of Deductible Expenses

Items of investor's expenses which have been held deductible include investment counsel fees, statistical services, safe-deposit box rental, custodian fees, legal and accounting advisory services, office expenses, and secretary's salary.[587] However, for post-1975 years an investor cannot deduct a portion of the expense of his residence used for investment activities unless he qualifies as a trader and meets other tests, including that the portion of the dwelling be used exclusively and on a regular basis for business purposes.[588] Home expenses

---

[579] Code: 453 (f).
[580] Code: 453 (b)(1)(B) and 453 (b)(2)(B), repealed.
[581] Code: 453 (h).
[582] Rev. Rul. 82-227, C.B. 1982-2, 89.
[583] Code: 453 (d).

[584] Code: 453 (f)(3).
[585] *Pozzi*, 49 T.C. 119 (1967).
[586] Code: 212.
[587] Reg. 1.212-1 (g).
[588] Code: 280A.

of a full-time investor were held not deductible because the taxpayer was not engaged in a trade or business as a trader.[589]

Carfare to visit a broker for consultation is deductible,[590] but not trips to a broker's office to watch the "ticker tapes."[591] Expenses incurred in searching for new investments have been disallowed.[592] Travel expenses incurred by an investor while making planned systematic investigations of publicly held corporations in which he held substantial interests were deductible because it was not a disguised personal trip.[593]

The Treasury has ruled that expenses incurred by stockholders in attending stockholders' meetings for the purposes of securing information on which to base future investment decisions are not deductible.[594] This questionable ruling is based on the theory that the expenses were not sufficiently related to the shareholder's investment activity so as to be deductible for income tax purposes. However, where the investor incurs reasonable expenses which are directly related to *present* investment interests, as, for example, the attendance at a stockholders' meeting in which the value of the investor's stock or the amount of the dividends payable may be affected, the deduction of such expenses should be allowed.[595] Expenses incurred in stockholders' proxy fights have been held to be deductible.[596] The expenses are deductible although the anticipated proxy contest never materializes.[597]

.03 Effect of Receipt of Tax-Exempt Income

No deduction is allowed for expenses otherwise allowable under Section 212 which are allocable to tax-exempt income.[598] Thus, expenses, such as taxes or depreciation which are deductible pursuant to Sections 164 and 167 or 168, are fully deductible despite the relationship between the expenses and the investment in tax exempts.[599] A separate disallowance is provided for interest expense attributable to

---

[589] *Moller,* 83-2 USTC ¶9698 (CA-F, 1983).
[590] *Henderson,* T.C. Memo. 1968-22.
[591] *Walters,* T.C. Memo. 1969-5.
[592] *Weinstein,* 420 F. 2d 700 (Ct. Cl. 1970).
[593] *W. R. Kenney,* 66 T.C. 122 (1976).
[594] Rev. Rul. 56-511, C.B. 1956-2, 1970; however, see *Godson,* 5 TCM 648 (1946); *Goldner,* 27 T.C. 455 (1956).
[595] Cf. *Milner Est.,* 1 TCM 513 (1943).
[596] *Surasky,* 325 F. 2d 181 (CA-5, 1963); *Graham,* 326 F. 2d 878 (CA-4, 1964);

followed by Treasury if cost of proxy fight connected with production of income, Rev. Rul. 64-236, C.B. 1964-2, 64; however, see *Dyer,* 352 F. 2d 948 (CA-8, 1965).
[597] *Nidetch,* T.C. Memo 1978-313.
[598] Code: 265(1).
[599] *Manufacturers Hanover Trust Co.,* 431 F. 2d 664 (CA-2, 1970); Rev. Rul. 78-81, C.B. 1978-1, 57.

tax exempts.[600] Custodial fees are disallowed to the extent attributed to services performed for tax-exempt securities.[601] Expenses that are not clearly allocable to either taxable or tax-exempt income are generally apportioned on the basis of the ratio of each to the total gross income.[602] Inclusion of capital gains, before deduction of capital losses, in gross income for purposes of allocating indirect expenses between taxable and nontaxable income is acceptable to the Treasury because there is no material distortion of income.[603] Similar rules apply to tax exempts held in trust.[604]

.04 Transfer Taxes

State and local transfer taxes paid on the sale of securities were deductible against ordinary income if the taxpayer itemized his deductions and, therefore, should not have been deducted from the selling price in computing gain or loss on the sale.[605] Thus, taxpayers generally obtained greater benefit by offsetting the transfer taxes against ordinary income than by reducing capital gains (or increasing capital losses) which are taxed at lower rates. These transfer taxes have been phased out and are no longer imposed on the sale of securities.

.05 Interest

Limitations have been imposed on the deductibility of investment interest expense, including deductions allowed for payments made on short sales of personal property.[606] Since 1969 the investment interest expense has been exposed to different treatments. Beginning in 1976 the amount of deductible investment interest expense is $10,000 ($5,000 for a married individual filing separately), plus net investment income (dividends, interest, rents, royalties, short-term gains, and gains on sale of investment property that is taxed as ordinary income, less other investment expense).[607] Tax shelter losses should not be deducted from investment income in computing the limitations.[608] Any disallowed investment interest expense is carried over for an unlimited period to succeeding years subject to the interest expense limitation for that year.[609] Carry-overs from pre-1976 years

---

[600] Code: 265(2).
[601] *Alt*, 28 TCM 1501 (1969).
[602] Rev. Rul. 63-27, C.B. 1963-1, 57.
[603] Rev. Rul. 73-565, C.B. 1973-2, 90.
[604] Rev. Rul. 61-86, C.B. 1961-1, 41.

[605] Code: 164(a), Reg. 1.164-1(a); Rev. Rul. 65-313, C.B. 1965-2, 47.
[606] Code: 163(d)(3). See ¶51.06.
[607] Code: 163(d)(1).
[608] Priv. Rul. Doc. 8105007.
[609] Code: 163(d)(2).

and interest from certain pre-September 11, 1975, debts are still subject to the limitations in effect for 1975 (see below).[610] Proration of the net investment income is required if the investment interest expense is subject to both the old and the new limitations.[611] For example, if the net investment income is $50,000 and the investment interest expense is $100,000 of which $60,000 is attributable to pre-September 11, 1975, debt, $30,000 (60 percent of net investment income) of the net income is applied to determining the limitation for the pre-September 11, 1975, interest and the remaining $20,000 will be included in computing the post-1975 limitation. Thus, the post-1975 limitation is $30,000 ($10,000 + $20,000 net investment income) resulting in an excess investment interest of $10,000 ($40,000 interest less $30,000 limitation). The 1975 limitation is $57,500 ($25,000 + $30,000 net investment income + ½ of $5,000 excess), resulting in excess interest expense of $2,500 ($60,000 interest less $57,500 limitation). The result is allowable interest expense of $87,500, a carry-over of post-1975 disallowed interest expense of $10,000 and a carry-over of pre-1976 disallowed interest expense of $2,500.

Under the post-1975 limitations, long-term capital gains are not includible in net investment income. Capital gain distributions from regulated investment companies are treated as capital gains and not as dividend income for purposes of computing allowable interest expense.[612] On the other hand, for pre-1976 years, the 50 percent long-term capital gain deduction may not be taken to the extent the investment interest expense is allocated to the long-term capital gains. Any disallowed interest will be carried over to subsequent years, subject to the interest expense limitation for such year. As explained above, the carry-overs retain their character as pre-1976 disallowed interest expense when carried over to post-1975 years.

Interest expense incurred for personal reasons, such as a mortgage on the family home or installment obligations to purchase appliances, are not subject to the limitations, neither are loans incurred for business purposes.[613] However, if a second mortgage is taken on a home to purchase investment securities, rather than for personal noninvestment activities, the interest expense will be subject to the limitations. Borrowing to acquire a general partnership interest in a business partnership will not come under these limitations.[614] On the other

---

[610] 1976 TRA: 209(b).
[611] Code: 163(d)(3)(A).
[612] *Kocueck*, 456 F. Supp. 740 (W.D. Texas, 1978), aff'd 628 F. 2d 906 (CA-5, 1978).
[613] Rev. Rul. 82-163, C.B. 1982-2, 57.
[614] Priv. Rul. Doc. 8235004.

hand, a limited partner is not deemed to be in a trade or business for self-employment tax purposes. Accordingly, indebtedness incurred to purchase a limited partnership interest in a real estate syndicate or similar tax shelter may be treated by the Treasury as an investment borrowing and, therefore, the Treasury may limit the interest deductions on the indebtedness. Interest expense paid by a partnership to purchase a controlling interest in a bank was held to be investment interest expense despite the fact that one of the general partners was also an officer of the bank.[615]

Borrowings by the partnership itself for business purposes should not be subject to any limitations. Whether the real estate partnership is actively engaged in a trade or business will depend upon its activity. If it is in the business of renting real property, or operating a motel or hotel, then it is engaged in a trade or business. However, if it is merely holding vacant land for appreciation, it would not be considered engaged in a trade or business,[616] and, accordingly, any interest expense incurred would be subject to limitations. If an investor receives investment income from depreciable property, straight-line depreciation over the useful life of the investment property should be used in computing the amount of the investment expenses rather than the larger amount of ACRS (accelerated) depreciation which may have been deducted in computing taxable income.[617] Property subject to a net lease will be treated as investment property rather than business property if (a) the deductions allowed under Section 162 are less than 15 percent of the rental income from the property, or (b) the lessor is either guaranteed a specified return on his investment or is guaranteed in whole or in part against loss of income.[618] Note that the investment interest limitation is increased by any excess deductions incurred on property subject to a net lease.[619]

In addition to the investment interest limitation, interest expense incurred to purchase or carry market discount bonds acquired after July 18, 1984 may be disallowed to the extent of the accrued market discount income for the year.[620] In any event, the interest expense will be deductible to the extent of the interest income earned on the market discount bond in that year. Similar limitations have also been imposed on interest expenses incurred in financing noninterest-bearing short-term obligations, such as Treasury bills.[621]

Interest on a margin account is deductible by a cash-basis investor

---

[615] *Miller*, 70 T.C. 448 (1978).
[616] Prop. Reg. 1.57-2(b)(2)(i).
[617] Code: 163(d)(3)(C); Priv. Rul. Doc. 8340023.
[618] Code: 163(d)(4).

[619] Code: 163(d)(1)(B).
[620] Code: 1277(a). (See ¶46.09(c) for additional details.)
[621] Code: 1282(a). (See ¶46.09(b).)

in the year in which credits are made to the account sufficient to absorb the interest charge.[622] No deduction is allowed for interest paid on indebtedness incurred or continued to carry tax-exempt bonds, interests in a unit trust or partnership, or shares in a municipal bond fund.[623] This would include a purchase of tax-exempts for cash in one brokerage account and a purchase by the same investor of taxable securities on margin in another account.[624] The disallowance provision has been expanded to include interest expense incurred by the taxpayer's spouse or an 80 percent controlled corporation if the requisite borrowing purpose can be established.[625] It is not necessary to trace the loan to the tax-exempts, but merely to show a "sufficiently direct relationship."[626] Interest expense incurred on loans for business purposes, or personal purposes, such as to purchase a home, automobile, or home appliances do not have a sufficiently direct relationship.[627] Note that refinancing an existing mortgage in order to purchase tax-exempts will result in a disallowance of the mortgage interest expenses.[628] Disallowance will result from borrowings to acquire nonbusiness portfolio investments, such as stock and securities (other than substantial ownership interest, such as 80 percent control), real estate investments, or limited partnership interests in real estate, farm, or gas and oil syndications, or similar tax shelters.[629] Once a direct relationship is shown, the interest expense will be disallowed even if it exceeds the tax-exempt income.[630] Generally, where an individual's investment in tax exempts is insubstantial (i.e., average adjusted basis of tax exempts does not exceed 2 percent of average adjusted basis of investment portfolio) and there is no direct relationship between the borrowings and the tax exempts, including the use of tax exempts as collateral, there will be no disallowance.[631] Nor should there be a disallowance where the spouses file a joint return and one spouse purchases tax-exempts with his or her funds and the other spouse incurred investment interest expense.[632] How-

---

[622] Rev. Rul. 70-221, C.B. 1970-1, 33.

[623] Code: 265(2) and (4); *Illinois Terminal Railroad Co.*, 375 F. 2d 1016 (Ct. Cl., 1967); *Wisconsin Cheeseman, Inc.*, 388 F. 2d 420 (CA-7, 1968).

[624] *B. H. Jacobson*, 28 T.C. 579 (1957) (Acq.); *Bernard P. McDonough*, T.C. Memo. 1977-50.

[625] Code: 7701(f), effective July 18, 1984.

[626] *Wisconsin Cheeseman, Inc.*, supra; *Ball*, 54 T.C. 1200 (1970).

[627] Rev. Proc. 72-18, Section 4.02, C.B. 1972-1, 740.

[628] *Amedeo Louis Mariorenzi*, T.C. Memo

1973-141, aff'd. 490 F. 2d 92 (CA-1, 1974).

[629] Rev. Proc. 72-18, Section 4.04, C.B. 1972-1, 740.

[630] *J. S. Wynn, Jr.*, 411 F. 2d 614 (CA-3, 1969), cert. den. 396 U.S. 1008 (1970).

[631] Rev. Proc. 72-18, Section 3.05, C.B. 1972-1, 740.

[632] *Levitt*, 368 F. Supp. 644 (1974), rev'd. on other issues, 517 F. 2d 1339 (1975); *Bernard P. McDonough*, T.C. Memo. 1977-50, aff'd 577 F. 2d 234 (CA-4, 1978); Priv. Rul. Doc. 8135084.

ever, interest will be disallowed on funds borrowed by one spouse and used by the other spouse to purchase tax exempts.[633] Similarly, there should be no disallowance where an estate or trust owns tax exempts, and a nongrantor beneficiary has incurred investment interest expense. Where an investor is also a partner in an investment partnership, however, his average investment in tax exempts and total investments must be aggregated with his pro rata share of the partnership's average investment in tax exempts and total assets in computing the amount of disallowance of investment interest expense for both the investor and his partnership.[634] Note that the disallowance applies only to interest expense and investment expenses deductible under Section 212. Other items, such as taxes, deductible under Section 164, are fully deductible even though the activity is described in Section 212.[635] A purchaser of a life interest in a family trust was permitted to amortize and deduct the cost of the life estate over the life expectancy of the life tenant despite the fact that the trust had made substantial investments in tax exempts.[636] Note that an attempt to create an amortizable life estate by dividing an existing interest in property into two separate principal and income interests was not permitted by the courts.[637] An officer-stockholder did not constructively receive income on an interest-free loan from his corporation to pay estimated tax although the taxpayer had investments in tax exempts.[638] Similar interest-free loans to an officer-shareholder after June 6, 1984 may have adverse tax consequences for both the lender and the borrower.[639] The above disallowance rules will continue to apply to term obligations incurred before July 19, 1984 and demand obligations outstanding 90 days after July 18, 1984. With respect to interest expense on obligations incurred after these dates, the Treasury is authorized to prescribe regulations linking borrowing to investments through use of related persons, pass-through entities, or other intermediaries.[640] A related person would include a husband or wife, an individual and his 80 percent owned corporation or partnership, and in appropriate cases, minor children. The present rules are still to be applied along with these attribution rules in determining whether there should be a disallowance of interest expense.

---

[633] Rev. Rul. 79-272, C.B. 1979-2, 124.

[634] *Bernard P. McDonough*, T.C. Memo. 1977-50, aff'd 577 F. 2d 234 (CA-4, 1978).

[635] Rev. Rul. 78-81, C.B. 1978-1, 57.

[636] *Manufacturers Hanover Trust Co.*, 431 F. 2d 664, (CA-2, 1970).

[637] *Lomas Sante Fe, Inc.*, 74 TC 662 (1980), aff'd 693 F. 2d 71 (CA-9, 1982), cert. den. 103 S. Ct. 1773, (1983).

[638] *Baker*, 75 T.C. 166 (1980).

[639] Code: 7872.

[640] Code: 7701(f).

Interest paid on genuine indebtedness without collusion between the investor and the creditor to avoid income taxes will be allowed as a deduction.[641] There should be some economic substance to the transaction apart from income tax effect.[642] Interest deductions were denied where the court found that the transaction was not a "sham" but lacked a business purpose.[643] An interest deduction was also denied if the debtor obtained the funds from the lender.[644] In addition, the Treasury had reversed its prior position and would allow a deduction for interest prepaid for only a 12-month period after the end of the taxable year, provided there was no distortion of income. Any remaining prepaid interest had to be deferred and deducted over the term of the loan.[645] Since 1976, prepaid interest must be capitalized and deducted over the period of the loan as if the investor were on the accrued basis.[646] Thus, if an investor prepaid interest of $130 for one month in 1981 and the entire year of 1982, only $10 would be deductible in 1981 and the balance of $120 in 1982. The current provision will not apply to prepayments made before 1977 pursuant to a binding loan or contract in effect on September 16, 1975.[647]

.06 Dividends and Interest Paid on Short Sales

Prior to the 1984 Act, amounts paid by investors for the use of stock borrowed to effectuate short sales of stock or to reimburse the lender of the stock for ordinary dividends paid on the borrowed stock were deductible as nonbusiness expenses.[648] Payments made in lieu of regular dividends on stock sold short are still deductible if the short sale is closed more than 45 days after the date of the sale.[649] The short sale period must be held open for more than one year if the payments

---

[641] *L. L. Stanton,* 34 T.C. 1 (1960).

[642] *E. D. Goodstein,* 267 F. 2d 127 (CA-1, 1959); *Knetsch,* 364 U.S. 361 (1960); *Barnett,* 44 T.C. 261 (1965), aff'd 364 F. 2d 742 (CA-2, 1966); *Goldstein,* 364 F. 2d 734 (CA-2, 1966), Cert. den. This latter case denies deduction of prepaid interest on a "valid" indebtedness where there is no purpose for the transaction other than to obtain a tax deduction. See also *Gilbert,* 248 F. 2d 399, 411 (CA-2, 1957). Under the current volatile interest conditions, it would be more difficult for the Treasury to establish that interest paid on a loan to purchase discount bonds or Treasury instruments was not incurred for valid economic purposes.

[643] *Rothschild,* 407 F. 2d 404 (Ct. Cl., 1969).

[644] *Battelstein,* 80-1 USTC ¶9225 (CA-5, 1980).

[645] Rev. Rul. 68-643, C.B. 1968-2, 76, modified by Rev. Rul. 69-582, C.B. 1969-2, 29.

[646] Code: 461(g).

[647] 1976 TRA: 208(b)(2).

[648] Rev. Rul. 72-521, C.B. 1972-2, 178; Rev. Rul. 62-42, C.B. 1962-1, 133; *Dart,* 74 F. 2d 845 (CA-4, 1935); *Wiesler,* 161 F. 2d 997 (CA-6, 1947); contra, *Levis Estate,* 127 F. 2d 796 (CA-2, 1942).

[649] Code: 263(h)(1), effective for short sales after July 18, 1984.

are for extraordinary dividends (5 percent for preferred stock dividends, 10 percent for common stock dividends, and 20 percent for aggregate dividends in a 365-day period).[650] The more-than-45-days and one-year holding periods are suspended during any period in which the taxpayer has a Call or is under an obligation to buy substantially identical stock or securities, or there is a diminution of risk because the investor holds other substantially similar positions.[651] Failure to meet the new holding period requirement will result in a disallowance of the deduction for the payment, which, instead, will be added to the basis of the stock used to close the short sale. Allowable deductions for short sale payments are no longer treated as Section 212 expenses. Instead, they are treated as an investment interest expense subject to the investment interest expense limitations[652] and the disallowance of interest expense deductions for owning tax-exempt bonds.[653]

Although never specifically enunciated by the Treasury, interest paid on short sales of debentures should be deductible.[654] These payments now constitute investment interest expense.[655] (See ¶51.05 for limitations on investment interest expense.)

Due to the substantial economic risks involved in holding short sales open for more than one year, the new provision may have effectively stopped the use of short sales in extraordinary dividend situations. The Treasury had ruled under prior law that amounts paid with respect to stock dividends or liquidating dividends on stock borrowed incident to a short sale are capital expenditures and are not deductible.[656] However, an argument can be made for treating the payment of all short dividends, including stock and liquidating dividends, as an ordinary deduction, since they are merely contractual expenses incurred as a necessary cost of obtaining the borrowed stock.[657] The deduction for payments should apply equally to short sales of regular

---

[650] Code: 263(h)(2). (See Code: 1059(c) and ¶66 for a definition of extraordinary dividends.)

[651] Code: 263(h)(4). (See ¶66 for a discussion of substantially similar property.)

[652] Code: 163(d)(3)(D).

[653] Code: 265(2).

[654] I.T. 3989, C.B. 1950-1, 34 (replaced by Rev. Rul. 72-521, C.B. 1972-2, 178) has been cited for such proposition (although interest was disallowed on grounds of sham). *J. G. Gold*, 41 T.C. 419, 426 (1963). "It is, of course,

true that one who borrows securities in order to make a short sale may deduct the amount of interest or dividends which he pays to the lender in order to reimburse him for the interest or dividends that the lender would have received during the period of the loan."

[655] Code: 163(d)(3)(D)(ii).

[656] Rev. Rul. 72-521, C.B. 1972-2, 178.

[657] *Main Line Distributors, Inc.*, 321 F. 2d 562 (CA-6, 1963)—disallowed deduction on other grounds. Cf. *1955 Production Exposition Inc.*, 41 T.C. 85 (1963).

corporations or special corporations, such as regulated investment companies (mutual funds), dividends (including capital gains), although, as discussed above, the Treasury may contend that a large capital gain distribution is similar to a liquidating distribution.

Where the sole purpose for entering into a short sale transaction is tax avoidance without any expectation of financial gain, the short dividends paid will not be allowed as a deduction on the grounds that they are not ordinary and necessary expenses paid or incurred for the production of income.[658]

52 TAX–FREE EXCHANGES

.01 Reorganizations

Recognizing that normal commercial activities would be impeded if every exchange of securities were subjected to income tax despite the lack of any substantial change in the security holder's financial position, Congress has enacted through the years many special tax provisions exempting certain transactions from tax. An exchange of common or preferred stock for stock of another corporation in a statutory merger or consolidation,[659] or the exchange of common or preferred stock for other common or preferred stock of the same corporation in a recapitalization[660] falls within this class. The receipt of preferred stock in a reorganization may be treated similar to a dividend of preferred stock and, therefore, may result in ordinary income on its sale or redemption.[661] Other exempted transactions include an exchange by a corporation of its voting stock for stock of another corporation which it controls after exchange,[662] a "triangular merger" using stock of the parent of one of the merged corporations,[663] and exchange of bonds for bonds (not in excess of the principal amount surrendered) or stock of the same corporation,[664] the conversion of convertible bonds into stock of the same corporation,[665] and, in appropriate cases, the receipt of stock upon division of a corporation.[666]

---

[658] *Hart,* 41 T.C. 131 (1963) aff'd 338 F. 2d 410 (CA-2, 1964); cf. *Carl Schapiro,* 40 T.C. 34 (1963). In the *Hart* case, the transactions were mere "bookkeeping" entries with no borrowing of securities, no payment of margin, lack of investment interest, price adjustments to prevent economic substance, and no delivery of stock to cover the sale.

[659] Code: 368(a)(1)(A).
[660] Code: 368(a)(1)(E) and 1036.
[661] Code: 306(c)(1)(B).
[662] Code: 368(a)(1)(B).
[663] Code: 368(a)(2)(D),(E).
[664] Code: 354, 368.
[665] Rev. Rul. 72-265, C.B. 1972-1, 222.
[666] Code: 355, 368(a)(1)(D).

Notwithstanding the tax-free treatment accorded exchanges of stock, an exchange of warrants for warrants of another party to the reorganization has been ruled by the Treasury to be a taxable exchange.[667] Published Capital Changes services generally contain the information the investor needs to determine the proper tax treatment of exchanges of publicly held securities.

With respect to the basis and holding period of the securities acquired in the exchange, see ¶33.02 and ¶34.02(b).

.02 Involuntary Conversions—Governmental Orders

Special provisions deferring the recognition of gain or loss are applicable to investors who were compelled to surrender their securities or receive distributions from their corporations pursuant to an order issued by the FCC,[668] SEC,[669] or the Board of Governors of the Federal Reserve System.[670] Pro rata distributions of stocks and securities to shareholders of qualified bank holding companies required to divest their interests pursuant to the Bank Holding Company Act are also nontaxable.[671] Published Capital Changes services generally describe the proper tax treatment in these situations.

.03 Exchange Funds

Holders of appreciated marketable securities formerly were able to diversify their holdings without recognition of gain by exchanging these securities for stock of a mutual fund which was specifically organized for this purpose. As a result of a change in the law, such exchanges will be treated as taxable exchanges.[672] Similar legislation was enacted to deny tax-free treatment on transfer of appreciated assets to an unincorporated investment company (partnership, trust, common trust fund), or where an undiversified investment company (more than 25 percent of its assets invested in one corporation or more than 50 percent invested in up to five corporations) enters into a reorganization with one or more investment companies.[673]

.04 Other Types

For discussion of tax-free exchanges of government bonds, see ¶2.09 and ¶46.10.

---

[667] Rev. Rul. 78-408, C.B. 1978-2, 203; Priv. Rul. Doc. 7949056.
[668] Code: 1071.
[669] Code: 1081.
[670] Code: 1101.
[671] Ibid.
[672] Code: 351(a), (d).
[673] Code: 368(a)(1)(F).

53 SALES TO RELATED PERSONS

Sales between related parties are viewed with suspicion by the Treasury and are strictly regulated by the Internal Revenue Code.[674] Gains realized in such transactions are generally recognized for tax purposes. Losses incurred will be disallowed for tax purposes if a member of the investor's family (spouse, descendant, ancestor, or sibling) buys the securities directly from the investor or buys them indirectly on an exchange on or about the same date and at approximately the same price.[675] The losses are not offset by gains realized on other sales.[676] The disallowed loss may be used by the purchaser to the extent the purchaser sells the security at a gain.[677] Whether the wash sale provisions can be avoided by having a related person reacquire the security is discussed in ¶36.07.

Intrafamily sales of securities can qualify for installment sales treatment, but both the Internal Revenue Service and the judiciary will closely scrutinize the transaction. An installment sale of securities to the seller's husband was approved by the court where the husband sold the securities after holding them for five months and used the proceeds to satisfy contractual obligations.[678] However, the Tax Court in a subsequent case upheld the Treasury's contention that the sale lacked substance because of the absence of a business or personal purpose other than tax avoidance where the wife sold the securities on the same day and reinvested the proceeds in mutual funds.[679] The tax court has since emphasized that interspousal installment sales will be recognized when there are independent nontax reasons for the sales transaction.[680] An installment sale to the taxpayer's son was invalidated because the son was found to be acting as an agent for his father.[681] Prior to these cases, the Fifth Circuit approved an installment sale to trusts created for the benefit of the seller's children of stock of a corporation which was to be liquidated.[682] This case was followed by a rash of cases that approved, distinguished, and disagreed with the *Rushing* case. As a consequence, the installment sale rules were amended with respect to sales or dispositions to related parties.[683] If an investor sells marketable securities to a related party who then sells the securities before paying the entire amount due on the first sale, then the investor will be deemed to have received the

---

[674] Code: 267.
[675] *J. P. McWilliams*, 331 U.S. 694 (1946).
[676] *Reddington*, 131 F. 2d 1014 (CA-2, 1942); *Englehart*, 30 T.C. 1013 (1958).
[677] Code: 267(d).
[678] *Nye v. U.S.*, 407 F. Supp. 1345 (D.C. N.C., 1975).

[679] *Philip W. Wrenn*, 67 T.C. 576 (1976).
[680] *Bowen*, 78 T.C. 55 (1982).
[681] *Lustgarten*, 71 T.C. 303 (1978).
[682] *Rushing*, 441 F. 2d 593 (CA-5, 1971).
[683] Code: 453(e). Related parties includes the taxpayer's spouse, children, grandchildren, and parents.

remaining sales proceeds at the time of the second sale.[684] With respect to an intrafamily sale of nonmarketable securities, the investor will be treated as having received the remaining sales proceeds at the time of the sale unless the second sale is more than two years after the original sale.[685] The two-year holding period cannot be avoided by acquiring a Put, selling the property short, giving a right to a third party to acquire the property, or any similar transactions.[686] However, these intrafamily sales provisions will not apply if the investor can show that neither the first nor second sale was done for tax avoidance purposes.[687]

54 SMALL BUSINESS INVESTMENT COMPANY STOCK

A magic formula of capital gains and ordinary losses applies to sales of small business investment company stock.[688] Losses are fully deductible by any stockholder without limitation and, if in excess of the current year's income, may be carried back or forward as a business loss. Transactions with regard to SBIC stock do not have to be "netted" with one another.[689] Therefore, if a taxpayer had gains and losses in the same year on SBIC stock, the gains would be accorded capital gain treatment, while the losses would be deductible as ordinary losses. The Treasury has ruled that a loss sustained on the closing of a short sale of stock of a small business investment company is treated as a short-term loss and not as an ordinary loss.[690] The beneficial tax treatment will be denied unless there is strict compliance with the tax provisions.[691] Losses on sale of small business stock are also treated as ordinary losses.[692] The maximum amount allowed as an ordinary loss in one taxable year is $50,000 ($100,000 for joint returns). Certain requirements must be met, such as: (1) the total amount paid for the small business corporation's stock cannot exceed $1 million, and (2) at least 50 percent of the gross receipts for the previous five years were from an active trade or business.

55 CURRENT DISTRIBUTIONS ON STOCK

.01 Dividend Income

Dividend income is not limited to periodic distributions of cash or property. Also included in the definition are stock redemptions, which

[684] Code: 453(e)(1).
[685] Code: 453(e)(2).
[686] Code: 453(e)(2)(B).
[687] Code: 453(e)(7).
[688] Code: 1242.

[689] Rev. Rul. 65-291, C.B. 1965-2, 290.
[690] Rev. Rul. 63-65, C.B. 1963-1, 142.
[691] *Childs*, 408 F. 2d 531 (CA-3, 1969).
[692] Code: 1244.

have the effect of dividends;[693] certain sales or redemptions of shares of preferred stock, which were received as stock dividends on common stock;[694] stock distributions received in lieu of cash dividends;[695] sale of stock to a related corporation;[696] distributions of stock in a corporation other than the distributing corporation;[697] cash or other property received in a reorganization that has the effect of a dividend[698] and, according to the Treasury, cash paid in lieu of fractional stock dividends unless shareholders approve sale of fractional shares on their behalf.[699] However, a distribution is a taxable dividend only to the extent it is paid out of either accumulated or current earnings and profits.[700] Distributions received from a regulated investment company can qualify as a dividend, nonqualifying dividend, capital gain dividend, a distribution of tax-exempt interest, or as a return of capital.[701] Capital gain distributions in a year the regulated investment company had capital loss carry-overs are treated as regular dividends.[702] Distributions from a real estate investment trust may qualify as nonqualifying dividends, capital gain dividends, or return of capital.[703]

Published Dividend Records indicate the tax status as well as the total amount of dividends paid annually by publicly held corporations. The same information, with greater detail regarding distributions in property, is available in published Capital Changes services.

Prior to 1981, the first $100 of dividends received from most domestic corporations in a taxable year was exempt from tax.[704] (The exemption was increased to $200 if a joint return was filed and the spouse also had at least $100 of dividend income.) This exclusion was expanded for the year 1981 to $200 of dividends or interest income ($400 for a joint return, even if the entire interest or dividend income is earned by one spouse). The $100 dividend exclusion ($200 for joint returns) was reinstated for post-1981 years, except that a $200 exclusion is allowed for joint returns, even if all the dividend income is earned by one spouse. The dividend received credit provisions are

---

[693] Code: 302.

[694] Code: 306. The ordinary income taint can no longer be eliminated because of the death of a shareholder after 1976. Code: 306(c)(1)(C).

[695] Code: 305.

[696] Code: 304.

[697] *Cheley,* 131 F. 2d 1018 (CA-10, 1942).

[698] Code: 356.

[699] Rev. Rul. 69-15, C.B. 1969-1, 95. Cash distributed in lieu of fractional shares resulting from stock dividends, stock splits, corporate reorganizations, and the like, will be treated as received on the sale of the fractional shares if undertaken solely to save the expense and consequence of issuing and transferring fractional shares and is not separately bargained for consideration. Rev. Proc. 77-41, C.B. 1977-2, 574.

[700] Code: 316.

[701] Code: 852. A foreign tax credit may be allowed the shareholder with respect to the nonqualifying dividends. Code: 853.

[702] Rev. Rul. 76-299, C.B. 1976-2, 211.

[703] Code: 857(b) and (c).

[704] Code: 116.

no longer in effect, but dividends received by investors who have attained age 65 are eligible for the credit for the elderly.[705]

Distributions in excess of the current and accumulated earnings and profits of the distributing corporation are treated as a return of capital, reducing the basis of the stock, and, after the investor has fully recovered his cost, any excess distributions are generally taxed as capital gains.[706]

During the period 1982–85, investors in common or preferred shares of qualified public utilities may elect to exclude from income up to $750 ($1,500 for joint returns) of qualified common stock dividends received in lieu of cash dividends.[707] Since the stock dividends will have a zero basis, the entire proceeds received on a subsequent sale will be taxed at capital gains rates. However, if the investor sells or otherwise disposes of the shares within one year from the time of any stock distribution, the proceeds will be taxed as ordinary income to the extent of the stock distributions made within one year of the disposition.[708] This election is available only to shareholders owning less than 5 percent of the voting stock (or value) of the public utility.

.02 Stock Dividends

A distribution of stock of the issuing corporation is generally not taxed to the stockholders. Distributions will be taxed as ordinary dividends if the stockholders have an option to receive cash or property in place of the stock dividend; or the distribution is made in discharge of preference dividends for the current year or the preceding year.[709] With respect to stock distributions in place of cash dividends, the Tax Reform Act of 1969 has expanded these provisions to include (a) disproportionate distributions among the holders of various classes of common stock, (b) constructive distributions where one class of common stock receives cash dividends and another class obtains an increased interest in the corporate assets and earnings and profits or an increase or decrease in the ratio in which one class of securities may be converted into another class of stock, or (c) a disproportionate distribution of convertible preferred stock.[710] Cash received in lieu of fractional stock dividends will be treated as ordinary income.[711] However, if the

---

[705] Code: 22.
[706] Code: 301(c).
[707] Code: 305(e).
[708] Code: 305(e)(9).
[709] Code: 305.

[710] Code: 305(b)(2)-(5) and (c). The rules are complex with various transitional dates but generally will not apply before 1991 to distributions on stock outstanding on January 10, 1969.
[711] Special Ruling, Dec. 21, 1960.

investor is given an option either to buy or to sell fractions, and the fractional dividends are sold, capital gain or loss treatment will follow.[712] The issuance of cash for fractional shares for convenience of the distributing corporation will not cause the stock distributions to be taxable under the Section 305 rules.[713] Distributions of stock of other corporations generally are taxable as ordinary dividends. Certain distributions of stock of other corporations may qualify as tax-free "spin-offs." [714] (For discussion of tax basis and holding period of stock received as a stock dividend, see ¶33.04 and ¶34.02(i).)

.03   Stock Rights

The receipt of stock rights in the issuing corporation, by itself, is not a taxable event.[715] However, distributions of stock rights will be taxed as ordinary income if the stockholders have an option to receive cash or property in place of stock rights.[716]

The issuance of rights to subscribe to the issuing company's convertible bonds is also a nontaxable distribution.[717] No income would be realized either on the acquisition or exercise of the convertible bonds.[718] The Treasury has ruled that the receipt of rights to purchase the issuing company's nonconvertible bonds is taxable.[719] A distribution of short-term transferable rights, convertible into two long-term warrants and a $100 debenture upon payment of $100, is not a taxable distribution.[720] The warrants are treated as stock for purposes of Section 305,[721] and the $100 is in payment for the debentures. Thus, this ruling is compatible with the prior ruling concerning rights convertible into debentures.

Sale of a nontaxable stock right results in capital gain or loss. In determining such gain or loss or the basis of stock acquired upon exercise of a stock right, the basis of the "old" stock is allocated to the nontaxable right based upon the fair market value of the rights received in relation to the fair market value of the stock (including the rights) at the time of distribution.[722] Reference to a published Capital

---

[712] Rev. Rul. 69-15, C.B. 1969-1, 95.
[713] Reg. 1.305-3(c).
[714] Code: 355.
[715] Code: 305.
[716] Code: 305(b).
[717] *Powel*, 27 B.T.A. 55 (1932) (acq.).
[718] G.C.M. 13275, C.B. XIII-2, 121.
[719] G.C.M. 13414, C.B. XIII-2, 124. Note that in a private ruling concerning the issuance of A.T.&T. rights to acquire a unit consisting of warrants and deben-

ture bonds of the issuing corporation, the issuance and exercise were held to be nontaxable. The ruling permitted the entire option price to be attributed to the purchase of the bond with the warrant receiving the same basis as the right.
[720] Rev. Rul. 72-71, C.B. 1972-1, 99.
[721] Code: 305(d).
[722] Code: 307(a), Reg. 1.307-1.

Changes service will provide the necessary percentages of allocation. However, where the fair market value of the rights at the time of distribution is less than 15 percent of the value of the stock, no allocation is made, and the basis of the rights is zero, unless the investor elects to make the allocation.[723] (See ¶33.04.)

Stock rights received in a nontaxable distribution take on the same holding period as the stock held.[724] Thus, when the rights are sold, the holding period of the stock is "tacked-on" in determining the holding period of the rights. However, securities acquired through the exercise of the rights will not take on a tacked-on holding period. The holding period will start on the date of exercise.[725]

Generally, no loss is recognized as a result of the failure to exercise nontaxable rights, unless the rights were acquired for a valuable consideration (e.g., acquired by purchase). No adjustment is made to the basis of the stock with respect to which the expired rights were distributed.[726]

Distributions by a corporation of rights to acquire stock of another corporation have been held under the pre-1954 law to be taxable at the time of exercise or sale and not at the time of issuance.[727] The amount that was taxable as a dividend could not exceed the lower of the spreads between option price and fair market value of the stock purchased at the time the rights were issued and at time of exercise.[728] It would appear that the amount received upon sale of the right, in excess of the spreads, should be taxable as capital gains,[729] but the Treasury's position was that such amount was taxable as ordinary income.[730] The Tax Court rejected the Treasury's contention that the proceeds of sale constitute ordinary and not dividend income.[731]

With the change of the statutory language in the 1954 Code, the Treasury and the Seventh Circuit have questioned the validity of the old cases. The Treasury has ruled that, under the 1954 Code, the issuance of rights to acquire stock of another company is taxable as a dividend at the time of issuance.[732] This ruling has been followed by

---

[723] Code: 307(a), Reg. 1.307-2.

[724] Code: 1223(5).

[725] Code: 1223(5); Reg. 1.1223-1(f); Rev. Rul. 56-572, C.B. 1956-2, 182.

[726] Reg. 1.307-1; Special Ruling, Dec. 4, 1946.

[727] *Palmer,* 302 U.S. 63 (1937); *Choate,* 129 F. 2d 684 (CA-2, 1942); *Baan,* 451 F. 2d 198 (CA-9, 1971).

[728] Ibid.

[729] *Gibson,* 133 F. 2d 308 (CA-2, 1943).

[730] GCM 25063, C.B. 1947-1, 45 (declared obsolete by Rev. Rul. 71-498, C.B. 1971-2, 434).

[731] *Tobacco Products Export Corporation,* 21 TC 625 (1954); *Baan,* 45 TC 71 (1965), rev'd on other grounds 382 F. 2d 485 (CA-9, 1967).

[732] Rev. Rul. 70-521, C.B. 1970-2, 72.

the Seventh Circuit.[733] Similarly, the issuance of stock rights by a wholly owned subsidiary to shareholders of the parent company was ruled to be a tax-free transfer of the rights to the parent company followed by a taxable distribution to the parent company's shareholders.[734] Pursuant to these rulings, noncorporate shareholders would realize dividend income at the time of receipt to the extent of fair market value (corporate shareholders realize no income), and this amount would also increase the shareholder's basis in the rights. Upon exercise, no gain or loss would be realized by the shareholders, and the basis of the acquired stock would be the option price plus the tax basis of the stock rights. A sale or lapse of the rights would result in capital gain or loss. The distributing corporation will realize gain or loss on the exercise of the rights, depending upon whether the option price is more or less than its tax basis.

The courts are split as to whether a distribution of rights to stock of another corporation may qualify as a tax-free spin-off[735] resulting in no gain or loss or dividend income when the rights are exercised. In the most recent case a distribution of rights to acquire stock of a wholly owned subsidiary was held to be a tax-free spin-off by the Tax Court, but it was reversed on appeal.[736] Consequently, the distribution of the stock rights was held to be taxable to the parent company's shareholders at the time of the distribution. (See above discussion.) If the distribution of the stock rights were held to be tax-free, dividend income may result upon the sale of such rights.[737]

56 LIQUIDATIONS

Upon complete liquidation of a corporation, a shareholder will realize capital gain or loss depending upon the value of the liquidating distributions and the tax basis of the shareholder's stock.[738] The capital gain or loss treatment also applies to a one-year liquidation, al-

---

[733] *Redding,* 80-2 USTC ¶9637 (CA-7, 1980), rev'g. 71 T.C. 597 (1979). The Tax Court discussed the Palmer doctrine but refused to give an opinion as to its current validity. In *Baumer,* 580 F. 2d 863 (CA-5, 1978), the Fifth Circuit limited the Palmer decision to its own set of facts (i.e., no spread exists on the date of issuance and the option period is so short that there is no expected appreciation in the stock before the options must be exercised).

[734] Rev. Rul. 80-292, C.B. 1980-2, 104.
[735] Code: 355; see *Gordon,* 382 F. 2d 499 (CA-2, 1967), rev'd 391 U.S. 83 (1968) and *Baan,* 382 F. 2d 485 (CA-9, 1967), aff'd 391 U.S. 83 (1968). The Supreme Court did not resolve this point.
[736] *Redding,* 71 T.C. 597 (1979), rev'd 80-2 USTC ¶9637.
[737] See *Bann* and *Gordon,* supra.
[738] Code: 331(a). The installment method of reporting gain is not available.

though the corporation may escape tax on sales of property during the liquidation period.[739] Installment obligation received by the shareholders as part of the liquidation distribution will qualify for installment sale treatment if the obligations were received on sale of property during the one-year liquidation period.[740] Where the one-month liquidation provision is elected, any gain realized by an individual shareholder will be taxed as dividend income to the extent of his ratable share of the corporation's earnings and profits, and any remaining gain will be taxed as capital gain to the extent the cash and marketable securities (acquired after 1953) received on liquidation exceed the ratable share of earnings and profits.[741] In the case of a partial liquidation, capital gain or loss will be realized depending upon the value of the liquidating distribution and the tax basis of the stock surrendered or deemed surrendered in the exchange.[742] While ordinarily not applicable to a publicly held corporation, capital gain treatment upon sale or liquidation will be denied if the corporation is a "collapsible corporation."[743] A liquidation of a foreign investment company or foreign controlled corporation may result in part or all of the gain being treated as dividend income.[744] (See ¶58.02.)

57 SECURITY LOANS

Many investors, including regulated investment companies and tax-exempt organizations, lend their securities to brokers to be transferred to purchasers in short sales transactions or when the seller fails to deliver the security on the settlement date. In exchange for the security loan, the borrower agrees to fully collateralize the loan with cash or securities of equivalent value adjusted daily, return an identical security on five business day's notice, and compensate the lender by paying an amount equal to the dividend or interest payment on the borrowed security as well as a fee for the use of the security.

The initial exchange of a security held for investment for the borrower's contractual obligation and subsequent return of an identical security will not result in gain or loss to the lender if the agreement:[745]

1. Provides for the return of an identical security (or equivalent se-

---

[739] Code: 337.
[740] Code: 453 (h).
[741] Code: 333. This election is made only when the corporation has little or no earnings and profits and thus enables a shareholder to defer reporting gain on liquidation. He is also eligible to elect the installment method on sale of the property.

[742] Code: 302 (e); Rev. Rul. 57-334, C.B. 1957-2, 240.
[743] Code: 341 (a) (2).
[744] Code: 1246 and 1248.
[745] Code: 1058, effective for transfers after 1976, does not apply to "Repos." Committee Report on P.L. 95-345.

curity in the case of a reorganization of the issuer of the security during the loan period).

2. Requires payments to the lender in amounts equivalent to the dividend, interest, or other distributions the lender would otherwise be entitled to during the loan period.
3. Does not reduce the risk of gain or loss opportunity to the lender.
4. Provides that the lender may terminate the agreement upon notice of not more than five business days.[746]

Transfers of securities in compliance with Section 1058 will be tax-free and the basis of the security returned to the lender (or the borrower's contractual obligation) will be the same as that of the originally transferred security.[747] The holding period of the returned security will include the initial holding period of the lender plus the loan period.[748] Any payments received by the lender in lieu of dividends or interest will lose their character and will be treated as a fee for temporary use of property.[749] Thus, a corporate lender of stock will not be entitled to an 85 percent dividends-received deduction. Similarly, a lender of a tax-exempt bond will be deemed to have received ordinary income instead of tax-exempt interest. It is unclear whether a lender of a zero-coupon bond or other discount bond will escape or defer reporting the original issue discount on the transferred bond during the loan period, since Section 1058 and the proposed regulations only discuss distributions received on the transferred security and are silent as to the treatment of original issue discount.

Failure to comply with the requirements of Section 1058 will ordinarily result in gain or loss on transfer of the security to the borrower.[750] If the terms of the agreement are proper but the borrower fails to return an identical security or otherwise defaults under the agreement, gain or loss generally will be recognized by the lender on the day of default.[751]

58 FOREIGN SECURITIES AND FOREIGN CURRENCY

.01 Foreign Income Tax Withheld

An investor may at his option claim foreign income tax withheld on income received from a foreign investment as a deduction, or as a

---

[746] Prop. Reg. 1.1058-1(b)(3).
[747] Code: 1058(c); Prop. Reg. 1.1058-1 (c)(2).
[748] Prop. Reg. 1.1223-2(a).
[749] Prop. Reg. 1.1058-1(d). The purchaser of the security will obtain the tax bene-

fit from any special characteristic of the dividend or interest income received from the security.
[750] Prop. Reg. 1.1058-1(e)(1).
[751] Prop. Reg. 1.1058-1(e)(2).

credit against the federal income tax.[752] The latter is normally more advantageous. In either case, the full amount of the dividend before withholding must be included in income.

.02 Foreign Investment Companies

Long-term gain from the sale of a foreign investment company stock is treated as ordinary income to the extent of the investor's ratable share of the company's undistributed earnings and profits after 1962.[753] The gain will be treated as capital gain if the foreign investment company elects to distribute its income currently.[754]

.03 Foreign Currency Transactions

Investors in foreign currencies will realize capital gains or losses upon culmination of the transaction.[755] Foreign currency held for investment is considered a capital asset and generally is subject to the same tax rules as securities.[756] Losses on sales of foreign currencies are not subject to the wash sales rules (see ¶36.03).[757] However, if the foreign currencies come under the new straddle rules, they may be subject to rules similar to the wash sales rules.[758] Similarly, the short sale rules may also apply when there are offsetting positions in foreign currencies.[759] Foreign currency contracts can now qualify as regulated Futures contracts and will be subject to the mark-to-market rules, including 60/40 capital gain treatment.[760] Prior to the Technical Corrections Act of 1982, a sale of a short Forward contract could result in a long-term capital gain.[761] Gain on retirement of foreign debt was held to be ordinary income.[762] However, exchange of Mexican gold coins for Austrian gold coins, whose values were based on gold content and were not used as currency, qualified as a tax-free exchange under Section 1031.[763] On the other hand, an exchange of U.S. $20 gold coins (numismatic-type coins) for South African Krugerrand gold coins (bullion-type coins) was ruled to be a taxable exchange.[764] Losses incurred

---

[752] Code: 164(a); 27; 901 et seq.
[753] Code: 1246. Similar rules apply to gains realized by an investor who owns at least 10 percent of a foreign corporation's stock. Code: 1248.
[754] Code: 1247.
[755] Rev. Rul. 74-7, C.B. 1974-2, 198; Rev. Rul. 75-479, C.B. 1975-2, 44.
[756] Cf. *Frank C. LaGrange*, 26 T.C. 191 (1956).
[757] Rev. Rul. 74-218, C.B. 1974-1, 202.

[758] Code: 1092(b) and (c).
[759] Ibid.
[760] Code: 1256(b). (See ¶44 for additional discussion.)
[761] *American Home Products Corp.*, 601 F. 2d 540 (Ct. Cl., 1979); *Hoover Co.*, 72 T.C. 206 (1979); *Carborundum Co.*, 74 T.C. 730 (1980) (Acq.).
[762] *Gillin*, 423 F. 2d 309 (Ct. Cl., 1970).
[763] Rev. Rul. 76-214, C.B. 1976-1, 218.
[764] Rev. Rul. 79-143, C.B. 1979-1, 264.

in foreign Futures transactions were disallowed for lack of substantiation.[765] Trading has commenced in foreign currency Futures and options. The Treasury has reversed itself and now holds that an exchange of silver bullion for gold bullion constitutes a taxable exchange.[766] The rules applicable to these transactions are identical to the general rules of commodity Futures and are covered in ¶41.03.

59 INSIDER'S SHORT–SWING PROFITS

An officer, director, or 10 percent (or greater) stockholder of a listed corporation or other corporation required to file annual reports with the SEC may be required to turn over to the corporation the gains realized on the sale of its stock if he sells and purchases (or purchases and sells) the stock of the corporation within a six-month period.[767] Ordinarily, the executive will realize a capital loss on repayment.[768] Tax Court decisions allowing an ordinary deduction where the payment was made solely to protect the executive's reputation have been reversed on appeal.[769] The problem is particularly likely to arise where the executive is in need of funds to exercise a stock option.[770] Instead of selling his stock, he should borrow the funds, with his stock as collateral, and sell the stock after the six-month period expires. Many employee stock option plans now permit an employee to pay the amount due on exercise of the options by surrendering stock of the employer that the employee currently owns. Apparently, this is permissible under the short-swing provisions, and for tax purposes it was not treated as a sale of the surrendered stock. However, payment for stock acquired through exercise of incentive stock options after March 15, 1982 by use of other statutory option stock will now be a taxable event.[771] A voluntary conversion of convertible bonds or preferred stock into common stock followed by a sale of the common stock within six months of the conversion date also comes within the short-swing profits provisions.[772] Advice of counsel should be obtained in all doubtful cases.

---

[765] Rev. Rul. 80-324, C.B. 1980-2, 340.

[766] Rev. Rul. 82-166, C.B. 1982-2, 190. It had previously ruled privately in Priv. Rul. Doc. 8020107 that the exchange was tax-free. This points out the risk of relying on a private ruling without obtaining your own ruling.

[767] Section 16(b) of the Securities Exchange Act of 1934.

[768] Rev. Rul. 61-115, C.B. 1961-1, 46.

[769] *Mitchell*, 428 F. 2d 259 (CA-6, 1970), rev'g. 52 T.C. 170 (cert. den. 401 U.S. 909 (1971); *Brown*, 529 F. 2d 609 (CA-10, 1976).

[770] Cf. *Greene* v. *Dietz*, 247 F. 2d 689 (1957); *Babbitt Inc.* v. *Lachner*, S.D. N.Y. 12/13/63.

[771] Code: 425(c)(3).

[772] *Park & Tilford, Inc.* v. *Schulte*, 160 F. 2d 984 (1947); *Heli-Coil Corp.* v. *Webster*, 222 F. Supp. 831 (1963).

60 VALUATION OF STOCK AND SECURITIES

Determining the market value of a stock or security is important not only for estate and gift tax purposes but in determining the amount of gain or loss in a taxable sale or exchange. These values are readily obtainable with respect to stock or securities sold over an exchange or over-the-counter market. A transfer of a restricted security (e.g., not registered with the SEC or subject to SEC sales restrictions), cannot be equated with the transfer of the same security that is not subject to "an investment letter" or similar SEC restriction. There is no automatic or mechanical solution. Rather, all material facts and circumstances must be considered in determining the fair market value of such restricted securities.[773]

61 ALTERNATIVE MINIMUM TAX

Since 1983, the alternative minimum tax and add-on minimum tax have been combined into one alternative minimum tax.[774] In computing the alternative minimum tax, the investor's adjusted gross income (AGI) before any net operating loss deduction is first reduced by the alternative tax net operating loss deduction and trust throwback income under Section 667, and is increased by the following tax preference items:[775]

1. The $100 dividend income exclusion ($200 for joint returns).
2. The all-savers' certificate exclusion.[776]
3. Excess accelerated (ACRS) depreciation on real property.
4. Excess accelerated (ACRS) depreciation on leased personal property.
5. Excess amortization on pollution-control facilities.
6. Excess mining exploration and development costs.
7. Excess research and development and circulation expenses.
8. Excess of depletion deduction over adjusted cost.
9. The 60 percent capital gain deduction.
10. The bargain element on exercise of incentive stock options.
11. Excess oil and gas intangible drilling expenses in excess of net oil income.

---

[773] Rev. Rul. 77-287, C.B. 1977-2, 319.
[774] Code: 55. The minimum tax will be included in computing estimated tax payments for taxable years after 1984. Code: 6654(d)(2)(B) and (C).
[775] Code: 57(a).

[776] Code: 128. Not effective for post-1983 taxable years. This provision was to have been replaced by a partial exclusion of interest, but the change provision was withdrawn by the 1984 Tax Reform Act.

This adjusted gross income amount is then reduced by the following items:[777]

1. Casualty losses in excess of 10 percent of AGI.
2. Charitable contributions.
3. Medical expenses in excess of 10 percent of AGI.
4. Personal housing interest expense.
5. Investment interest expense to the extent of investment interest income.[778]
6. The Section 691(c) estate tax deduction.

Note that other itemized deductions such as real estate taxes, state and local income taxes, sales taxes, other investment expenses, and miscellaneous expenses are not deductible in arriving at the alternative minimum taxable income. A flat 20 percent tax rate is imposed on the minimum taxable income in excess of $40,000 for joint returns, $30,000 for single returns, and $20,000 for married persons filing separate returns. The alternative tax is imposed only if it exceeds the regular income tax. Only the foreign tax credit and certain refundable credits can be offset against the alternative minimum tax.[779] As a consequence, taxpayers with large investment tax credits, but with little or no foreign tax credits, may become liable for the alternative minimum tax. Investment credit, WIN credit, and the new employee credit cannot be offset against the alternative minimum tax even if they are attributable to an individual's active trade or business as contrasted to a tax shelter investment. However, the unused credit may be carried back or over to the extent that it did not reduce the individual's tax in the current year. For example, assume an individual had a regular income tax of $12,000 which was offset by an investment tax credit of $5,000, resulting in a regular tax of $7,000. The alternative minimum tax was $9,000. Since the individual reduced his tax liability by only $3,000 through use of the credits ($12,000 − $9,000), the remaining $2,000 of credits can be carried back or over to applicable years.

The consequences of oversheltering, whether through losses or credits, is that the alternative minimum tax will become applicable,

---

[777] Code: 55(e).
[778] Limited partners and inactive shareholders of S corporations should aggregate their share of investment income, such as dividends and rents, together with their share of all other income, including trade or business income, in computing their net investment income

for purposes of the alternative minimum tax. The same amounts are not necessarily used in determining the investment interest expense limitations under Section 163(d). (Announcement 84-39.)
[779] Code: 55(c).

and the investor will end up with only a 20 percent tax reduction for his excess sheltering. An individual may wish to reduce his taxable income but should limit the amount of the deductions to avoid the application of the alternative minimum tax. It might be advisable to enter into an investment that produces an investment tax credit which, although not beneficial in the current year due to the alternative minimum tax, would be available as a carryback, and thus effectively recoup tax from the previous three years.

62 MAXIMUM TAX ON PERSONAL SERVICE INCOME

The maximum rate for both personal service income and unearned income has been reduced to 50 percent for post-1981 years. Consequently, the provision dealing with the maximum tax on personal service income has been repealed for post-1981 years.[780] With the repeal of the maximum tax provision, one of the major disincentives to investing in tax shelters that generate tax preferences has been removed.

63 INCOME AVERAGING FOR CAPITAL GAINS

Investors who have substantial net capital gains in the current taxable year may realize considerable savings in income tax by electing the income averaging provisions and thereby compute their tax as though the bunched income was earned over a four-year period. Income averaging is also available with respect to most types of ordinary income.[781] Some of the benefits of income averaging have been eliminated for years after 1983 with the shortening of the base period from four to three years and increasing of the percentage of average base income taken into account from 120 percent to 140 percent.

64 "SHAM" TRANSACTIONS

An investor may make his investments in any legitimate manner in order to obtain the maximum tax savings, and he will not be punished for choosing the avenue that produces the lesser tax.[782] This rule does not give tax effect to mere paper transactions where, in lieu of actual purchases and sales, the alleged transactions are merely entries on the broker's books.[783] Nor can an investor have recognized for tax pur-

---

[780] Code: 1348, repealed.
[781] Code: 1301-1305.
[782] *Gregory* v. *Helvering*, 293 U.S. 465 (1935); *Karl F. Knetsch*, 364 U.S. 361

(1960).
[783] *Eli D. Goodstein*, 267 F. 2d 127 (CA-1, 1959); *George G. Lynch*, 273 F. 2d 867 (CA-2, 1960).

poses a transaction he enters into solely for tax reasons (e.g., to obtain interest deductions in the current year) with no expectation of ever realizing a profit on the transaction.[784] Through proper planning, an investor can obtain maximum tax savings without resort to "sham" transactions.

65 PARTNERSHIPS

A partnership can take the form of a general business partnership, an investment club, a hedge fund, or a limited partnership with a general partner making the investment decisions. It is not a taxable entity,[785] but a conduit through which dividends, capital gains, tax exempt income, and other items of income and deductions are passed through and allocated among the partners in accordance with the partnership agreement.[786] The income of a partnership can be allocated among the partners based upon a partner's pro rata share of the partnership total income for the period the investor was a partner or the actual income of the partnership (including cash basis accounting method) during the period the investor was a partner.[787] Thus, losses incurred for periods before the investor became a partner cannot be allocated to the partner unless the expenses were paid while the investor was a partner. However, for periods after March 31, 1984, certain cash-basis items must be allocated among the partners based on their proportionate interests for each day during the period.[788] This will prevent the use of the cash method in allocating expenses to newly admitted partners. An election may be made by all the members not to be treated as a partnership if the separate income and deduction can be adequately determined without the computation of partnership income.[789] It is important that the partnership avoid falling within the classification of an association which is taxed as a corporation.[790]

The Treasury has ruled that the investment activities of an investment club do not constitute business activities and therefore, the expenses of such partnership are deductible on a pro rata basis as itemized deductions by each partner on his personal income tax return.[791] This position is contrary to the general rule that partnership

---

[784] See *Kapel Goldstein*, 364 F. 2d 734 (CA-2, 1966); *Michael J. Ippolito*, 364 F. 2d 744 (CA-2, 1966) (Cert. Den. 385 U.S. 1005); *Rothschild*, 407 F. 2d 404 (Ct. Cl., 1969); Rev. Rul. 77-185, C.B. 1977-1, 22.

[785] Code: 701.

[786] Code: 702.

[787] *Richardson*, 76 T.C. 512 (1981).

[788] Code: 706(d)(2).

[789] Code: 761.

[790] Reg. 1.761-1(a)(2)(i); Code 7701(a)(3); Reg. 301.7701-2.

[791] Rev. Rul. 75-523, C.B. 1975-2, 257.

expenses are effectively deductible by the partners in arriving at adjusted gross income.

66 CORPORATIONS

A corporate investor generally is subject to the same rules as an individual with respect to tax basis, holding period for long-term capital gains, wash sales, and short sales.[792] The total amount of cash dividends are included in gross income, but dividends paid in property to U.S. corporate shareholders are included in gross income at the lesser of market value or the adjusted tax basis plus gain recognized to the distributing corporation.[793] Both cash and accrual basis corporations should report the dividend income when actually or constructively received, rather than when the dividend is declared or on the ex-dividend date.[794]

In lieu of a $100 exclusion for dividends, a corporate shareholder is entitled to an 85 percent dividends-received deduction.[795] The amount of the dividends-received deduction by a corporate investor will in effect be reduced if the corporate investor borrowed funds (including through margin accounts or short sales) to acquire or hold the stock, based on the percentage of the cost that was financed during the base period.[796] Thus, if 50 percent of the cost was financed by the purchasing corporation (or an affiliated corporation), then the dividends-received deduction would be reduced by 50 percent, but the amount of the reduction cannot exceed the interest expense attributable to the dividend income. The base period is the period from the previous ex-dividend date to the day before the current ex-dividend date. Only indebtedness during this period will operate to reduce the dividends-received deduction. Buying stock within five days of the ex-dividend date will result in the indebtedness being outstanding on the settlement date, which will be after the ex-dividend date. Accordingly, a literal reading of the statute would indicate no indebtedness during the base period, and therefore, no disallowance of the dividends-received deduction. A corporation must be the owner on the

---

[792] A nondealer corporation was not allowed a deduction for dividends paid on a short sale. See footnote 657.

[793] Code: 301(d)(2).

[794] Rev. Rul. 78-117, C.B. 1978-1, 214.

[795] Code: 243(a)(1).

[796] Code: 246A, effective for stock purchased after July 18, 1984. The provision does not apply to certain con-

trolled corporations, including a 50 percent controlled subsidiary or a 20 percent interest in a closely held corporation, stock held by a small business investment company, or to the 100-percent dividends-received deduction for dividends received from members of the same affiliated group.

record date and not on the ex-dividend date in order for the dividend to qualify for the 85 percent deduction.[797] In general, common and preferred stock must be held for more than 45 days, and preferred stock in arrears for more than 366 days must be held for more than 90 days, in order for the particular dividends to qualify for the 85 percent dividends-received deduction.[798] The required holding period is suspended during the time the corporation owns a Put or sells the stock short.[799] Thus, the simultaneous purchase of a preferred stock and acquisition of a Put will prevent the commencement of the 45- or 90-day holding period, thereby preventing the dividend received from qualifying for the 85 percent dividends-received deduction. The required holding period is also suspended for any period in which the corporation "is under a contractual obligation to sell the stock."[800] A recent amendment will reduce the holding period for any period in which the corporation has sold Calls (options to buy) on a substantially identical stock or security other than qualified covered Calls.[801] Thus, covered option writing, especially in high-dividend-paying stocks, remains attractive for corporations, since 85 percent of the dividend income may still be received tax-free. Prior to this amendment, writing a Call would not affect the holding period unless the Call was exercised by the holder.[802] An attempt to diminish risk of loss by holding other substantially similar positions could also reduce the holding period.[803]

In general, a corporate investor does not reduce the basis of the stock of the distributing corporation when it receives dividends payable out of earnings and profits. Thus, if the stock is sold shortly after the qualifying dividend, a corporation will have received a dividend with an effective tax rate of up to 6.9 percent because of the dividends-received deduction, and a capital loss approximately in the

---

[797] Rev. Rul. 82-11, C.B. 1982-1, 429; Priv. Rul. Doc. 7840002.

[798] Code: 246(c)(1),(2). The increase in the holding period requirement from more than 15 days to more than 45 days applies only to stock acquired after July 18, 1984. 1984 Act: 53(e)(2).

[799] Code: 246(c)(4)(A). The 85 percent dividends-received deduction will be also disallowed if the corporate investor is obligated to make corresponding payments with respect to substantially similar stock or securities. Code: 246(c)(1)(B). Prior to the 1984 Act, the corresponding payment had to be with respect to a substantially identical stock

or security. Thus, the restriction will now apply to a short sale of a convertible preferred stock or convertible bond that does not qualify as a substantially identical security.

[800] Code: 246(c)(4)(A).

[801] Code: 246(c)(4), effective for stocks acquired after July 18, 1984.

[802] Priv. Rul. Doc. 7836066. But see Rev. Rul. 80-238, C.B. 1980-2,96, in which the Treasury indicated that the holding period may be suspended if the corporation writes an in-the-money Call (call price less than market value of the underlying stock).

[803] Code: 246(c)(4)(C).

amount of the dividend, which can be offset against short- or long-term capital gains. To rectify this tax advantage, a basis reduction will now be required to the extent of the untaxed portion of the extraordinary dividends for stock held for not more than one year.[804] For this purpose, a preferred stock dividend will be considered extraordinary if the amount of the dividend is equal to at least 5 percent of the basis of the preferred stock; 10 percent is extraordinary for common stock dividends.[805] Dividends exceeding 20 percent of basis are also considered extraordinary if their ex-dividend dates are within a 365-day period.[806] Note that where a dividend consists of appreciated property, the fair market value, and not tax basis, is to be used in computing the amount of the reduction.[807] This is to discourage the practice of distributing low-basis property, such as oil royalty interests, to the corporate shareholders. This low-basis property can be immediately sold at long-term capital gains while a short-term loss is realized on sale of the stock. Long-term capital gains treatment on the distributed property may also be denied by another amendment that prevents the holding period of the distributed property from beginning earlier than the date the holding period in the stock began.[808]

Dividends received from affiliated members may qualify for an 100 percent dividends-received deduction or are excluded from gross income if both corporations join in a consolidated return.[809] Thus, ordinarily, a corporation would prefer to realize dividends rather than long-term gains because the maximum tax rate on dividends is 6.9 percent (15 percent of 46 percent corporate rate), whereas long-term capital gains are taxed at 28 percent.

Payments in lieu of dividends received by a corporate investor who had loaned stock to be used to close a short sale, do not qualify for the dividends-received deduction.[810] To avoid possible loss of the dividends-received deduction, a corporate investor should avoid having its shares used to effectuate short sales or otherwise loaned out at the ex-dividend date. This would include stock loans by the stock broker who holds the corporation's shares in street name. Dividends received by a corporation from a regulated investment company (mutual fund) may qualify, in part or in whole, for the 85 percent dividends-

---

[804] Code: 1059, effective for distributions after March 1, 1984.

[805] Dividends with ex-dividend dates within an 85-day period are aggregated. Code: 1059(c)(3)(A).

[806] Code: 1059(c)(3)(B).

[807] Code: 1059(d)(2).

[808] Code: 301(e) and 1223(14), effective for distributions ending after July 18, 1984.

[809] Code: 243(a)(3); Reg. 1.1502-14(a).

[810] Code: 1058; Rev. Rul. 60-177, C.B. 1960-1, 9. (See ¶57.)

received deduction.[811] Net short-term capital gains are included in gross income for purposes of determining the amount of qualifying dividends from the mutual fund.[812] Since only true dividends received by a mutual fund will qualify, dividend-received deductions are not allowed on distributions from money market funds whose gross income consists principally of interest income.

Net long-term capital gains received in taxable years after 1983 can either be taxed at regular corporate tax rates (15 percent on the first $25,000 of taxable income, 18 percent, 30 percent, and 40 percent respectively on each additional $25,000, and 46 percent on more than $100,000) similar to short-term capital gains, or be taxed at a rate of 28 percent by means of the alternative tax computation.[813] Note that while the maximum capital gains rate for individuals has been reduced to 20 percent for net capital gains after June 9, 1981, the corporate capital gains rate remains at 28 percent. The 60 percent long-term capital gain deduction is not available to corporations. Unused capital losses cannot be offset against ordinary income but can be carried back three years and carried forward for five years as short-term capital losses.[814] However, a capital loss cannot be carried back if it will create or increase a net operating loss for the taxable years to which the loss is being carried. Note that a capital loss must be carried back to a year in which the capital gains could be offset by net operating losses from other years.[815] Accordingly, a corporation with expiring net operating losses in 1985 should not use a commodity straddle (i.e., close out the profitable position in the year the net operating losses will expire and establish a short-term loss by closing out the loss position in the subsequent year), because any unused capital losses in the three subsequent years must be carried back and applied against the capital gain created in the expiring year before the net operating loss carry-over can be offset against the capital gain. A

---

[811] Code: 854(b). Unless 100 percent of the mutual fund's gross income is from dividend income (replaces 75 percent requirement) for taxable years of the mutual fund beginning after July 18, 1984, only the portion of the gross income attributable to the dividend income will qualify for the 85 percent dividends-received deduction.

[812] Despite the fact that previous law excluded gains from disposition of securities from gross income, the Treasury ruled that short-term gains from unexecuted options are treated as ordinary income. Priv. Rul. Doc. 7813075.

[813] Code: 11(b). The graduated rates are phased out for large corporations with taxable income exceeding $1 million, by imposing a 5 percent surcharge on the first $405,000 of taxable income in excess of $1 million or an additional maximum tax of $20,250. Thus, if a corporation had taxable income of $1.2 million, the surcharge would be $10,000.

[814] Code: 1212(a).

[815] Reg. 1.1212-1(a)(3)(iv), Example (6).

corporation can not enter into straddle positions in order to create capital losses for carry-back purposes.[816]

Corporations are subject to an add-on minimum tax. The add-on minimum tax rate is 15 percent and the allowable deduction in computing the tax is the greater of $10,000 or regular federal income tax for the current year.[817] The list of tax preferences differs from that applicable to individuals. (See ¶61.) Approximately 39 percent ($^{18}/_{46}$) of long-term capital gains constitute a tax preference if the alternative tax method is utilized.[818] In addition to the minimum tax, corporations face a 20 percent reduction in benefit from certain tax preferences, such as Section 1250 capital gains and intangible drilling costs.[819] With respect to these preferences, only a portion of the amount is exposed to the minimum tax.[820]

Many corporations, being unaware of or disagreeing with adverse decisions in two fairly old cases,[821] have entered into short sales of preferred stock or common stock for the primary purpose of obtaining an ordinary deduction for the payments made to reimburse the lender for the dividend paid on the stock and give a short-term capital gain upon closing of the short sale. In a typical transaction, the corporation would sell a preferred stock short and buy a preferred stock in a similar industry to reduce the risk of loss. (These preferred stocks are not considered substantially identical but may be substantially similar.) Aside from overcoming the effects of these two cases, in order to obtain the deductions, a corporation must now hold the short sale position open for at least 46 days for ordinary dividends (not to exceed 5 percent preferred stock, 10 percent common stock, and an aggregate of 20 percent for dividends in a 365-day period).[822] Short sales must be held open for more than one year for extraordinary dividends. In addition, there must be valid economic reasons for entering into the short sales besides the potential tax benefits. (See ¶51.06 for additional discussion of the short sales rules.)

Interest received from tax-exempt securities is excluded from the corporation's taxable income.[823] However, it is includible in earnings and profits of a corporation and constitutes a taxable dividend when distributed to shareholders.[824] Despite this detriment, investment in

---

[816] Code: 1092 and 1256.
[817] Code: 56(a).
[818] Code: 57(a)(9)(B).
[819] Code: 291.
[820] Code: 57(b).
[821] Main Line Distributors, Inc., 321 F. 2d 562 (CA-6, 1963); 1955 Production Exposition, Inc., 41 TC 55 (1963). The

Senate Committee Report for the 1984 Act (April 2, 1984) in discussing extraordinary dividends, states that non-dealer corporations do qualify for the deduction.
[822] Code: 263(h).
[823] Code: 103.
[824] Reg. 1.312-6(b).

tax-exempts may be advisable for corporations that may be liable for tax on unreasonable accumulation of earnings,[825] or the personal holding company tax.[826] Tax-exempt income is excluded in calculating the amounts subject to tax. Corporations investing in tax-exempts suffer the risk that some of their interest expense and investment expense allocable to the tax-exempt income will be disallowed, thereby reducing the tax benefits of this type of investment. Nevertheless, interest will not be disallowed if not directly attributable to the tax-exempts or the tax-exempts constitute not more than 2 percent of the average adjusted basis of the total business assets.[827]

A cash-basis corporation can defer interest income by investing in noninterest-bearing short-term obligations, such as Treasury bills.[828] However, accrual-basis corporations must now include in income currently a ratable portion of the acquisition discount.[829]

Closely held corporations, with five or less individuals directly or indirectly owning at least 50 percent of the value of the outstanding stock and whose personal holding company income (dividends, interest, royalties, and the like) constitute at least 60 percent of its adjusted ordinary gross income, may be subject to a personal holding company tax of 50 percent on its undistributed personal holding company income. All capital gains are excluded in making the 60 percent test.[830] Net long-term gains, after adjustment for capital gains tax, are deducted in computing the personal holding company tax.[831] Personal holding company tax can be avoided by distributing all of the personal holding company income or by electing consent dividends.[832] The use of a personal holding company as a vehicle to hold the family's investments is recommended for estate planning since a large discount from the value of the underlying assets may be taken for gifts of minority interests to other family members or where the shareholder, including the original grantor, owns a minority interest at time of death.

A corporation (Subchapter S corporation) may elect to be treated similar to a partnership, whereby the shareholders report on their tax returns their share of the undistributed ordinary income, long-term capital gains, or net operating losses.[833] There is no longer any disqualification as an S corporation if the corporation's passive investment income (including dividends, interest, rents, and gains from

---

[825] Code: 531.
[826] Code: 541.
[827] Rev. Proc. 72-18, C.B. 1972-1, 740.
[828] Code: 454.
[829] Code: 1281. (See ¶46.09(b).)

[830] Code: 543(b).
[831] Code: 545(b).
[832] Code: 565.
[833] Code: 1361–1368.

sales of securities) exceeds 20 percent of its gross income.[834] These S corporations with earnings while they were regular corporations will have their special status terminated if their investment income exceeds 25 percent of their gross receipts for three consecutive taxable years.[835] In those cases, care should be taken to limit passive income to 25 percent of gross receipts. Investment in tax-exempts may be suitable for this purpose. The tax-exempt income may then be distributed tax-free to the shareholders.[836]

67   ESTATES AND TRUSTS

Estates and trusts compute their taxable income in a manner similar to individuals and pay a tax on undistributed income using the tables of an unmarried individual.[837] The investment interest expense limitation is applicable, but trusts are not entitled to the $10,000 minimum deduction.[838] A deduction is allowed for distributions to beneficiaries, who must report the income in the year the estate's or trust's taxable year ends.[839] The character of the income will be the same as in the hands of the estate or trust.[840] Thus tax-exempt income received by an estate or trust will retain its exempt status when received by the beneficiary.

Ordinarily, the estate or trust will pay a tax based on its income on any capital gains realized unless the governing instrument provides for distribution of capital gains.[841] However, a sale of appreciated property that was transferred within two years from the date of sale will be taxed to the trust at the same rates as if the transferor had sold the property and reported the gain realized on the sale, but not in excess of the appreciation at the time transferred to the trust.[842] The two-year period cannot be avoided by a short sale of the property ("short against the box").

A capital gain could have been avoided on discretionary distributions before June 1, 1984 of appreciated property to a beneficiary where there was no obligation to make the distribution either in a specific dollar amount or in other property.[843] For example, if a fiduciary has the discretionary power to accumulate or distribute the income, a distribution of appreciated stock or securities would not be taxed to the estate or trust, but the estate or trust would have received

---

[834] Code: 1372(e)(5).
[835] Code: 1362(d)(3).
[836] Code: 1366(a)(1).
[837] Code: 641.
[838] Code: 163(d)(1).

[839] Code: 651 and 662.
[840] Code: 652 and 663.
[841] Code: 643(a)(3).
[842] Code: 644(a)(1).
[843] Reg. 1.661(a)-(2)(f).

a deduction equal to the value of the property. The beneficiary would report income based on the value of the property received in a manner similar to that for a cash distribution, and the market value would be the beneficiary's tax basis for the property. With respect to distributions of property after May 31, 1984, the estate or trust can either elect to report the appreciation as capital gain income or receive a distribution deduction equal to the income taxed to the beneficiary (the tax basis of the property in the hands of the estate or trust adjusted for any gain or loss recognized on the distribution).[844] The trust or estate will be liable for tax under either alternative. The tax and liquidity position of the estate or trust and the beneficiaries should be considered before making the property distribution and deciding whether to have the estate or trust report the appreciation income. Note that the estate or trust should not distribute property that has depreciated in value since it will not receive any tax benefit from the reduction in value. In this situation, when feasible, the estate or trust should sell the property and distribute the cash proceeds.

A tax-planning device that was not affected by the various tax acts is a 10-year reversionary trust.[845] Under this arrangement a high-tax-bracket individual places assets in a trust, with the income to be distributed to a dependent parent or other family members who pay little or no tax on the income because of the allowable deductions, exemptions, and low tax bracket of the dependent. With the increase in the annual gift tax exclusion for gifts made after 1981 from $3,000 to $10,000 per donee ($6,000 to $20,000 for joint gifts) a grantor can contribute over $30,000 to a short-term trust without being exposed to gift taxes.[846] In the case of a minor child it is recommended that the income be accumulated in a custodian account with the grantor's spouse as the custodian. Any capital gains realized by the trust will be taxed currently to the grantor although not received until termination of the trust unless the trust instrument provides that capital gains are to be distributed to a beneficiary other than the grantor or his spouse.[847] Upon termination of the trust, the trust principal, including any unrealized appreciation, reverts back to the grantor. Instead of making support payments or accumulating funds for the future needs of his children with after-tax dollars, through this arrangement the same needs are met with half the outlay due to the savings of tax. For example, if an individual in the 50 percent tax bracket makes yearly support payments of $3,000 to his dependent parents, he will have to

---

[844] Code: 643 (d).
[845] Code: 673.

[846] Code: 2503 (b).
[847] Code: 677.

earn $6,000 of before-tax income in order to make the payments. By distributing to a short-term trust sufficient funds to earn $3,000, the trust distributions are not taxed to the grantor and the beneficiaries escape tax by means of their exemptions and deductions. Therefore, the grantor saves $3,000 of tax annually or $30,000 over a 10-year period.

A U.S. grantor could defer tax until expiration of the trust by creating a foreign trust, preferably with a situs in a tax-haven country, invest the funds in foreign securities, and provide for income to be accumulated and paid to U.S. beneficiaries upon expiration of the trust.[848] The advantage of creating a foreign trust is that income could be earned on the funds which otherwise would have been used to pay taxes by a U.S. trust. Foreign trusts created before May 22, 1974, do not come within the new grantor trust provisions discussed below, but a U.S. beneficiary will be liable, on receipt of the accumulated income, for a nondeductible interest charge of 6 percent per annum for the year the distributed income was accumulated.[849] Foreign trusts created by a U.S. grantor after May 21, 1974, with at least one U.S. beneficiary will be treated as a grantor trust for post-1975 years.[850] The grantor is treated as the owner of the property and must include the income earned by the foreign trust in his tax return in the year earned. Income from a foreign trust still will be excluded from U.S. tax if there are no U.S. beneficiaries. An excise tax of 35 percent of unrealized gain will be imposed on any appreciated property transferred by a U.S. person to a foreign trust, foreign corporation, or foreign partnership unless the transferor treats the contribution as a taxable exchange.[851]

An investor can accelerate his charitable deductions by creating and transferring funds to a less than 10-year charitable lead trust, with the income payable to charitable beneficiaries in the form of guaranteed annuities and the securities held by the trust reverting to the grantor at the end of the trust term.[852] By having the trust invest in tax-exempts, the grantor avoids paying a tax on the trust income. The charitable deduction should not exceed 20 percent of his adjusted gross income for the year the charitable trust is created.[853] The grantor must also limit the amount of his investment interest expense to prevent a partial disallowance because of the tax-exempt income from

---

[848] Code: 665(c).
[849] Code: 667(a) and 668.
[850] Code: 679.

[851] Code: 1491 and 1057.
[852] Code: 170(f)(2).
[853] Code: 170(b)(1)(B).

the trust that he is deemed to have received.[854] Some of the advantages of a charitable lead trust have been eliminated when as of December 1, 1983, the Treasury increased the percentage factor for valuing the charitable income interest and remainder interest of the trust from 6 percent to 10 percent. The effect is to reduce the value of the charitable income interest, thereby reducing the amount of the charitable deduction by more than 15 percent.

68   TAX-EXEMPT ORGANIZATIONS

Qualified pension, profit sharing, and stock bonus plans, and religious, educational, charitable, and other tax-exempt organizations are not taxed on their investment income.[855] An exempt private foundation is subject to a 1 or 2 percent excise tax on its net investment income consisting of dividends, interest, rents, royalties, and net capital gains less applicable investment expense.[856] Note that capital losses are deductible only against capital gains and any excess capital losses cannot be carried to another year. Tax-exempt income is also exempt from the excise tax. Notwithstanding their tax-exempt status, any unrelated business income is subject to a regular corporate or unincorporated tax depending upon whether the exempt organization is a corporate or unincorporated charity.[857] Investment income normally is not considered unrelated business income unless derived from debt-financed property.[858] Thus, if securities are purchased on margin, the income from the securities is taxed to the extent of the percentage of the property that is debt financed, less a deduction for a similar percentage of related investment expense. Income from lapse of options regularly written by a tax-exempt organization was held by the Treasury to constitute unrelated business income,[859] but this has been rectified by recent legislation.[860] Organizations which were hesitant to write "covered" Calls (Calls in which they own the underlying stock) are now free to utilize Calls as an investment technique to maximize income on their investments. However, income on lapse of options now constitutes short-term gains and is subject to the excise tax when earned by private foundations.[861] Income derived from temporary

---

[854] Code: 265.
[855] Code: 501.
[856] Code: 4940.
[857] Code: 511.
[858] Code: 512(b)(1) and (4), and 514.
[859] Rev. Rul. 66-47, C.B. 1966-1, 149.

Many authorities have questioned the accuracy of this ruling, feeling its conclusion is erroneous.
[860] Code: 512(b)(5).
[861] Code: 1234(b).

loans of stock to a brokerage house to cover short sales also does not constitute unrelated business income.[862]

69 NONRESIDENT ALIENS

A nonresident alien investor may be subject to U.S. tax only on certain types of income from U.S. sources. The ensuing general discussion may be superseded by a treaty between the United States and the investor's country.

In general, a 30 percent tax will be withheld on fixed income received from U.S. sources, including dividends, rental income, and interest.[863] There is no withholding tax on U.S. Treasury bills unless held by a foreign investor for more than six months.[864] Original issue discount on obligations with a maturity of more than 183 days is currently taxable. However, the tax withheld is limited to the tax on the amount of original issue discount since the last payment of interest, but cannot exceed the actual interest payment less the 30 percent tax imposed thereon.[865] Thus, if the OID computed under the compound interest method (see ¶46.09(b)) is $300 and an interest payment of $70 ($100 less 30 percent withholding) is due, then a withholding tax of 30 percent would be imposed on the original issue discount but would be limited to the $70 net payment. No withholding tax is imposed on zero-coupon bonds since interest is not paid until maturity. On sale or retirement of the discount obligation, a tax will be imposed on the gain realized but limited to the untaxed earned original issue discount.[866] These original issue discount rules also apply to stripped coupons or bonds.[867] (See ¶46.09(f).) Interest income from deposits with banks[868] or from corporations who derive less than 20 percent of their income from U.S. sources[869] is not taxable. Generally the 30 percent tax is computed without deductions, such as interest on a margin account, or personal exemptions. Nonresident alien investors may avoid the 30 percent withholding tax on investment interest, including original issue bond discount income, by purchasing registered bonds issued by U.S. borrowers (this includes U.S. bonds).[870]

---

[862] Rev. Rul. 78-88, C.B. 1978-1, 163.
[863] Code: 871 and 1441.
[864] Priv. Rul. Doc. 7838070.
[865] Code: 871(a)(1)(C)(ii) and 871(g)(1), applies to payments made at least 60 days after July 18, 1984 with respect to bonds issued after March 31, 1972. Tax is not imposed on other discount obligations until the bonds are sold or retired.
[866] Code: 871(a)(1)(C)(i).

[867] Code 871(g)(4).
[868] Code: 861(c).
[869] Code: 861(a)(1)(B).
[870] Code: 871(h), effective for registered bonds issued after July 18, 1984. Certain unregistered bonds that will be sold only to nonresident aliens, with interest payable only outside the United States and its possessions, may also qualify for exclusion.

Capital gains are not taxed unless the foreign investor is personally present in the United States for at least 183 days or the gain is in connection with a trade or business carried on in the United States.[871] Merely buying or selling securities or commodities through a broker or agent in the United States is not considered doing business in the United States. However, a nonresident alien, who was a limited partner in a partnership doing business in the United States that carried on the business of its corporate predecessor, was taxable on the gain realized on liquidation of the corporation and on other sales of stock during the taxable year.[872]

Options written after September 1, 1976, will be accorded short-term gain or loss treatment upon expiration or upon closing of the transaction, and, accordingly, will be generally exempt from U.S. taxation. If the capital gain is taxable, the 30 percent tax is imposed on the entire net capital gain, after taking into account any capital losses realized in the taxable year but without any 60 percent capital gain deduction.[873] A foreign investor who is present in the United States for only a short period of time can escape U.S. tax by selling on the installment basis and receiving the income after he has left the United States.[874] If an investor owns real property in the United States, he may be able to reduce his U.S. tax by electing to treat the real property income as being connected with a United States business.[875] A disposition of an investment in U.S. real property is now subject to U.S. tax.[876]

A 30 percent tax will also be imposed on fixed income from U.S. sources received by a foreign corporation not connected with a United States business.[877] The rules are similar to those discussed above for nonresident alien investors.

70 SECURITIES DEALERS

.01 In General

A securities dealer can be a corporation, partnership (including a limited partnership), or a proprietorship. The general rules will apply to all forms of dealers, but the dealer's form of doing business may affect the tax treatment of special items, such as dividends-received deductions, which are applicable only to corporate dealers. Additionally, a corporate dealer can pick any fiscal year, whereas a

---

[871] Code: 871(a)(2).
[872] *Vitale,* 72 T.C. 386 (1979).
[873] Reg. 1.871-7(c)(3).
[874] Reg. 1.871-7(d)(2)(iv).

[875] Code: 871(d).
[876] Code: 897, effective for dispositions after June 18, 1980.
[877] Code: 881.

partnership is more limited in its choice of a fiscal year. Some firms are dealers in only one product—e.g., stock, bonds (including tax exempts), options, or commodities—whereas more diversified investment houses will deal in many, if not all, of these investment products. An investment house may be a dealer in some products and trade for its own account (e.g., arbitrage trading) in the same or other products. The tax treatment is not necessarily the same for all of these varied activities. However, if these activities are not segregated and separately identified, adverse tax consequences may ensue for the investment firm.

.02 Dealer Defined

Activities as a dealer must be distinguished from activities as a trader, broker, investor, or speculator. A dealer's profits must be derived from a merchant's markup of the products it sells to its customers in the ordinary course of its business and not from market appreciation.[878] Thus, a dealer in securities is a merchant of securities, with an established place of business, regularly engaged in the purchase and resale of securities to customers with a view to the gains or profits that may be derived therefrom.[879] A "specialist" on a stock exchange who accepts orders in selected stocks from other members of the exchange will be treated as a dealer with respect to the selected stocks,[880] but a specialist who merely matches buy or sell orders received from other brokers will not.[881] Other securities held by a specialist for speculation purposes are treated as capital assets and should not be inventoried.[882] Similarly, securities held by a stock or bond dealer for investment or speculation purposes will not be treated as inventory.[883] Note, however, if the so-called investment securities are consistently sold to customers in the same manner as inventory securities are sold, they will receive ordinary income treatment.[884] A trader actively engaged in the business of buying and selling securities on his own account will be treated as being in business for certain

---

[878] George R. Kemon, 16 T.C. 1026 (1951).

[879] Reg. 1.471-5; William D. Stevens, 78 F. 2d 713 (1935).

[880] Helvering v. Fried, 299 U.S. 175 (1936); Rev. Rul. 60-321, C.B. 1960-2, 166.

[881] Lowell, 30 B.T.A. 1297 (1934).

[882] Brendle, et al., 31 B.T.A. 1188 (1935), aff'd per curiam 87 F. 2d 998 (CA-2, 1937).

[883] Stephens, Inc., 464 F. 2d 53, (CA-8, 1972), cert. denied, 409 U.S. 1118; Franklin Brown, 9 B.T.A. 965 (1927), Holton & Co., 44 B.T.A. 202 (1941).

[884] J. C. Bradford, 22 T.C. 1057 (1954), rev'd on other issues 233 F. 2d 935 (CA-6, 1956).

tax purposes, but will not qualify as a dealer.[885] An investment company that holds securities for long-term investment or for trading purposes will also not be treated as a dealer.[886]

.03 Accounting Methods

Ordinarily, a dealer must compute its taxable income using the same method of accounting regularly employed in keeping its books.[887] In order to clearly reflect income, dealers with substantial inventory must use the accrual method of accounting.[888] However, dealers engaged in more than one business may use a different method of accounting for each separate and distinct business.[889] Hence, the acrual method may be used for the businesses requiring inventories and the cash method used for separate service or commission businesses. Sometimes these various businesses will be conducted through separate subsidiaries or partnerships to ensure different accounting treatment.

.04 Inventory Methods

Inventory on hand at the end of a year may be valued for both book and tax purposes at (1) cost; (2) cost or market, whichever is lower; or (3) market value.[890] Securities held for investment or speculation and not for resale to customers may not be included in inventory. In the first year of business, the opening inventory should be valued at cost even when the closing inventory is marked-to-market.[891] In lieu of these valuation methods, a securities dealer may elect to use the last-in, first-out (LIFO) method of valuation.[892] In times of rising prices, the use of the LIFO method can significantly reduce a dealer's taxable income. A dollar-value method of valuation instead of a unit value method can be used in conjunction with the LIFO election.[893] Hedges against inventory losses, whether in the form of Futures con-

---

[885] *C. E. Wilson, et al.*, 76 F. 2d 476 (CA-10, 1935).

[886] *Leach Corp.* v. *Blacklidge*, 23 F. Supp. 622 (DC, 1938); *Oil Shares, Inc.*, 29 B.T.A. 664 (1934).

[887] Code: 446.

[888] Reg. 1.446-1(c)(2).

[889] Reg. 1.446-1(d).

[890] Reg. 1.471-5. The use of market value, although in excess of cost, to value a closing inventory of securities or com-

modities, has been expressly permitted in Rev. Rul. 74-226, C.B. 1974-1, 119 and I.T. 3123, C.B. 1937-2, 114.

[891] *Claude Neon Electrical Products Corp., Ltd.*, 35 B.T.A. 563 (acq.) (1937).

[892] Reg. 1.472-1(a); Rev. Rul. 60-321, C.B. 1960-2, 166. See Reg. 1.472 for conformity rules and other requirements that must be met before a proper election can be made.

[893] Reg. 1.472-8.

tracts or options, are not part of inventory and must be treated separately.[894] Where it was customary for commodity dealers to include the market value of the inventory and the hedging contracts in determining book income, gain or loss on the hedging contract determined by marking them to market at year-end was permitted.[895] Speculative contracts are not eligible for the mark-to-market treatment. Dealers not using the mark-to-market method for the hedging transactions will report a gain or loss when the hedging contract is sold or terminated. In cases where the value of the inventory has decreased and there are unrealized profits in the hedging contracts, a dealer using the lower of cost or market method would report the inventory losses in the current year and the hedging gains in the following year. If the losses are in the hedged positions, a dealer may recognize the loss in the earlier year by closing out the loss positions, but the dealer should not enter into new positions that are substantially identical to the closed positions.

.05 Investment Securities

Securities dealers may obtain capital gain treatment on sales of securities (including stock, bonds, stock rights, and options) provided each security is clearly identified in the dealer's records by the close of the acquisition day as being held for investment, and the security is not held at any subsequent time primarily for sale to customers.[896] Once a security has been designated as held for investment, any loss on disposition will be a capital loss even if the security is sold in the ordinary course of business.[897] Securities placed in a trading account or an arbitrage account that is clearly separated from the dealer operation should qualify for capital gain treatment. A failure to meet both requirements of Section 1236 could result in ordinary income or capital loss on disposition of the security. Thus, a failure to segregate certain stocks does not justify inventory treatment where other factors indicate that the shares were held primarily for investment purposes.[898] It is sometimes difficult to determine whether the security is held for investment. In one case, part of a sale of a large lot was

---

[894] *Bacon Grain Co.*, 2 B.T.A. 558 (1925); Rev. Rul. 74-227, C.B. 1974-1, 119.

[895] Rev. Rul. 74-223, C.B. 1974-1, 23.

[896] Code: 1236(a). The Treasury may, by regulations, require identification prior to the close of the acquisition day. Floor specialists must identify within seven days following the date of ac-

quisition. Code: 1236(d). See Rev. Rul. 64-160, C.B. 1964-1, 306 for an amplification of the stock identification requirements.

[897] Code: 1236(b), Reg. 1.1236-1(b).

[898] *Stephens, Inc.*, 464 F. 2d. 53 (CA-8, 1972), cert. denied, 409 U.S. 1118.

treated as a sale of inventory, and the balance of the lot was held to be investment property.[899] A security acquired by a dealer upon exercise of an option may be designated as investment property only if the option was identified as held for investment on the day the option was acquired by the dealer.[900] Stock acquired in a reorganization in exchange for inventory stock may also be identified as investment stock under Section 1236.[901] Note that investment stock may be used as collateral for a loan without adversely affecting its investment status.[902]

.06 Wash Sales

After 1984, losses on sales of stock or securities by a securities dealer will not be disallowed despite the purchase of substantially identical stock or securities in the prohibited 61-day period, provided the loss is sustained in a transaction made in the ordinary course of business.[903] For sales made prior to 1985, noncorporate taxpayers need not be dealers in order to avoid the wash sales rules as long as the sales were made in connection with the taxpayer's trade or business. Corporate dealers were previously permitted to enter into wash sales only if the sales were made in the ordinary course of their business as dealers.[904] Traders will be subject to the disallowance rules for post-1984 sales. These disallowance rules will also apply to the non-dealer activities of a securities dealer. Arbitrage or trading accounts in which the dealer is trading on its own behalf rather than for resale to customers may now be subject to the wash sales rules. Even where these activities are performed by different individuals in separate divisions of the dealer's establishment, these separate accounts will be combined in determining whether there was a violation of the wash sales rules. If these activities are conducted in separate subsidiaries, the losses should not be disallowed unless one subsidiary acted as an agent for the other or the sales and purchases were part of a coordinated transaction.[905] Note that with the inclusion of stock and Listed options in the tax straddle provisions, dealers may come under rules similar to wash sales rules unless one of the exceptions, such as qualified covered Calls or hedging transactions, applies.[906] Commodities

---

[899] *E. Nielsen,* 333 F. 2d. 615 (CA-6, 1964). But see *J. C. Bradford,* 444 F. 2d. 1133, where the taxpayer was held to be a trader in a similar transaction.
[900] Code: 1236(e).
[901] Rev. Rul. 76-392, C.B. 1976-2, 249.
[902] Rev. Rul. 73-403, C.B. 1973-2, 308.

[903] Code: 1091(a). (See discussion of wash sales rules starting with ¶36.01.)
[904] Reg. 1.1091-1(a).
[905] *J. P. McWilliams,* 331 U.S. 694 (1947); *Jacob M. Kaplan,* 21 T.C. 134 (1953).
[906] Code: 1092. (See ¶39.11.)

dealers, who ordinarily are not subject to the wash sales provisions, may come under the tax straddle rules.

.07 Short Sales

Dealers may enter into short sales by selling a security, borrowing the security from a third party for delivery to the purchaser, and then closing the short sale by returning a substantially identical security to the lender. Purchasing a Put may also be treated as a short sale that is closed when the Put is exercised or terminated except when the Put is acquired on the same day as the security to be used on exercise of the Put (married Put). The tax consequences of a short sale generally are that (1) the capital gain on the sale would be short-term if substantially identical property was held for less than the applicable long-term capital gain period at the time of the short sale; (2) the holding period of such substantially identical property owned at the time of the short sale or acquired in the interim short sale period starts anew at the time the short sale is closed; and (3) any loss on the short sale is a long-term capital loss if substantially identical property was held for the applicable long-term holding period at the time of the short sale.[907] These short sales rules do not apply to dealers unless the stock used to close the short sale was a capital asset in the dealer's hands.[908] Thus, while these rules will not apply to inventoried securities (including stock, bonds, and commodity Futures that are not part of a hedging transaction), they would apply to investment securities held in identified Section 1236 accounts and securities used for trading or arbitrage operations. Where applicable, these rules will apply to securities held in different divisions of the security dealer's operation. These rules may be avoided by placing the operations in different subsidiaries.

Dealers entering into short sales (or acquiring Puts) with respect to their stock (or convertible securities, stock rights, or options) held for resale to customers may lose the holding period of substantially identical securities held in a noninventory account if the short sale is held open for more than 20 days.[909]

> **Example.** Assume a dealer has 100 shares of ABC stock that has been held in an investment account for five months. The dealer then sells short 100 shares of ABC stock and closes the short sale after 30

---

[907] Code: 1233(b) and (d). (See discussion of short sales starting with ¶37.01.)

[908] Reg. 1.1233-1(a)(2).
[909] Code: 1233(e)(4).

> days with ABC stock held in its inventory. The general short sales rules will not apply to this transaction, except that the investment shares will have a new holding period starting with the date the short sale is closed.

Many dealers enter into arbitrage transactions expecting to make a profit from the differences in price among the securities acquired. Examples are buying stock of the acquired corporation and selling short stock of the acquiring corporation, or combining stock and convertible bonds or options. These securities have an economic relationship, although they may not be substantially identical securities. In the case of a short sale entered into as part of an arbitrage operation, the loss of holding period rules in Section 1233(b)(2) are first applied to the substantially identical property acquired for the arbitrage operations and held at the close of the day of the short sale. The holding period of other substantially identical securities owned by the dealer will be affected by the short sale only to the extent that the amount sold short exceeds the amount acquired for the arbitrage operations.[910]

> **Example.** Assume a dealer, on September 1, purchases for investment 100 bonds convertible into 100 shares of XYZ stock. On November 1, for arbitrage purposes, the dealer purchases another 100 bonds and on the same day sells short 100 shares of XYZ stock. The dealer closes the short sale on December 15 with 100 shares of XYZ stock purchased on that day. Only the bonds purchased as part of the arbitrage operations will receive a new holding period starting on December 15. There would be no change in the holding period of the investment bonds even if the bonds acquired later were converted into stock to be used to close the short sale. If in the above example, only 60 bonds were acquired for arbitrage, the holding period of 40 of the investment bonds would be lost and a new holding period would start when the short sale is closed.

Sometimes the related securities purchased for arbitrage operations are disposed of with part or all of the short positions remaining. The net short position on the day the related securities were disposed of would constitute a short sale made on that day.[911] In that event, the

---

[910] Code: 1233(f)(1).   [911] Code: 1233(f)(2).

holding period of substantially identical securities acquired for investment and held for less than the applicable long-term period on the day
of the deemed short sale would be terminated and a new holding period would begin on the day the deemed short sale is closed.[912] For
example, assume in the above example that the 100 bonds acquired
for arbitrage operations were sold and the short position remained
open. This net short position would affect the holding period of the
bonds purchased for investment.

For purposes of these arbitrage rules, at the close of a business day
a dealer is deemed to own property which it is entitled to receive
or acquire through ownership of other assets acquired for arbitrage
operations, such as convertible securities, or because of a contract
entered into in the arbitrage operation.[913] The arbitrage transactions
must ordinarily be identified on the dealer's records on the day of the
transaction.[914]

Example.   Assume a dealer, on August 1, acquires 100 shares of
ABC for investment purposes. On October 1, the dealer sells short
100 shares of ABC stock identified on that day to be part of arbitrage
operations. As part of the same identified arbitrage, the dealer contracts to purchase 100 preferred shares of ABC, convertible into 100
shares of common stock. Delivery of the preferred shares is not made
until November 1. Since the dealer had contracted to acquire substantially identical assets on the same day as the short sale, the dealer is
deemed to own substantially identical property for purposes of the
above arbitrage rules. Accordingly, the holding period of the investment stock is not disturbed.

Dealers in stock, Listed options and other securities may also be
subject to the tax straddle rules, which include rules similar to the
short sales rules.[915]

.08   Section 1256 Contracts

Holders of Section 1256 contracts are subject to both the mark-to-
market rule (report gain or loss on contracts held at year-end based
on their closing market values) and 60/40 long-term/short-term capital gains or losses on actual or deemed dispositions of the contracts.[916]

---

[912] Reg. 1.1233-1(f)(1)(ii).
[913] Code: 1233(f)(3).
[914] Reg. 1.1233-1(f)(3).

[915] Code: 1092. (See ¶38.02.)
[916] Code: 1256(a). (See ¶38.03 for further
discussion.)

These rules generally apply to all holders of regulated Futures contracts (e.g., Futures in commodities, government bonds, and cash
settlement contracts), foreign currency contracts, and any nonequity
options. In addition, only dealers can enjoy the 60/40 capital gain
treatment for any dealer equity options, including Listed (but not Unlisted) stock options and narrow-based stock index options.[917] A
dealer equity option is an equity option purchased or granted by an
option dealer in the normal course of its options business, and listed
on the national securities exchange on which the options dealer is
registered.[918] Only persons registered on the appropriate national securities exchange as a market maker or specialist in Listed options or
traders performing similar services as determined by the Treasury
qualify as options dealers.[919] Note that these options dealers have in
effect, abandoned their usual method of valuing these Listed options
held at year-end in favor of the mark-to-market method. The mark-to-
market and 60/40 capital gain rules do not apply if the Section 1256
contract is part of a hedging contract.[920] Once personal property has
been identified as part of a hedging transaction, any gain (and presumably loss) will be taxed as ordinary income (or loss).[921] With respect to mixed straddles, an election may be made not to apply the
mark-to-market and 60/40 capital gains rules for Section 1256 contracts that are part of the mixed straddle.[922] It may be advisable to
make this election because net Section 1256 gains from the mixed
straddles are currently taxable but net losses would be deferred under
the tax straddle rules. Section 1256 contracts that would normally
receive ordinary income or loss treatment on disposition are excluded
from the 60/40 capital gain rules but still remain subject to the mark-
to-market rules.[923] This includes inventory items or ordinary income
items under the Corn Products doctrine.[924] However, the rule is inconsistent with the dealer equity option provision, and the authors believe

---

[917] Code: 1256(b), generally effective for
positions established after July 18, 1984.
An October 31, 1983 effective date applies to options on regulated Futures
contracts.

[918] Code: 1256(g)(4).

[919] Code: 1256(g)(8).

[920] Code: 1256(e). A hedging transaction
is a transaction in a dealer's normal
course of business to reduce the risk of
price changes or interest changes with
respect to property held by, or liabilities of, the dealer, where ordinary gain
or loss would result from the transac-

tion, and the transaction is clearly identified as a hedging transaction before
the close of the day of the transaction.
The identification requirement does not
apply to any stock options or stock acquired within 60 days of the date of
enactment of the 1984 Act (July 18,
1984).

[921] Code: 1256(f)(1).

[922] Code: 1256(d). (See ¶38.04.)

[923] Code: 1256(f)(2).

[924] *Corn Products Refining Co.*, 215 F. 2d
513 (CA-2, 1954), aff'd 350 U.S. 46
(1955).

it should not apply to dealer equity options. Additionally, limited partners (or limited entrepreneurs) in dealer equity options partnerships will report their share of the gain or loss on the options as a short-term gain or loss instead of receiving 60/40 treatment.[925] Traders in Section 1256 contracts generally will receive 60/40 capital gain treatment unless a hedging loss with respect to the offsetting property would be an ordinary loss.[926]

An election can be made to apply the mark-to-market and 60/40 capital gains rules to (1) all Section 1256 contracts held on July 18, 1984 (the date of enactment of the 1984 Act) or (2) all such contracts held at any time during the taxpayer's taxable year in which the 1984 Act was enacted (1984 for calendar year taxpayers).[927] If an equity options dealer elected the latter full-year election, it can also choose to pay the additional 1984 tax attributable to the appreciation, as of the close of the preceding year, on the dealer equity options and any offsetting stock position in the options straddle in two to five installments.[928] The first installment would be due with the return filed for the election year. Interest will be charged on the unpaid installments at regular rates.

.09 Tax Straddles

Many investment houses engage in straddle transactions in their trading and arbitrage operations, as well as through their dealer activities. The nondealer activities will be subject to the same loss deferral rules as those covering investors or traders.[929] Rules similar to the wash sales and short sales provisions are also applicable.[930] Interest and carrying charges on these straddles (e.g., cash and carry transactions) may have to be capitalized and added on to the basis of the property in lieu of being deducted currently.[931] When at least one of the offsetting positions consists of a Section 1256 contract, these tax straddle rules may apply to all positions, including the Section 1256 contracts.[932] Dealership activities will be excluded from these tax straddle rules if they are engaged in as part of a hedging transaction.[933]

---

[925] Code: 1256(f)(5).
[926] Code: 1256(f)(4).
[927] 1984 Act: 102(g).
[928] 1984 Act: 102(h).
[929] Code: 1092(c). (See ¶38.02.)
[930] Code: 1092(b).

[931] Code: 263(g). (See ¶38.05.)
[932] Code: 1092(d)(5).
[933] Code: 1092(e). (See Code: 1256(e) and footnote 920 for a definition of hedging transactions.)

.10 Short-Term Obligations

As part of their normal business operations, investment houses purchased short-term discounted Treasury bills (T-bills) and borrowed to finance the purchases (Repos). These transactions (sometimes referred to as T-bill rolls) resulted in a current deduction for the interest expense and a deferral of the discount income in the T-bills until maturity or disposition.[934] Under the 1984 Act, bond dealers and other accrual-basis taxpayers will now have to include in income a ratable daily portion of the acquisition discount based on the portion of the term of the T-bill that is included in the current taxable year.[935] Thus, if the acquisition discount in the T-bill was $1,000 and three months of a one-year T-bill expired in the tax year, then 25 percent of $1,000, or $250, would be included in gross income in the current year. The remaining $750 would be taxed in the following year. Since a holder of a T-bill will report more income in the first year under the ratable (straight-line) method than under the compound interest method used for original issue discount on long-term obligations, the holder may elect to use the compound interest method for all T-bills acquired in the election year and subsequent years.[936] Any interest expense incurred to purchase the T-bills is currently deductible under the regular rules.[937] Moreover, the basis of the T-bill is increased by the amount of the acquisition discount income includable in income.[938]

Many taxpayers were faced with the problem of reporting in one year all of the accumulated interest income on the T-bill rolls. To mitigate this potential hardship, they are permitted, under a complex formula, to report the accumulated income over a five-year period as a change of accounting method. Unlike the installment payment rules for equity option straddles (see ¶70.08) no interest is payable on any of the deferred income.[939] An election can be made by bond dealers and other accrual-basis taxpayers for their first taxable year ending after July 18, 1984 to accrue acquisition discount income on all T-bills held at any time during the taxable year. An offsetting net adjustment representing the excess of the amount of discount income includable in income under the former cash method over the amount includable under the current accrual method is then spread over a five-year period starting in 1984 for calendar-year taxpayers. However, to

---

[934] Code: 454 (b). (See ¶46.09 (b).)
[935] Code: 1281 (a), applies to T-bills acquired after July 18, 1984.
[936] Code: 1283 (b) (2).

[937] Code: 1282 (b) (1).
[938] Code: 1283 (d) (1).
[939] 1984 Act: 44 (e).

prevent a possible reduction in tax by electing this five-year spread provision, the taxpayer must earn additional T-bill discount income for the first four years of the five-year period. Accordingly, the annual adjustment is reduced to the extent that the actual accrued discount is less than the required amount.

Example. Assume that in 1984 an accrual-basis calendar-year taxpayer had an excess of cash-basis discount income from T-bills over accrual basis of $10,000 resulting from a T-bill roll. One fifth of $10,000 can be deducted in 1984 provided the accrued amount for the year is at least $8,000 (80 percent of net adjustment). Additional deductions of $2,000 can be taken in the second year if the accrued discount amount is at least $6,000. As can be seen, the required accrued discount amount each year is reduced by the amount of adjustments deducted in the previous years and the current year. The amount of deductions taken for the current and prior years plus the required accrued discount income for the current year should equal the net adjustment amount under Section 481 ($10,000 in this example). Thus, no accrued discount income is necessary for the last year of the spread period since the total deductions will be $10,000.

Note that if in the above example, the taxpayer recognized $10,000 of income from the 1983 T-bill roll and did not acquire any T-bills in 1984, the excess of cash over accrual basis discount would be zero and, therefore, no deduction could be made under Section 481. The same would apply to each of the other years of the five-year period. The adjustment allowed each of these years, other than the last year, would also be one fifth of excess discount income. Thus, if in the second year the excess cash discount were only $1,000, the negative adjustment would be limited to $1,000.

.11 Expenses Disallowed under Section 265

The disallowance of interest and other expenses for holding tax exempts applies to dealers in tax exempts as well as to investors.[940] Dealers will be denied interest deductions even where the tax-exempt securities constitute a minor part of the business and the dealer borrowings were not specifically made to purchase or retain bonds.[941] A

---

[940] Code: 265(2). (See ¶51.05.) Certain banks are excepted from these provisions. Reg. 1.265-2(b).

[941] J. E. Leslie, 413 F. 2d 636 (CA-2, 1969); J. C. Bradford, 60 T.C. 253 (1973).

2 percent *de minimis* rule, applicable to corporations investing in tax-exempt bonds, does not apply to corporate dealers.[942] Moreover, the fact that the tax exempts were acquired primarily for resale or trading purposes and that the interest expense greatly exceeded the interest income was held to be immaterial.[943] Any amounts directly traceable to the purchase or carrying of tax exempts will be disallowed. In addition, if there is no special account for the dealings in tax exempts and borrowing is incurred for the general purpose of carrying on a brokerage business, an allocable amount of the interest expense will be disallowed.[944] In practice, the Internal Revenue Service has established elaborate rules for determining exclusion and inclusion in the general formula. Some brokerage firms are not in full agreement with the inclusion of certain items.

.12 Bond Premiums

Traders and investors may elect to deduct bond premiums paid on taxable bonds, but are required to annually reduce the basis of tax-exempt bonds by nondeductible amortizable amounts.[945] Bond dealers are not subject to these bond premium provisions with respect to their bonds held for sale to customers.[946] Dealers in tax exempts, however, may have to amortize any premiums paid as if the tax exempts were held for investment.[947] If the dealer does not inventory the tax exempts or uses the cost method of valuation, the basis of the tax exempts sold during the year is reduced by the total bond amortization for the period the bonds are held.[948] Dealers valuing their bond inventories under any valuation method other than cost (e.g., market value) must annually reduce their cost of securities sold by the amount of the annual bond premium amortization on tax exempts held during the taxable year.[949] No amortization adjustment need be made for tax exempts sold at a gain if either (1) they were held for less than 30 days after acquisition, or (2) the earliest maturity or call date of the bond is more than five years after the date the bonds were acquired.[950] With respect to the more-than-five-year bonds that are not sold at a gain, the entire amortization during the period the bonds are held will reduce the cost of securities sold in the year of sale.[951]

---

[942] Rev. Proc. 72-18, Section 3.05, C.B. 1972-1, 740.
[943] *J. S. Wynn Jr.,* 411 F. 2d 614 (CA-3, 1969).
[944] Rev. Proc. 72-18, Section 5, C.B. 1972-1, 740.
[945] Code: 171(a); *R. F. Brown* 426 F. 2d

355 (Ct. Cl., 1970). (See ¶46.02.)
[946] Code: 171(d); Reg. 1.171-4(c).
[947] Code: 171(e) and 75.
[948] Code: 75(a)(2).
[949] Code: 75(a)(1).
[950] Code: 75(b)(1).
[951] Code: 75(a).

.13 Dividends Received Deduction

Corporate investment houses may be entitled to an 85 percent dividends-received deduction on qualifying dividends received on stock held for investment, trading, arbitrage operations, or dealer activities.[952] The increase in the required holding period from 16 to 46 days for most stocks (one year for extraordinary dividends) will make it more difficult to qualify for the dividends-received deduction.[953] Additionally, the amount of the dividends-received deductions will be reduced if the firm borrowed funds to acquire or hold the stock; the reduction is based on the percentage of the cost that was financed during the base period.[954] Note that the use of cost instead of market value in making the computations can have an impact on the amount of disallowance if the stock has substantially increased in value in a short period after acquisition and the dividend amount was based on the increased market price for the stock. The practice of reducing tax liability by means of dividend rollovers (85 percent dividends-received deductions in the current year and capital or ordinary loss on sale of the stock in the next year) will also be curtailed by the requirement that the basis of the stock be reduced to the extent of the untaxed portion of the extraordinary dividend for common stock dividends.[955] Moreover, the practice of issuing appreciated property with low tax basis (e.g., oil royalty trust interests) will no longer be feasible with fair market value, and not tax basis, being used in determining the amount of the stock-basis reduction.[956] Long-term gain on the future sale of the distributed appreciated property may also be prevented by another provision limiting its holding period to the holding period of the stock.[957]

71 TAX SHELTERS

The types of tax shelters are varied. Included among the principal tax shelters are real estate, including commercial, residential, and subsidized housing, oil and gas, coal royalties, cattle feeder and breeder programs, other agricultural products, motion picture film, research and development, and leased personal property. Some of these shelters—such as movie ventures, coal royalties, master recordings, gems, and Bibles—have been diminished as viable tax shelters

---

[952] Code: 243. (See ¶66.)
[953] Code: 246.
[954] Code: 246A.

[955] Code: 1059.
[956] Code: 1059(d)(2).
[957] Code: 301(e) and 1223(14).

for individual investors because of prior changes in the tax law or because of a toughened Treasury tax posture.

Recent case law has also denied tax deductions where excessive prices were paid for the tax-oriented property, drilling of oil was delayed or there was no firm commitment to drill, the financing did not meet the "at risk" requirements, no income was received in the current year with respect to depreciation of film, prepayment of fees represented a deposit rather than a binding agreement, or there was failure to show an economic purpose for the transaction other than tax avoidance. Aside from the Treasury's intensified efforts to uncover abusive tax shelters and take appropriate action, some of the benefits obtained from the 1981 ERTA provisions—such as increased depreciation deductions and tax credits, and nullifying the effect of tax preferences on the maximum tax on personal service income—have been offset by the provisons of the 1982 Tax Equity and Fiscal Responsibility Act (TEFRA) and the 1984 Tax Reform Act. These include an expanded alternative minimum tax, additional penalties for engaging in abusive tax transactions, deferring deductions until economic performance occurs, limiting deductions for prepaid expenses, tightening the partnership rules to prevent the deduction of expenses that should be capitalized and limiting the expenses that can be deducted by a new partner, a reduction in basis for investment credit allowed, and a decrease in the depreciation allowed in the early years for most investment real property.

These changes will make it more difficult for an investor to obtain a valid "two-for-one" write-off and, therefore, will expose the investor's own funds to the economic risks of the tax-oriented investment. Therefore, at a minimum, an investor should investigate the promoter's background to ascertain whether he or she is reputable, whether the promoter's prior offerings were profitable before taxes, and whether the price paid for the property is not exorbitant, as well as the results of any previous tax examinations of the promoter's offerings by the Internal Revenue Service. In addition, investors should reevaluate their tax strategy. New projections should be made to ascertain whether greater after-tax income can be obtained from investing in tax shelters such as real estate, oil, personal property leasing, or research and development projects; or from conventional investments, such as tax-exempt securities, taxable bonds, stocks, deferred annuities; or from special tax deferral provisions such as IRAs, Keogh plans, and employee salary reduction plans. Any investment, including a tax shelter, should be judged on its risk-reward ratio. In the past, many tax shelters were poor investments but could still result in a substantial after-tax rate of return on investments due to favorable tax treatment. Real estate is an example of a favored tax shelter, where through leverage, an investor could get deductions of $3 to $4 for every dollar invested because of nonrecourse financing. While "at-risk" rules still do not apply to real estate, the increase in the depreciable life of real estate means smaller deductions in the earlier years. This will reduce the value of real estate shelters and, accordingly, will reduce the amounts the present investors will receive on sale of their real estate investments. Furthermore, tax shelters provide tax deferral until the shelter is sold; a complete escape of tax if the investor were to die holding the tax shelter; and for many tax shelters, long-term capital gain on ultimate disposition. Aside from the current tax provsions, an investor should consider the possibility of a flat tax on income and its effect on tax shelters and other tax-oriented investments.

Below is a discussion of some of the relevant provisions incorporated in recent tax legislation and their effect on specific tax shelters.

.01 "At Risk" Capital

Increased leverage generally can no longer be obtained through nonrecourse financing whereby the debtor is not personally liable.[958] The effect of this provision is to limit the total amount of allowable deductions to actual cash or property contributions and recourse financing. Previously, nonrecourse financing would result in a higher tax basis, resulting in greater depreciation deductions in the early years and, more importantly, in larger investment credits. This is still true for commercial real estate, especially qualified rehabilitated buildings.[959]

Investment credit in qualifying personal property, such as breeding cattle, personal property leasing, and motion picture film, may be limited to the amount the investor is "at risk" (cash outlay plus recourse financing).[960] Increased investment credit can no longer be obtained in personal property investments from the use of nonrecourse financing unless the activity qualifies as an active trade or business or the lender is a bank, insurance company, or other lending institution. All tax shelters other than real estate will be affected by these at-risk limitations with respect to losses and investment credits. As stated

---

[958] Code: 465 (a).
[959] Code: 46 (a)(2).
[960] Code: 46 (c)(8).

previously, efforts to increase the tax basis of the property by means of inflated prices or disguised nonrecourse financing have been frustrated by both the Treasury and the courts. Requiring a basis reduction for investment credit allowed has further reduced the tax benefits of these types of investments.

.02 Upfront Deductions

Prior to the 1976 Tax Reform Act (TRA), the Treasury permitted a deduction for one year's prepaid interest expense where there had been no distortion of income. Cash-basis taxpayers are in effect now placed on an accrual basis and can only deduct prepaid interest ratably over the duration of the loan.[961] (See ¶51.05.) Attempts to increase interest deductions by computing the amount of interest expense under the Rule of 78s will no longer be permitted by the Treasury except for short-term consumer loans.[962] Deferring deductions until economic performance occurs and restricting the use of prepaid expenses will also deny certain shelters the advantages of current deductions. These restrictions will affect most tax shelters involving financing. In the same vein, interest and taxes incurred during the real estate construction period will now have to be capitalized.[963] Real estate taxes and interest expense can still be deducted during the construction of low-income housing.[964] The costs of producing motion picture films cannot be deducted when incurred, but are deferred until income is earned.[965] Farming syndicates can deduct expenses for feed, fertilizer, seed, and other farm supplies only when consumed.[966] Tax shelters can not deduct expenses before economic performance occurs, which in many cases must be within 90 days after the close of the tax year.[967] Thus, cattle feed not consumed or oil drilling not commenced within 90 days after year-end are not deductible in the current year. In addition, the cost of planting, cultivating, maintaining, and developing a citrus or almond grove, an orchard, or a vineyard must be capitalized where incurred prior to the productive stage.[968] Investors in oil and gas drilling programs can usually deduct between 60 and 75 percent of their cost by electing to deduct intangible drilling and development expenses.[969] Part of the remaining cost is attrib-

---

[961] Code: 461 (g).
[962] Rev. Rul. 83-84, C.B. 1983-1, 97.
[963] Code: 189.
[964] Code: 189 (d).
[965] Code: 280.
[966] Code: 464 (a).

[967] Code: 461 (h) and (i), generally effective for amounts incurred after July 18, 1984.
[968] Code: 278 (b).
[969] Code: 263 (c).

utable to machinery and equipment and can be depreciated over a five-year period.[970] The overall tax benefits of the oil and gas investment can further be increased by placing the investment in a 10-year reversionary trust, with the investor retaining the right to the oil income in an amount equal to the percentage depletion allowed on the oil income (and also the depreciation on the machinery and equipment); the balance of the income is payable to family members in lower tax brackets.[971] Thus, the investor receives the initial tax benefits from the oil and gas investment and any subsequent taxable income will be reported by the lower-tax-bracket trust beneficiaries.

.03 Tax Preferences

In the past, the tax preference items created by the tax shelters were not considered important because of the exemptions and deductions allowed in computing the minimum tax on tax preferences, but had a substantial effect on maximum tax on personal service income. (See ¶61 and ¶62 respectively.) With the repeal of the maximum tax on personal service income in 1982, investors, such as professionals and corporate executives, no longer will need to be concerned that the tax preferences could substantially increase the tax on their earned income. On the other hand, combining the alternative minimum tax with the add-on minimum tax into one alternative minimum tax will expose more investors to the 20 percent alternative minimum tax and also limit the benefits of excess tax preferences to 20 percent. (See ¶61.) Future shelters will depend more on accelerated depreciation, intangible drilling expenses, and tax credits, but investors should not ignore the economic aspects of the shelter. They must bear in mind that they are now sheltering only "50 percent" income rather than "70 percent" income and, therefore, can suffer a greater after-tax loss from the investments. In addition to obtaining less tax benefit for each dollar of loss thrown off by the tax shelter, the investor should also consider that the Treasury may question the validity of the tax shelter if it lacks a profit potential.

.04 Capital Gains on Disposition

The maximum capital gains rate of 20 percent for post-June 9, 1981, transactions increases the tax benefits of certain tax shelters and must be contrasted with other shelters that generate ordinary income on

---

[970] Code: 168. Investment credit may also be taken on the machinery and equipment.

[971] Rev. Rul. 84-14, I.R.B. 1984-4, 7.

disposition subject to tax rates up to 50 percent (70 percent pre-1981). Investors no longer have to be concerned that the deductions created by the tax shelter may be offset against income subject to a maximum tax rate of 50 percent and can be recaptured at 70 percent tax rates. Gain on sale of residential property, other than certain low-income housing, will be taxed as ordinary income to the extent of accelerated depreciation.[972] This ordinary income treatment previously applied to sale of commercial real estate, leased personal property, motion picture film, and breeding cattle. A gain on sale of oil and gas property will also be taxed as ordinary income to the extent of excess intangible drilling costs.[973] In lieu of a sale, many investors have made charitable contributions of the oil and gas property. A charitable contribution deduction will not be allowed to the extent ordinary income would have resulted from a sale of the property.[974]

.05 Increased Basis at Death

Due to the inability of disposing of a tax shelter during lifetime without incurring substantial tax liability, many investors had retained their tax shelters until death. At death, the deceased investor's estate or beneficiary would obtain a new tax basis for the property equal to its market value and thereby escape tax for the excess deductions previously allowed. The ability of the estate or beneficiary to obtain a new increased basis for the shelter has been retained with the repeal of the basis carry-over rules.[975] For many investors this will represent the only means of avoiding the adverse tax effects of a burned-out shelter other than investing in another shelter to offset the income flowing from the burned-out shelter.

72 DEFERRED ANNUITIES

A variation of the variable annuity policy has recently received a good deal of publicity. The main selling points of these deferred annuities appear to be high guaranteed interest rates in the first years of the policy, deferral of income taxes on the income earned by the investments, and flexibility in receiving the deferred income and the principal contributed by the investor. The terms of the policies will vary among the different insurance companies.

One type of annuity is the savings annuity whereby an investor will contribute $30,000 or more in savings bank certificates, or certifi-

---

[972] Code: 1250(a).
[973] Code: 1254(a)(1)(A).
[974] Code: 170(e).
[975] Code: 1023.

cates of deposit. The insurance company takes title to these certificates and the income is not taxed to the investor until he receives his annuity payments. Because the certificates do not mature for a period of time, the investor has less flexibility in making withdrawals.

Investment annuities, on the other hand, give more flexibility to the investors. Funds are contributed to the insurance company in the form of cash, mutual fund shares, or securities. These annuities also provide for high guaranteed interest in the earlier years and either a lower interest rate thereafter or an interest rate dependent on the yield from investments in the investor's custodian account. An initial contribution of securities by the investor will result in gain or loss to the investor. Any gains realized after the insurance company takes title are taxed to the insurance company, but the costs are passed on to the investor by a charge to his custodian account. For this reason investment of long-term, high-yield bonds is better than low-yield stock. Prior to the 1982 TEFRA, the income earned on these investments was passed through to the investor as a tax-free return of investment on the theory that the annuity had not started, but this resulted in larger income when the investor starts receiving annuity payments. For these services an investor may be charged an original sales charge plus annual handling charges varying from 0.5 percent to 2 percent. Penalties may also be charged for premature distributions.

Inherent in the investment annuity policies and other deferred annuities is the requirement that the investor must make the investment decision or must hire investment counselors to make them. Any additional costs for investment advisory services are borne by the investor. Originally, the Treasury approved these investment annuities, but it has since ruled that the investor would be treated as the owner of the assets held in the custodian account if he had full control over future investments.[976] In this event, the investor would be taxed on the income generated by the investments as if he retained ownership.

The rulings by the Treasury with regard to investment control casts

---

[976] Rev. Rul. 77-185, C.B. 1977-1, 12. A court action to prohibit the Treasury from enforcing this ruling has failed. *Investment Annuity, Inc.,* 609 F. 2d 1 (CA-DC, 1979), cert. den. The Treasury has ruled that the investor is currently taxable on the wraparound annuity contract in Rev. Rul. 80-274, C.B. 1980-2 CB, 27, and Rev. Rul. 81-225, C.B. 1981-2, 12. An investor would not be currently taxed on income from a wraparound annuity if the funds are invested in mutual funds that are not available to the public at the time of purchase. Rev. Rul. 82-55, C.B. 1982-1, 12. In addition, controlling broad general strategies with respect to investments in stock, bonds, or other money market instruments would not constitute sufficient control to cause the investor to be currently taxed on the income. Rev. Rul. 82-54, C.B. 1982-1, 11.

clouds over annuity policies that fail to meet the Treasury requirements. The attractiveness of these investments has been further diminished because the ability to make current tax-free distributions was curtailed with respect to distributions after August 12, 1982. Any distributions received before the annuity starting date, including loans or partial surrenders, will be treated as income to the extent the cash surrender value of the policy exceeds the net premiums paid by the annuitant.[977] Early withdrawal afer 1982 can also result in a 5 percent penalty.[978]

In other respects, this type of annuity usually offers larger income yields than regular insurance policies and a deferral of the income until later years when the investor may be in a lower tax bracket; in the meantime, the investor receives additional income from funds that otherwise would have been used to pay the income tax imposed on the investment income. As stated previously, annuity payments made after the annuity date (i.e., the date annuity payment commences) are taxed under the normal annuity rules,[979] and the percentage of the annuity payments that will be subject to tax will increase if prior principal payments were made. A lump-sum payment to the investor's beneficiary upon the investor's death before the annuity date would be tax-free, similar to a payment of life insurance.[980] However, the insurance proceeds would be subject to estate taxes.[981] Before investing in these deferred annuities, an investor should compare the economic and tax results with those of other types of investments, including tax-exempt bonds.

---

[977] Code: 72 (e). This provision applies to annuity contracts entered into before August 14, 1982, but not to income allocated to investments made before such date.

[978] Code: 72 (q).

[979] Code: 72.

[980] Code: 101 (a).

[981] Code: 2042.

Index of Citations

TREASURY DEPARTMENT RULINGS

General Counsel's Memoranda

*Proposed Reg.

228

COURT DECISIONS

232

MISCELLANEOUS

Subject Index